S0-BXV-731

The Greatest Players and Moments of the Philadelphia Flyers

Revised Through 2002

by
Stan Fischler

SPORTS PUBLISHING L.L.C.
804 N. Neil
Champaign, IL 61820

©2002 Stan Fischler
All Rights Reserved.

All cover and interior photos provided by Bruce Bennett Studios.

Director of Production, book design: Susan M. Moyer
Dustjacket design: Joe Buck & Margaret Rogers
Developmental editor: Noah Amstadter
Research editors: Dan Saraceni, Michael Casey, Edward Salib
Copy editor: Cynthia L. McNew

ISBN: 1-57167-234-6
Library of Congress Catalog Card Number:

Sports Publishing L.L.C.
804 N. Neil
Champaign, IL 61820
www.SportsPublishingllc.com

Printed in the United States

To all the Philadelphia hockey people who made my coverage of The Game more pleasurable over the years—Larry Zeidel, Bob Clarke, Joe Kadlec, Mark Piazza, Bernie Parent, Eric Lindros, Bill Barber, Tim Kerr, Rick Tocchet, John LeClair, Rod Brind'Amour, The Watson Brothers—Joe and Jimmy—Dave Poulin, Dave Schultz, Ed Van Impe, Ron Hextall (all class), Paul Holmgren, Doc Emrick, Chico Resch, Brad Marsh, Mark Recchi, Murray Craven, Doug Favell, Dave Brown, Ron Sutter, Kevin Dineen, Bob Froese, Peter Zezel, Pete Peeters, Scott Mellanby,

Terry Crisp, Bill Clement, Gene Hart, Ed and Jay Snider, Ron Ryan, Fr. Casey, Tim Panaccio, Zack Hill, Roger Neilson, Keith Acton, Wayne Cashman, Les Bowen, Bill Fleischman, Steve Coates, Gary Dornhoefer, Bruce Cooper, Al Morganti, Jay Greenberg, Bobby Taylor and Diane Gerace, and any others I have inadvertently forgotten.

Contents

Acknowledgments

Compiling a list of the 50 greatest players of a team that featured so many memorable performers and provided so many sparkling moments over the last 30 years is a difficult but not impossible task. Not if you have good wingmen.

Without the assistance of many gracious individuals, this work could not have even been discussed, let alone completed.

Thanks to the Philadelphia Flyers public relations staff for providing us with a wealth of information: Zack Hill, Jill Lipson, Joe Kadlec, Joe Klueg, Linda Held, Kevin Kurz and Kerrianne Brady, at the CoreStates Complex Archives.

Pivotal in sorting the mounds and mounds of Flyers files, our staff of researchers, who put aside their own team alliances to learn more about the Broad Street Bullies: G. P. Aroldi, Christina Attardo, Thomas Berk, Michael Casey, Edward Salib, Dan Saraceni, Jonathan Scherzer, Darren Siegel, Amy Spencer, Josh Liebman, Dan Rice, Jon Kars, Patrick Hoffman and David Kolb. Casey and Salib, in particular, worked tirelessly ferreting through old clippings, magazines and other research resources to round out the production.

We would also like to thank longtime Flyers fan Eric Servetah for his insight and our editors at Sports Publishing, Noah Amstadter and Joseph Bannon Jr., for their devotion and enthusiasm.

In addition, a number of books on the Flyers were invaluable research resources. During the Stanley Cup years, Jack Chevalier authored *The Broad Street Bullies—The Incredible Story of the Flyers*. It was a superb chronicle of the early Flyer years.

In 1990, Philadelphia broadcast legend Gene Hart—with Buzz Ringe—published *Score—My Twenty-Five Years With The Broad Street Bullies*. It was an anecdote-filled gem that did exactly what the title said it would do.

New York Post columnist and former *Philadelphia Daily News* reporter Jay Greenberg wrote the definitive Flyers history, *Full Spectrum—The Complete History of the Philadelphia Flyers*, covering the saga of the orange and black from the beginning to the present. It was a reference tool that helped us constantly.

Each of the above was an aid in our research and development of this product.

Last but not least, a debt of gratitude to the NHL's archivist John Halligan, who steered us toward Mike Pearson, who had the faith in this project and gave us the green light to do it.

Thanks to all!

Introduction

My connection with Philadelphia hockey predates the Flyers by more than two decades. As a youth, I attended many Sunday afternoon Eastern Amateur Hockey League games at Madison Square Garden.

The New York Rovers—the top Rangers farm team—were the home club. They frequently hosted the Philadelphia Falcons, who distinguished themselves in many ways to my eyes.

For one thing, future NHL goalie (and later coach and general manager) Emile Francis played his first game at the Garden for the Falcons, and I was there to witness it.

Another time, the Falcons came to New York with a goaltender named Dave Kemp. I can say without fear of contradiction that Dave Kemp was the worst goaltender I have ever witnessed in my entire life.

After the Falcons departed our midst, my connection with Philadelphia hockey was reestablished when old pal Larry Zeidel was signed for Philadelphia's first NHL team in 1967.

That was the year of the NHL's expansion from six to twelve teams. Like others I doubted whether the City of Brotherly Love could support major league hockey. Happily I was proven wrong.

I visited the Spectrum in November, 1967 for the first time, catching a Flyers home game while preparing a magazine piece on Zeidel.

Several aspects of the visit still are vivid in my memory. One was the relatively luxurious trappings of the home dressing room. Another was the extensive game notes prepared by likeable publicist Joe Kadlec. And, finally, the enthusiasm of Philadelphia fans.

Another vivid memory was my first sighting of owner Ed Snider at the annual governors' meeting. He stood out because he was dressed in a sharper, more sophisticated manner than any of his brethren and seemed out of place. Snider later proved to be ahead of the game in many ways. He was among the first to recognize the World Hockey Association as a threat, and, along with Bill Jennings, he suggested a reasonable settlement. Ed and I have disagreed over the years, but my respect for him has never abated.

As the Flyers matured as a team, I continued to follow them as both a hockey writer and a broadcaster. The result was a trio of books about the team. My first, *Bobby Clarke and the Ferocious Flyers*, was followed by a photo-text album for Prentice-Hall and then the autobiography of Dave Schultz, *The Hammer: Confessions of a Hockey Enforcer*.

Through my *Hockey News* column and broadcasting, my association with the team continued through the decades of the 1980s and then the 1990s.

As such I have interviewed—and battled with—the likes of Ron Hextall and Schultz. Happily, we settled our differences and became friends. To this day, I number Hextall and Schultz among the classiest people I have encountered.

This book is not meant to be definitive nor infallible. It is merely one man's view of a hockey club–from its inception in 1967 through 2002–that has been intimidating, inimitable and always intriguing.

Hopefully, the book won't be intimidating but perhaps engaging or intriguing.

Stan Fischler,
New York, New York
July, 1998

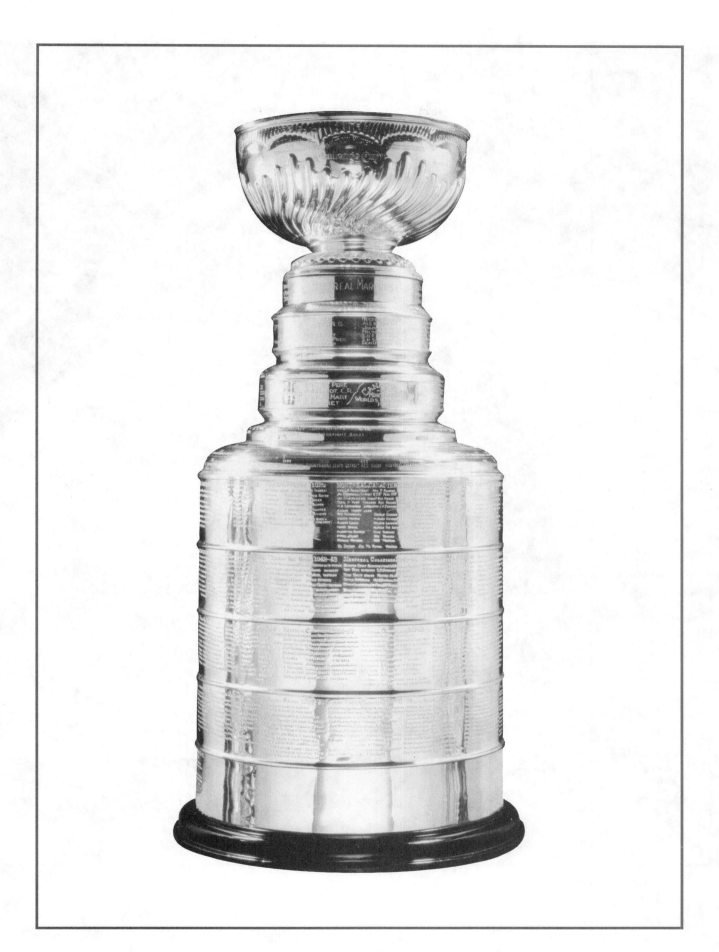

The ultimate Flyer—an ultimate Philadelphia captain, Bobby Clarke.

Bobby Clarke

There is no question in anyone's mind that Bobby Clarke is Mister Hockey in Philadelphia. He has earned that niche mostly as a player, but he fortified his legendary status in later years serving in the Flyers' high command.

But it is a combination of Clarke's playing skills and leadership qualities that has earned him a position at the very top of the list of all-time Broad Street aces.

Although less skilled than other Hall of Famers such as Mike Bossy and Wayne Gretzky, to name a pair who played against him, Clarke brought so many other dimensions to the game that he is recognized as the dynamo behind the Flyers' two Stanley Cup championship teams in 1974 and 1975 and, more recently, as a front office leader ranking with the best of them.

ROBERT EARL "BOBBY" CLARKE

Born: Flin Flon, Manitoba, August 13, 1949

Position: Center

NHL Teams: Philadelphia, 1969-84

Awards/Honors: Hart Trophy, 1972, 75, 76; Lester B. Pearson Award, 1973; Lester Patrick Award, 1980; Selke Trophy, 1983, First Team All-Star, 1975,76; Second Team All-Star, 1973, 74; Played in All-Star Game, 1970-75, 1977-79; Captain,1979 Challange Cup Team, Captain, Philadelphia, 1972-79, 1982-84; Reached Milestone Award for 600 Assists, 1000 Points, 1000 Games Played, 1983; Hockey Hall of Fame, 1987; Flyers Hall of Fame, 1988

Management: General Manager, Philadelphia, 1984-90, 1995-present; General Manager, Minnesota, 1990-92; General Manager, Florida, 1993-94 season

The legendary Philly captain and Hall of Famer, Bobby Clarke, stands at attention.

Challenge Cup.

It has never been easy for Clarke. A diabetic since his youthful years in Flin Flon, Manitoba, he lacked the smooth skating skills of a Bobby Orr or a Guy Lafleur. His shot was less than overwhelming, but he made the most of his attributes.

"Guts is what he had in abundance," said original Flyer Larry Zeidel. "Not everybody saw his qualities at first, but after a while it was evident that Bobby was a winner."

If anyone had suggested to Flyers boss Ed Snider that the seventeenth player claimed in the 1969 amateur draft would someday be the NHL's most valuable player, it is quite possible that Snider would have fallen over backwards in his chair with

---

What Pete Rose meant to any baseball team with which he had been affiliated, Clarke was to the Flyers.

---

laughter. Yet in September, 1969, while the Flyers' first-year men were working out in Quebec City, someone detected that rare quality of utter superiority in the young man. It was Bud Poile, then gen-

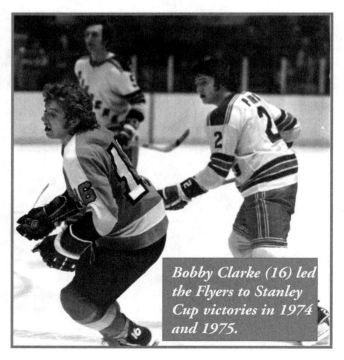

Bobby Clarke (16) led the Flyers to Stanley Cup victories in 1974 and 1975.

What Pete Rose meant to any baseball team with which he had been affiliated, Clarke was to the Flyers.

Beginning in 1969, when he made his National Hockey League debut, the gap-toothed center was regarded as the Charlie Hustle of hockey.

"Clarke," said Dave Schultz, who played with him on the Cup-winning teams, "was the heart and soul of our club."

Like Rose, Clarke displayed a fervor for his pastime that never diminished with age. In 1982, more than a decade after he had broken into the big time, he was clawing for position with greater zeal than rookies ten years his junior.

Clarke's contributions became apparent and acknowledged in a very short time. He was awarded the Hart Trophy as the NHL's most valuable player in 1973, 1975 and 1976. He was First All-Star center in 1975 and 1976 and a Second Team All-Star in 1973 and 1974. Bobby starred for Team Canada in the eight-game series against the Soviet All-Stars in 1972 and captained the NHL All-Stars against the Soviet Selects in the 1979

eral manager of the Flyers, whose radar uncovered the greatness in Clarke.

"Within three years," said Poile, "that 20-year-old boy will be the best in the league. And if he's not the best, I'll guarantee that he will be in the top three."

Poile was talking to his heir apparent as general manager, Keith Allen, about Clarke, who then was a rather awkward center about whom little was known. Precisely what it was about Clarke that inspired Poile's raves was somewhat of mystery. But as the 1972-73 season wound down to a playoff conclusion, it was evident that Poile either knew what he was talking about or had made an awfully good guess. By the time the Flyers went up against the Montreal Canadiens in April 1973, Bobby had irrevocably become Philadelphia's favorite hockey player.

Veterans such as defenseman Ed Van Impe knew it as well as the man in the street.

"He was tireless and always fought a little bit harder for the puck than anyone else," said Zeidel. "Bobby was the kind of player you would have wanted to go to war with if you had to march into the firing line."

Clarke was one of the best faceoff men the NHL has known and arguably as good a captain as any club ever had. In Philadelphia's hockey history dating back to 1967, there have been two Stanley Cups delivered to Broad Street, both by Bobby Clarke.

Robert Earle Clarke was born August 13, 1949 in the mining town of Flin Flon in northern Manitoba. Hockey was big in Flin Flon, and the local junior team, known as the Bombers, was where the action was. They played in a frontier atmosphere that was rife with brawling and intimidation.

"Flin Flon," as former Flyer Orest Kindrachuk once joked, "is five miles north of where civilization ends."

Clarke survived the battles in junior hockey, captained the Bombers and seemed destined for professional hockey when word of his diabetic condition circulated through the NHL scouting grapevine.

Fortunately for Bobby, his coach, Paddy Ginnell, was determined to see that his crack center got a fair chance to reach the top. He arranged for his young captain to visit the famed Mayo Clinic in Rochester, Min-

A diabetic, Bobby Clarke was bypassed by every NHL team but the Flyers, who correctly gambled that he had the right stuff.

nesota. Following a battery of tests, the doctors agreed that there was no reason why Clarke could not play pro hockey, provided that he took care of himself.

"What's more, the doctors put it in writing," said Ginnell.

Skeptical though they were, the Flyers decided to gamble on Clarke. He was picked seventeenth overall by Philadelphia in the 1969 amateur draft and made the big club on his first try, and by the 1972-73 season he had exceeded the 100-point mark. During a game against the Montreal Canadiens at The Forum, Philadelphia came away with a 7-6 victory. Bobby scored a hat trick, the winning goal achieved with only 3:39 remaining in the game.

"I'd hate to think where the Flyers would have been without him," said Keith Allen, who had become general manager of the team. "He certainly had become Hart Trophy material."

Nevertheless, Clarke continued to be bedeviled by

Bobby Clarke was unquestionably the most perservering player of the 1970s and early 1980s despite his diabetes.

physical ailments. In addition to his chronic diabetes, he also suffered optical problems. He was diagnosed with 200-100 myopia.

"That meant," said Clarke, "that I had trouble seeing far away. I never wore lenses in junior hockey. If I'm on top of the play, I'm okay. It's when the puck is in the air that I have trouble judging it."

Bobby made the adjustments and continued to excel on a team that was fast becoming notorious for its brawling style as well as its artistic ability. Clarke's growth as a player paralleled the development of the Flyers as an NHL power. By playoff time 1973, Clarke had fulfilled the promise of his September press clippings when he surprised everyone in the Team Canada camp. He had finished second in the scoring race behind perennial leader Phil Esposito of the Boston Bruins with 37 goals and 67 assists for 104 points in 78 games. In 1974-75 and 1975-76, he led the NHL in assists with 89 both seasons. He also led in playoff assists in both years with 12 and 14, respectively.

There was a voracious quality to his pursuit of the puck as well as his attitude toward the enemy. Clarke's tenacity knew no limits and there were times—many

times—that he resorted to indelicate means to win hockey games. He was unsparing of his body, and by the late 1970s the wear and tear of battle had taken a toll on his physique. Not surprisingly, his point production began a downward spiral—90, 89, 73, 69 and 65 in the 1980-81 season. His last meaningful chance for a third Stanley Cup came in 1980 when the Flyers battled the New York Islanders in a six-game final round before the Nassaumen triumphed.

During the early 1980s, the Flyers attempted to relieve Clarke by making him an assistant coach while limiting his playing time, but his will to play was overwhelming, and in 1981-82 he helped regenerate the Flyers' rebuilding process with a gallant show of energy. He finally retired in May, 1984, and in a natural progression became Flyers general manager. Critics mocked the move, claiming that Clarke was but a novice at a job for which he was unqualified. He fooled them, turning the club into a powerhouse, and Philadelphia reached the Stanley Cup finals in 1985 and again in 1987.

Then came a depression of sorts, and by 1989-90, the Flyers not only were below .500 but also were out of the playoffs. Clarke left Philadelphia and became general manager of the Minnesota North Stars in 1990-91, and they responded by going directly to the Stanley Cup finals before being eliminated by Pittsburgh in a tough six-game series.

Many of Clarke's maneuvers in Minnesota turned into brilliant decisions. He oversaw the drafting of future NHLers such as Richard Matvichuk and Jere Lehtinen as well as defenseman Derian Hatcher, who would later become the Stars' captain in 1994.

Success in Minnesota had its shortcomings, the most significant of which was that it was not Pennsylvania—Philadelphia in particular. He missed Broad Street, and Ed Snider missed him. Finally, in June 1992, Snider persuaded Clarke to return to The Spectrum as vice president of the Flyers. The title looked good, but the action was otherwise. Clarke was not in the hands-on position that his psyche demanded, and when an opening developed with the expansion Florida Panthers, Bobby left Broad Street once more, this time to become general manager of the Miami-based team.

Once again his brilliance leading the general staff was evident. He orchestrated the signing and drafting of a team that would not only be instantly competitive but

actually challenged for a playoff berth—and nearly made it—in Florida's maiden season.

Meanwhile, the Flyers were failing without him, and Snider waited for the moment when he could make the inevitable change and return Clarke as his president and general manager. The time came exactly one month after the 1993-94 season had ended, and Clarke promptly hired Terry Murray as head coach.

Once again, Bobby delivered. The Flyers would make the playoffs in each of the next three seasons and climb all the way to the Stanley Cup finals in 1997 before losing to the Detroit Red Wings. During that span, Clarke engineered one of the best trades in Philadelphia sports history, when in 1995 he acquired future 50-goal scorer John LeClair and playoff-hardened defenseman Eric Desjardins from Montreal in exchange for Mark Recchi and a third-round draft pick. LeClair, along with Eric Lindros and Mikael Renberg, combined for the famed Legion of Doom line, which quickly became one of the most feared in the league.

Clarke's wheeling and dealing continued through the 1997-98 season but with less luck. He fired Murray and hired Wayne Cashman as head coach. When that move failed in midseason, he then brought in Roger Neilson. The Flyers played well but not well enough, and though they made the playoffs, their first-round playoff defeat at the hands of Buffalo was regarded as an embarrassment.

Following Neilson, Clarke hired and fired Craig Ramsay (1999-2000 to 2000-2001) and Bill Barber (2000-2001 to 2001-2002). Meanwhile, his running battle with Eric Lindros finally led to the estrangement of his superstar from the hockey club. Eventually Clarke solved the dilemna by trading Lindros's rights to the New York Rangers in the summer of 2001.

Clarke's move was justified by the fact that, depite Lindros, the Rangers failed to make the playoffs whereas the Flyers finished first in the Atlantic Division. After his club was eliminated in the first 2002 playoff round, Clarke hired Ken Hitchcock as new head coach. As always, Flyers fans stuck behind their leader. After all, Bobby Clarke is not Mister Hockey in Philadelphia for nothing.

Bobby Clarke (16) did whatever it took to win—just ask Walt Tkaczuk (18) of the New York Rangers.

Bernie Parent winces in pain after getting hit in the eye; it would prove to be a career-ending injury.

Bernie Parent

I t would have been literally, figuratively and practically impossible for the Philadelphia Flyers to have a Stanley Cup—let alone two straight championships—sitting in The Spectrum without Bernie Parent. If he was not the greatest goaltender in National Hockey League history, Parent certainly was the very best in the early and mid-1970s when Broad Street was the hub of a pair of championship parades. While Bobby Clarke supplied the heart and Rick MacLeish the pivotal goals, none of those meaningful assets could have produced a title without the virtually airtight goaltending of Parent.

A disciple of the immortal Jacques Plante, Parent was an original Flyer. Drafted from the Boston Bruins organization in 1967, he already had been touted as a future star and became the first player to join Philadelphia in the NHL's first expansion year, 1967. The Flyers were fortunate, because Boston had to choose between two fine netminders, Parent and veteran Gerry Cheevers. When the Bruins opted for Cheevers—he also delivered a pair of Stanley Cups—Parent was left unprotected in the draft, and Philadelphia snatched him. When he reported to training camp in 1967, Parent competed for the top goaltending job with equally young Doug Favell whose acrobatic style starkly contrasted with Bernie's classic stand-up puck-stopping. The Favell-Parent tandem paced the Flyers to

BERNIE PARENT

BORN: Montreal, Quebec, April 3, 1945

Position: Goaltender

NHL Teams: Philadelphia, 1967-71, 1973-79; Toronto 1971-73.

Awards/Honors: Conn Smythe Trophy, 1974, 75; Vezina Trophy 1974, 75; First Team All-Star 1974, 75, Played in 1974, 75, 77 All-Star Games; Jersey #1 retired by Flyers, October 11, 1979

Coaching: Goaltending Instructor, Philadelphia, 1981-93

first place in the NHL's expansion division while Bernie turned in an impressive 2.49 goals-against average and four shutouts.

"When the Flyers made the playoffs," said Oakland Seals coach Fred Glover, "it was mostly thanks to Parent."

Scott Bowman, who then was coaching the St. Louis Blues, became an instant Parent fan.

"Bernie is the best young goalie in the league," said Bowman. "And when Glenn Hall and Jacques Plante retire, he'll be the best in the game."

Reaching the top was not easy. Like so many of his goaltending colleagues, Parent was a worrier. Once, during the 1967-68 season, he was scheduled to play against the Montreal Canadiens at The Forum. Flustered, Bernie spent a sleepless night, nervously questioning his roommate, defenseman Larry Zeidel.

"We don't have a chance, do we? How many shots do you think they'll take at me?" questioned Parent.

Zeidel, the cagey veteran, was reading *Psycho-Cybernetics: A New Way to Get More Living Out of Life*. He turned to the goalie. "Bernie, you've got to think positive. Just let the old subconscious work for you."

Four hours later the Flyers were on the way home with a 4-1 win under their belts and a goalie with a new outlook on life. That game was a turning point for Parent's career. Slowly but relentlessly he established himself as Philadelphia's premier goaltender. During the 1969-70 season he posted a respectable 2.79 goals-against average in 62 games. But the Flyers had trouble scoring goals in those early years, and to remedy the problem, they traded Parent to the Toronto Maple Leafs midway through the 1970-71 season for center Mike Walton and goaltender Bruce Gamble. Walton then was dealt to Boston for Rick MacLeish.

Parent was shocked and disappointed. He had established firm roots in Philadelphia and had grown to be a favorite with the fans. That was the bad news. The good news was that Parent would be playing alongside his boyhood idol, Jacques Plante. For learning purposes, it was the best thing that could have happened to Bernie. With Plante an eager tutor, Parent honed his goaltending style to sharpness and in 1971-72 lowered his goals-against average to 2.56. The young French-Canadian had become not only recognized as a young Plante but also sought by other teams—and another league.

In 1972, a rival major league, the World Hockey Association, was launched and a team in Miami, known as the Screaming Eagles, was awarded a franchise. The club persuaded Bernie to sign with them for the inaugural 1972-73 season, but before the first puck was even dropped, the Florida franchise had dissolved and Parent found himself playing for the WHA's Philadelphia Blazers. Bernie played in 57 consecutive games and chalked up the most victories in the WHA, with 33. But by this time it had become apparent that the Blazers were a rinky-dink operation, and when Flyers owner Ed Snider suggested that Parent return, he was quick to agree.

"I never wanted to leave in the first place," said Parent as he inked a new, multiyear contract with the Flyers on June 22, 1973. "Now that I'm back, I couldn't be happier. I've always considered myself a Flyer."

Most importantly, Parent was welcomed by his teammates.

"Bernie," said the Flyers' Bobby Clarke, "is the most valuable player in all of hockey."

A case also could be made for Clarke—and it was—

This is what they meant by a "scramble" around Bernie Parent's net.

"Bernie is the best young goalie in the league," said Bowman. "And when Glenn Hall and Jacques Plante retire, he'll be the best in the game."

but Parent certainly bolstered his reputation during the 1973-74 campaign. Playing in 73 out of 78 games—more than any other goalie—Parent produced a dazzling 1.89 goals-against average which was the best in the NHL. Until this time an expansion team had never won a Stanley Cup, but the Flyers that season were driven—by coach Fred Shero, by Clarke at center and by Parent's goaltending, which took them to the finals against a Bruins team that had won championships in 1970 and 1972 and still were led by Bobby Orr and Phil Esposito.

Nevertheless, Philadelphia took a three games-to-two lead into Game 6 of the series, whereupon Parent blanked the Bruins, 1-0. The Flyers had their first Stanley Cup, and Parent won the Conn Smythe Trophy as the most valuable player in the playoffs.

Perhaps the most surprised person of all was Shero. He had suffered doubts about Parent long before Bernie had returned to Philadelphia.

"I really didn't know how good Bernie was," Shero confessed. "I had only coached against him six or seven times when we were both in the Central League, and I had seen him on television a few times. Whenever my team played against him, my team always beat him pretty badly. But when he came to Philly, I wanted to get a reading on him, to feel him out. I invited him over to our house and we spoke."

Shero delivered an important message that Parent instantly grasped.

"I told him," Shero recalled, "that he had to remember that he lived in Philadelphia now and that he'll have a lot of pressure. 'You're going to have some games when they're going to boo you,' I said. 'But if you're good, you won't have to worry about that for long.'"

Parent-watchers believe that his most decisive moment in winning over Spectrum fans occurred on opening night in October 1973. Philadelphia was facing Toronto, Bernie's former team.

"I knew I had to produce early to take off the pressure," Parent remembered.

He did. The Flyers scored twice, and the visitors never lit the light at all.

New York Ranger Pete Stemkowski scores a goal against the Flyers' Bernie Parent.

"That shutout took 500 pounds off my shoulders," Parent concluded.

Bernie compiled 12 shutouts that season, just three shy of a league record. He was looking more and more like a vintage Plante every night. Whenever Bernie would slump, he would recall the advice that the Old Master has given him.

"We had pretty much the same styles," said Parent. "I watched everything he did, how he handled himself on shots, and whatever he was doing, I tried to do."

Parent's finest hour was reserved for that moment on May 19, 1974 when the final buzzer sounded at The Spectrum and the Flyers had beaten Boston for The Cup, a feat duplicated the following year against the Buffalo Sabres. The significance of the accomplishments did not go overlooked by Bernie.

The Flyers over the years have been blessed with top goaltending, but nobody was better than Hall of Famer Bernie Parent.

"When I was a boy," he remembered, "I used to watch so many great Montreal teams win The Cup. In my mind, I would try to figure out what the feeling would be like to win it."

He got the chance when he and Clarke cradled the ancient silver mug in their arms during the traditional post-game rites.

"Winning the Cup is not like I thought it would be," Parent explained. "It is better than I thought it would be. It's a feeling you can't describe. I'll never forget this feeling; it will always be with me. So many guys play hockey and never win the Cup. I feel sorry for anyone who never experiences what I'm feeling."

Unfortunately for Bernie, his 1975 Cup-winning experience would be his last. He missed most of the 1975-76 season with back surgery and was never quite as sharp afterward, although he performed brilliantly in the 1978 playoffs. But in 1979 his career came to a crashing end.

During a game against the New York Rangers on February 17, 1979, Flyers defenseman Jimmy Watson was attempting to clear an opponent away from the net.

Watson's stick blade pierced the right eye hole in Parent's mask, permanently damaging the goaltender's right eye.

Bernie's career ended after just 36 games of the 1978-79 season. It was a tragedy of monumental proportions, particularly for a team that was preparing for another Stanley Cup challenge.

"You talk about money players," said Flyers backup goalie Bobby Taylor, "and let me tell you, whenever we needed a game, there was Bernie, ready to deliver it to us."

His credentials were more impressive than those of any goaltender to have worn the Flyers' orange and black. He finished his ten-year Philadelphia career with a goals-against average of 2.42 and an overall record of 232-141-103, including an amazing 50 shutouts.

His playoff numbers were equally impressive. His 35-28 record is supported by a 2.38 goals-against average and six shutouts.

In 1982, Parent became the Flyers' goaltending coach, a position he held until 1994. Bernie Parent was a classic, from style to performance.

Bill Barber

Playing in the shadows of Bobby Clarke and Bernie Parent was hardly a problem for Bill Barber. His industriousness, clever play and prodigious production during Philadelphia's glory years of the 1970s eloquently spoke for his right to be in the Flyers' pantheon. But as a Spectrum superstar, Barber also was an enigma. As a player, he was never known for ostentatious behavior nor rambunctiousness in the manner of teammates such as Dave Schultz or Bob Kelly. Still, to this day, he remains a somewhat controversial NHL figure in the eyes of historians.

There are two reasons for this unusual reaction. The first is the fact that Barber became notorious as one of the first top National Hockey League players to "perfect" the art of diving (i.e., inducing the referee to call undeserved penalties on the opposition). While this dubious distinction was considered clever in some quarters, it was viewed by devotees as a detriment to The Game and an unfortunate trend-setter.

No less debatable were Barber's nomination and acceptance into the Hockey Hall of Fame. Did his record earn him the honor? Some thought not, but Barber did make it to the shrine, and his credentials as one of the foremost Flyers

BILL BARBER

Born: Collander, Ontario, July 11, 1952

Position: Left Wing

NHL Teams: Philadelphia, 1972-85

Awards/Honors: First Team All-Star, 1976; Second Team All-Star, 1979, 81; Jersey #7 retired by Flyers, March 6. 1986; Flyers Hall of Fame, 1989; Hockey Hall of Fame, 1990; Flyers Class Guy Award, 1981; Flyers 100-Point Club, 1975-76; Flyers 50-Goal Club, 1975-76

Coaching: Flyers Head Coach, 2000-02

Despite leading all rookie scorers in 1972-73, Bill Barber (far left) lost out on Rookie of the Year honors to the Rangers' Steve Vickers.

are impeccable. He played 13 seasons, scoring 420 goals and 463 assists for 883 points, second best on the Flyers' all-time scoring list. Bill was a pivotal member of Philadelphia's two Stanley Cup-winning teams in 1974 and 1975. Although he did not win the Calder Trophy in 1972-73—Steve Vickers of the New York Rangers took the prize—many critics contend that Barber was more deserving of the award. Barber had topped all of the first-year players in scoring with 30 goals and 34 assists and was a better all-round player than Vickers, but some-how, the Ranger carried the day when the voting was completed.

How did it happen? Flyers coach Fred Shero had a theory.

"Vickers was a type—a good goal-scorer," Shero explained. "He had a good touch around the net. But Barber was a better all-round player."

Bill proved Shero right by thoroughly outplaying Vickers over their NHL careers and winning two Cups while the Ranger won none. But in the beginning there was no certainty that Barber would evolve into a star although Flyers general manager Keith Allen had faith that he would eventually excel. Allen supported Barber from the beginning, perceiving assets that others over-looked.

"Bill turned out to be a helluva player," said Allen. "It took a bit of time, but even in his rookie season Bill was recognized by the right hockey people. I remember at the end of the 1973 Cup series with Montreal, Jimmy Roberts of the Canadiens told me that he didn't realize what a great hockey player Bill was and what a good skater he was. That was quite a tribute."

Flyers bird dogs were not that surprised. They had touted Barber after watching him play junior hockey and made Bill Philadelphia's first choice in the 1972 NHL amateur draft. A native of Callander, Ontario, and one of five brothers, Bill had been encouraged to play hockey by his father, who hoped that at least one of his sons would make it to the NHL.

Bill recalled, "Just to make sure we had everything going for us, Dad built us a rink that was almost regulation size. He had hydro poles put up and lights strung out like a big-league arena. That's where I learned to play."

The homemade rink made a better player—and a better person—out of him.

"It snowed a lot up where I came from," Barber remembered. "We'd get through plowing a foot of it off the rink and then the snow would start again. So I had to clear another foot of it. All that ploughing was the thing that made my arms as strong as they were when I got to the NHL."

Barber cut his puck teeth with three years in juniors with Kitchener of the Ontario Hockey Association. He scored 127 goals and 171 assists playing all forward

Bill Barber is well-sandwiched by the Rangers.

positions. After the Flyers drafted him, he was dispatched to Richmond of the American Hockey League for seasoning.

"I never realized that checking in the NHL was so hard or important," Barber asserted. "I learned that there was a world of difference between Richmond and the NHL. You wouldn't believe all the breakaways I had in the AHL."

After a month in the minors, Barber was promoted to The Show, replacing Flyers stalwart Bill Flett, who

---

Bill recalled, "Just to make sure we had everything going for us, Dad built us a rink that was almost regulation size. He had hydro poles put up and lights strung out like a big-league arena. That's where I learned to play."

---

had been sidelined with a sprained knee. Barber failed to score in his first two games but played well enough to continue taking regular turns.

"Finally, I broke the ice in a game against Buffalo," Bill recalled. "We won the game, 5-3, and I got two goals and two assists. That clinched it for me."

For a couple of months, Barber played left wing on a line with Rick MacLeish and Gary Dornhoefer. Then he was teamed with Flett and center Bobby Clarke. By this time, everyone on Broad Street knew that he was here to stay.

After Barber's 64-point rookie year, he climbed to 69 points in 1973-74 and followed that with a career-high 50-goal season in 1975-76. He added 62 assists for a total of 112 points.

His scoring potency also was evident during the playoffs. In helping the Flyers to their second straight Cup in the spring of 1975, he totalled six goals and seven assists for 13 points in 16 games.

Although he never enjoyed another 100-point season after 1975-76, Barber continued to ring up impressive totals. His second best year was 1981-82, when he scored 45 goals and 44 assists for 89 points.

Bill's career lasted through 1985, and in that time he won the following honors: First Team NHL All-Star in 1976; Second Team NHL All-Star in both 1979 and 1981; Seven-time participant in the NHL's mid season All-Star Game and Flyers Class Guy Award in 1981.

Shero likened Barber to Rangers Hall of Fame right wing Andy Bathgate.

"As soon as Bill stepped out on the ice you knew he was a hockey player and was going to be better than most of the others. He had the same sort of class and finesse with the puck—and the hockey brains—that Bathgate had. And when some of the other teams started to challenge Bill, he fought back and fought back well. Bathgate, you'll remember, was quite a fighter himself; one of the best."

Yet Barber had only one season of more than 100 penalty minutes–1975-76, when he totalled 104 minutes. The sum total is a distinguished career that was marred only by the voting oversight in 1973 when Bill was denied the Calder Trophy he so richly deserved.

Barber: "I once was talking to my dad about it and he said that winning the Calder would have been nice. And I agree. Who wouldn't have wanted it? But my goal was never the trophies. My goal was to concentrate in every game, to be a better player and help Philadelphia win a Stanley Cup."

In that sense, Bill Barber succeeded—twice!

As intense as he was as a player, Bill was equally consumed as a coach, starting in 1984-85 at Hershey.

When the Flyers put a farm team in The Spectrum in 1996-97, Bill demonstrated that he was one of the best head coaches in the minors. For three straight years the Phantoms finished first in the Mid-Atlantic Division, and in 1997-98 his club won the Calder Cup, emblematic of the American League Championship.

He was named the fourteenth head coach in Flyers history during the 2000-01 season and led the club to second place in the Atlantic Division.

A year later his team finished first in the Atlantic with a record of 42-27-10-3.

Despite the fact that the Flyers' 97 points were just three shy of the top rank in the Eastern Conference, Barber was fired as coach after the Flyers were knocked out of the playoffs by the Ottawa Senators.

Reggie Leach

There is nothing more glamorous in sports than the power hitter. Babe Ruth demonstrated the point in baseball, and Bobby Hull would do likewise in the National Hockey League. The advent of the slap shot, the banana blade and the high-tech stick enabled attackers to fire the puck harder than it ever was delivered during the pre-expansion era of the 1950s, 1940s and earlier. Hence, such nicknames as Boom Boom and The Golden Jet accompanied the arrival of hockey's new power shooters.

One of the most devastating shooters of any NHL epoch was Reggie Leach of Philadelphia. Originally a right wing with the Boston Bruins (1970-72) and later the California Golden Seals, Leach did not blossom into a superstar until he reached Broad Street in 1974. Suddenly, all the gears began meshing in this scoring machine, and under the guidance of coach Fred Shero, Leach smoothed his rough edges and became a significant member of the Stanley Cup championship team.

But while teammate Bobby Clarke was more renowned for his tenacity and Bill Barber for his versatility, Leach dazzled goaltenders—including his own Bernie Parent—with a devastating slap shot.

REGGIE LEACH

Born: Riverton, Manitoba, April 23, 1950

Position: Right Wing

NHL Teams: Boston, 1970-72; California, 1972-74; Philadelphia, 1974-82

Awards/Honors: Conn Smythe Trophy, 1976; Second Team All-Star, 1976; Flyers 50-Goal Club, 1975-76; Flyers Hall of Fame, 1992

Arguably the hardest shot of any Flyer—Reggie Leach.

"He's murder on goaltenders," said Parent. "He gets his shot off so quickly, with so little body movement, that there's no time to get set. He has strong forearms and good balance with his body when he shoots. Any time he gets near the circles he can beat you. You give him a little opening and he puts the puck there and beats you. He is the most dangerous guy in the league shooting backhand or forehand."

The statistics added to the Leach legend. In eight seasons as a Flyer, he scored 306 goals and added 208 assists. The total of 514 points ranks him seventh on the club's all-time list. None of this could have been forecast when he skated for Boston or California. As a younger player, he was one-dimensional and given to periods of loafing.

"I'd play in spurts," he admitted. "I played when I wanted to and not bother when I didn't want to. I'd go for the bonus and then pack it in."

When Leach arrived at The Spectrum, Shero dedicated himself to turning the hard shooter into a more reliable performer.

Shero: "He had been used to doing whatever he wanted. Like most hockey players, he didn't have the slightest idea about playing a disciplined game in every zone."

The metamorphosis from indolent stick handler into a star did not come easy nor did it come fast. Leach started slowly with the Flyers but he was encouraged by Clarke and admonished by Shero. The coach's warning was explicit: "You have to go beyond yourself. Have you ever done that?"

"I don't think so," Leach softly responded.

Starting the 1974-75 season, Leach had scored just three times in his first 20 games. But after his chat with Shero, Leach fired 42 goals in his next 60 games and earned the nickname "Rifle." Considerable credit for the transformation belonged to Clarke, who had skated alongside Leach on the Flin Flon Bombers of the Western Canada Hockey League. It was Clarke who had insisted that general manager Keith Allen trade for Leach and it was Clarke, along with Barber, who fed Leach such delicious passes that led to the 45 goals from The Rifle. The idea was for either Clarke or Barber to carry the puck over the enemy blue line and then determine whether Leach was available for a pass.

"He's murder on goaltenders," said Parent. "... He is the most dangerous guy in the league shooting backhand or forehand."

Clarke: "I knew what he could do and where he was going to be. I knew what shots he liked and I also knew that there was no way that I was going to score from the blue line although Reggie surely could. He could take a pass and wrist the puck in one motion. I couldn't

Reggie Leach smiles as he skates past Boston's Johnny Bucyk.

score much from 25 feet out but I knew that Leach could, and I had seen him score goals from some impossible angles. So what was better for us, me going into the corners and digging out the puck for him or the other way around?"

Leach got the message and responded in kind.

"I knew that all I had to do was skate to an open spot on the ice and that I would get the puck from Clarkie, and usually right on my stick. Then, it was just a matter of pulling the trigger."

Barber was equally cooperative and understanding of his linemate's offensive skills. What impressed Barber most of all—as it did opposition goaltenders—was the potency and style of The Rifle's shot.

"Reggie didn't take the big windup," Barber revealed. "He didn't have to tee up the puck and slap it. He had such a great wrist shot—with real hardness to it —that he could wrist the rubber or slap it if the spirit moved him.

"The trick was that he would get himself in good position. He had the repertoire, including a deadly shooting backhand. And he could score from the right side or left side; it didn't matter which."

One episode spoke mightily about the Leach shot. On the night of May 6, 1976, the Flyers and Bruins were locked in a Game 5 playoff collision that was personally settled by Leach. He scored five goals to destroy the foe. On the first goal Leach streaked down the left side to beat the Boston defenders and fired a slap shot past goalie Gilles Gilbert. On goal two, Leach took a pass from Clarke on the right side and cracked a rising slapper past Gilbert. For number three, Leach displayed his puck handling skills. He started a rush from his own end of the ice, eluded Boston's Steve Langdon and from the circles flicked an off-balance backhander by the surprised Gilbert. Number four came on Leach's blazing wrist shot. Clarke dropped the puck to him—again on the right side—and Reg's far-corner wrist shot eluded the goaltender. For his fifth and final tally, Leach again teamed with Clarke. The two performed a give-and-go at center ice with Clarke zipping a nifty break-in pass on to Leach's stick. Leach fired home a heavy backhand shot from the left circle.

Leach led the way for Philadelphia when the Flyers aimed for a third straight Stanley Cup in 1975-76. He was able to take them to the finals against the Montreal Canadiens, but the Cup eluded their grasp.

Nevertheless, The Rifle would finish the 1976 playoffs with a league-leading 19 goals and 24 points. Although the Habs swept the Flyers out of the finals in four straight games, Leach still brought home the Conn Smythe Trophy as most valuable player of the playoffs.

For Reggie, it was a fitting end to a historic season. During the regular campaign he netted 61 goals. That coupled with his 19 in the playoffs made him the first ever big-leaguer to score 80 goals in one season, playoffs included.

Leach remained a Flyer through 1982 when he was dealt to the Detroit Red Wings. His NHL career concluded after that one season in the Motor City. In addition to the Conn Smythe Trophy, Reggie was named to the NHL Second All-Star Team in 1976 and in 1992 was placed in the Flyers Hall of Fame. More than anything, Reggie Leach was a sharpshooter who fully earned his sobriquet, The Rifle.

Rick MacLeish

Rick MacLeish. Mention the name to any Philadelphia hockey fan who happened to be in The Spectrum on the night when it finally happened, and he—or she—will immediately mention THE goal. The date was May 19, 1974. The Flyers were facing the Boston Bruins. It was the sixth game of the Stanley Cup finals and somehow, Philadelphia was leading the series, three games to two. Until that point in time, no expansion team had ever won a Stanley Cup. Few, if any, experts anticipated that Fred Shero's skaters could defeat a club that already had won championships in 1970 and 1972. The Big, Bad Bruins already had proven to be one of the most formidable teams in history. Paced by high-scoring Hall of Famers Phil Esposito and Bobby Orr, the Bostonians were favored to win again in 1974.

But they did not bargain for the amazing MacLeish. Heading into Game 6, he had collected a playoff-leading dozen goals, three more than Esposito. Fortunately for the Flyers, he was not finished with his work. With the score deadlocked at zero—and almost 15 minutes gone in the first period—MacLeish took a pass from defenseman Andre (Moose) Dupont and fired it past Bruins goaltender Gilles Gilbert.

RICHARD GEORGE "RICK" MacLEISH

BORN: Lindsay, Ontario, January 3, 1950

Position: Center

NHL Teams: Philadelphia, 1970-81; Hartford, 1981-82; Pittsburgh, 1982-83; Philadelphia, 1983-84; Detroit, 1984

Awards/Honors: Elected to Flyers Hall of Fame, 1990

Rick MacLeish is forever immortalized for his Stanley Cup-winning goals against Boston in 1974.

Rick MacLeish. *Mention the name to any Philadelphia hockey fan who happened to be in The Spectrum on the night when it finally happened, and he—or she—will immediately mention THE goal.*

Somehow—almost magically—the Flyers weathered the Bruins' endless assaults, and when the final green light signalled the game's end, Bernie Parent owned a shutout and MacLeish's "Shot Heard 'Round Broad Street" proved to be the Stanley Cup winner. As a neat postscript to the triumph, Rick also led all 1974 playoff scorers with 22 points.

This hardly was a fluke. A year later, as the Flyers defended their championship, MacLeish was at the head of the scoring pack with 20 points as the Broad Streeters defeated the Buffalo Sabres in six games.

In retrospect it's hard to imagine that the Flyers did not acquire MacLeish from the Bruins at the point of a gun. They simply sent goalie Parent to the Toronto Maple Leafs who, in turn, dispatched their left winger Mike Walton to the Bruins. Boston then sent MacLeish to Philadelphia. That was on February 1, 1970. Three years later, MacLeish was en route to a 50-goal season. In between there were some hard times for MacLeish, for the Flyers high command and especially for a Philadelphia scout named Les Moore.

On the day of the big trade, Moore went out on a limb.

"MacLeish," he said, "will score 15 goals between now and the end of the season."

Rick came up 13 goals short of Moore's prediction. Then, in the first 17 games of the 1971-72 campaign, MacLeish managed just one goal for the Flyers. The next thing he knew, he was toiling for Richmond in the American Hockey League. He had dropped from prospect to minor-leaguer. Somewhere along the way, Moore and the Flyers parted company, although the Spectrum general staff never quite gave up on MacLeish.

"We were willing to be patient," said general manager Keith Allen. "Rick needed some work and he wasn't getting it. In a way he was a victim of his own success in junior hockey. He was so good down there that he didn't have to bear down during his final year."

True, MacLeish had been a sensation in the Ontario Hockey Association. In his last season with Peterborough, he had 45 goals and 56 assists in 34 games. He was the fourth player selected in the year's amateur draft—by the Bruins—and spent his first professional season with Oklahoma City of the Central League.

At the time, Boston rated MacLeish as the best forward in the Bruins' farm system. That, however, was news to Rick, who was less than enthused about the treatment he received in the minors.

"I didn't learn a thing in Oklahoma City," he recalled. "The coach [Murray Davison] never told me anything. All he had us do was skate and do line rushes in practice."

In Oklahoma, MacLeish was playing at wing in-

Rick MacLeish counterattacks with Bill Barber bringing up the rear.

stead of center, his normal position.

"I don't want to knock anybody," Rick later reflected, "but my centerman was not the greatest and I never got on the ice on a power play."

Whatever the reason—or reasons—MacLeish had scored just 13 goals in 46 games with Oklahoma City when the Bruins, in effect, decided to sacrifice future possibilities for instant help in the form of an established NHL player, Mike Walton. On the other hand, the Flyers were under little pressure to win the Stanley Cup immediately. Thus, Keith Allen was able to say of the trade, "We dealt for youth and we're willing to wait for the kids, like Rick, to develop." But then he added, somewhat ominously, "Going to Richmond will be MacLeish's big test. It will prove whether or not he has the desire to play in the NHL."

As it happened, he did. In 42 AHL games he netted 24 goals. More than that, he showed a willingness to play defensive as well as offensive hockey. He hit people and he tried to excel in every phase of the game. He also had matured sufficiently to realize that while the Flyers were willing to be patient, they would not wait indefinitely for him to become a major-leaguer.

"I'm sure they were disappointed," Rick allowed.

At his next training camp, MacLeish found himself competing against a cerebral center named Bill Clement. It was an interesting test for MacLeish; was he getting the message? Would he respond to it?

Apparently, the answer was in the affirmative. He made the big club and never looked back. Centering for veteran Gary Dornhoefer and rookie Bill Barber, MacLeish scored 17 goals in Philadelphia's first 29 games.

"He can skate, pass and shoot," Dornhoefer said. "He also works as hard as

hell."

By season's end, MacLeish had 50 goals, making him—at age 21—the youngest player in NHL history to reach that magic figure. He also had 50 assists!

Putting it all in perspective, the numbers revealed that MacLeish finished only four points behind the NHL's Hart Trophy winner, Flyers captain Clarke.

"I've seen a lot of good hockey players but I've never seen anyone as loose as Ricky," Clarke recalled in tribute to his teammate. "They just can't get the puck away from him."

In true Flyers tradition, MacLeish also betrayed a tough side. Once, in junior hockey, he fought with Bob Kelly, a notorious pugilist. The two became teammates on Broad Street when MacLeish joined the club in 1971.

"Rick just stood there and slugged it out with me," Kelly recalled. "I can honestly say I never lost a fight in juniors, but that was one that I did not win."

A solid 5'11", 185 pounds, MacLeish claimed to have gone undefeated in the Central League.

"I had seven fights and never lost one."

Beyond his fighting ability, MacLeish displayed a

Rick MacLeish (19) and Jim Watson flank Islanders captain Eddie Westfall.

willingness to play hurt. Early one season he suffered an ankle injury in a game against the Pittsburgh Penguins. It was painful, but he insisted on playing through the hurt the next night against the Chicago Blackhawks.

"MacLeish shook off that ankle injury very well," coach Fred Shero remembered. "But against the Hawks he got rapped on the head by a stick and the doctor told me not to play him after the first period. Still, he did everything for us, including winning faceoffs. He showed me that he played okay even when he was dizzy."

MacLeish also scored three goals that night as the Flyers beat Chicago, 5-3. It was the portent of even bigger things to come in a career that has surprisingly been overlooked by many hockey historians.

In the opening game of the 1973 Stanley Cup semifinal pitting Philadelphia against Montreal, MacLeish scored the winning goal in a 5-4 victory at 2:56 of the first overtime period. But he missed the next two games because of a 101-degree fever, and even when he did return he was too drained to help the Flyers. Had MacLeish been fit, the outcome of that series might have been different. Even so, it was a highly successful season at The Spectrum and for MacLeish. It was the year he became a star, although he modestly has always maintained otherwise.

"It was just a matter of coincidence," he said in retrospect. "Once I realized I had a place on the team, I started to work harder."

Dornhoefer: "The kind of big build-up that Rick entered the league with isn't good for anybody because it's so hard to live up to. It just means so much additional pressure."

MacLeish accepted that pressure and handled it as well as anyone could have expected. He played for Philadelphia until 1981-82 when he moved on to the Hartford Whalers. He concluded his NHL career in 1984 with the Detroit Red Wings after a short stint in Pittsburgh with the Penguins.

In 1990 Rick MacLeish was elected to the Flyers Hall of Fame. Surely, the voters must have had that big, BIG goal against the Boston Bruins in 1974 on their collective minds. After all, it did produce the first Stanley Cup championship for Philadelphia, which should have been enough reason to enshrine the native of Lindsay, Ontario.

Tim Kerr wasn't the original power forward, but he was one of the best ever.

Tim Kerr

I n many ways the resemblance between Hall of Famer Jean Beliveau —one of the legendary Montreal Canadiens aces—and Tim Kerr is striking.

Beliveau was physically huge at the time he performed in the National Hockey League but less than physically intimidating in terms of aggressive play.

"Given his choice," teammate Dickie Moore once said of Beliveau, "he would prefer to play a finesse game than a fighting game. But there were times when Big Jean would get mad, and when that happened, look out."

Ditto for the 6'3", 230-pound Flyer. The Windsor, Ontario native could —and would—get angry from time to time, but those occasions were the exception rather than the rule. And the rest of the NHL was pleased about that state of affairs.

"The NHL was lucky that Kerr was easygoing," said Hall of Famer Bryan Trottier, who, as a New York Islander, played against Tim. "If he had ever been a mean player—or a goon—with his size and strength, we would all have been in big trouble."

As it happened, the rest of the NHL was in big trouble because of Kerr's scoring proclivities. In the 1984-85 season, for example, he reached the level of 54 goals and 44 assists for 98 points. It was his second 54-goal year, the first being 1983-84 when he reached 39 assists. What could he do for an encore? During the 1985-86 campaign he rang up 58 goals and did precisely that again in 1986-87.

TIMOTHY KERR

BORN: Windsor, Ontario, January 5, 1960

Position: Center

NHL Teams: Philadelphia, 1980-91; N.Y. Rangers, 1991-92, Hartford, 1992-93

Awards/Honors: Second Team All-Star, 1987; Masterton Trophy, 1989; Flyers Hall of Fame, 1994

Not bad for a young man who had been regarded as lazy when he skated for the Kingston Canadiens in the Ontario Hockey Association's Junior A division. Although he scored 40 goals during the 1979-80 season with Kingston, he was bypassed in the annual draft by each of the NHL clubs. Fortunately for the Flyers, he was signed as a free agent by Philadelphia on the advice of scout Eric Coville.

"I believed in him right from the start," said Coville. "You don't know the heat I took before we signed him. Not many people rated him high, but I thought he had the potential to be a first-round-calibre pick. He could skate, he was stronger than anyone we had at center, and he was a better faceoff man than anyone we had. His shot, with those powerful wrists and that good eye, was excellent."

Coville remained the unsung Flyers hero in the Kerr saga, not merely for fingering Kerr and his skills but also for encouraging the young man before he actually put on the skates in Philadelphia.

"I had seen him play many times, but I had never spoken to him," Coville recalled. "I told him that I was talking to him the same way I'd talk to my own son. I told him he could be as good as he wanted to be, as long as he was willing to work."

Kerr made his debut as a Flyer in 1980-81 and as an NHL rookie reached 22 goals, which didn't exactly qualify him for the Calder Trophy as the top freshman in the league. Suffering a slight "sophomore slump," Kerr dipped to 21 goals in 1981-82. A series of injuries the following year limited him to 24 games, but he managed almost a goal every other game and finished with 11 red lights. However, it was the season that set the stage for his great leap forward in 1983-84.

Kerr had come to realize that he should play the game in a manner reminiscent of Bruins scoring machine Phil Esposito. That is, camp in front of the net and pounce on loose pucks because few defenders will be able to legally move him out of the way.

"My style wasn't hard to figure," Kerr explained. "I wasn't the type of player who was going to skate around a couple of guys with the puck and go in and score. For me to be successful, the other guys on the ice had to get me the puck. They usually knew where I was. I wasn't too far from the same spot all the time."

"Given his choice," teammate Dickie Moore once said of Beliveau, "he would prefer to play a finesse game than a fighting game. But there were times when Big Jean would get mad, and when that happened, look out."

E. J. McGuire, who was assistant coach to Mike Keenan at the time of Kerr's emergence, helped develop Tim into an all-round player. Defense was stressed as much as offense, and the big guy listened.

"I knew he matured," said McGuire, "because he was willing to play defense and was willing to learn. I knew that the goals would come for him, but it was his ability to do the unglamorous things that had us pleased."

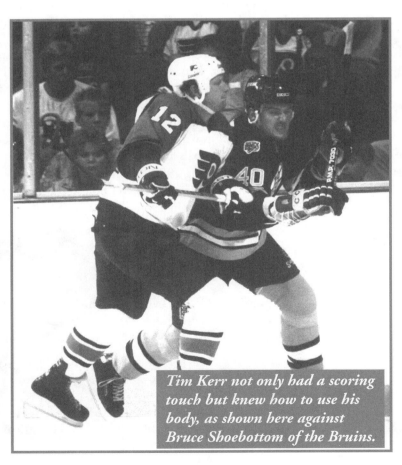

Tim Kerr not only had a scoring touch but knew how to use his body, as shown here against Bruce Shoebottom of the Bruins.

Equally pleasing were the numbers. He leaped from that 11-goal season to 54 the next year, a jump of 43 red lights.

"Actually," Kerr recalled, "I never set any goals for myself. I simply went out and tried to contribute to our success every game. At the end of the season, I would just add up the goals.

"Not that I would ever minimize goal-scoring. That was a very important part of the game, but I never wanted to say I was going to score this many or that many every year. But I did try to score every shift I was out there."

Ironically, after his first 54-goal year—during the summer of 1984—Kerr asked to be traded from Philadelphia.

"I felt that they might not have the confidence in me to offer me a good contract, and if that was true—if they felt my scoring 54 goals was a fluke that I couldn't repeat—then I wanted to be traded."

The Flyers stood by their man and re-signed him. He rewarded them with just the kind of production they had hoped for, and he also dispelled the notion that he could not be motivated enough to produce.

"The worry," said Bobby Clarke, "and the question was, would he work hard enough?"

Peter Zezel, who was a 19-year-old center for Kerr when Tim began popping goals regularly, knew that there should be no concern about the big fellow's work ethic.

"I remember the first time he scored four goals in a game," said Zezel. "Every time he would score, I would look over at Rick Tocchet and we would just shake our heads. We couldn't believe it. He was so strong and he had such great talent. You didn't have to be a fan to appreciate that.

"You had to wonder how the opposition was going to knock him off the puck. And that shot. The puck would come to him; he would put the stick down, and then, bam, before you could see it, it was in the net. Unbelievable!"

Opponents raved just as much as the Flyers. Ron Duguay, who played alongside Phil Esposito on the Rangers, perceived a distinct similarity in styles.

"Tim had the same instinct as Phil—to score goals."

Kerr starred for the Flyers clubs that reached the Stanley Cup finals in 1985 and 1987. He scored ten goals and four assists for 14 points in a dozen games in 1985. His 13 points in the 1987 round were comprised of eight goals and five assists. A severe shoulder injury sidelined him for all but eight games in 1987-88. He rebounded in 1988-89 to contribute 48 goals and 40 assists for 88 points as the Flyers reached the conference finals. During 19 playoff games he had 14 goals and 11 assists for 25 points. He also won the Bill Masterton Trophy that season.

Kerr's production began slipping the next season, and by 1991 the Flyers had concluded that it was best to leave Tim exposed to the Expansion Draft. He was claimed by San Jose but then dealt to the Rangers for Brian Mullen and future considerations. He played 32 games for New York, scoring only seven goals and eleven assists. In eight playoff games he managed one goal. The Rangers traded him to Hartford in July 1992 for future considerations. He collected six assists in 22 games for the Whalers but not a single goal.

Tim retired after that season. To this day he is remembered for many accomplishments, but a headline over a magazine story dating back to April 1985 says it all about Tim Kerr—IMMOVABLE IN FRONT OF THE NET.

Tim Kerr on location—threatening Toronto goalie Alan Bester.

Defenseman Mark Howe won the Barry Ashbee Trophy as the best Flyers defenseman in 1983, 1986, 1987, and 1988.

Mark Howe

One can only imagine how differently Mark Howe would have been viewed had he not been the son of immortal right wing Gordie Howe. Rather than being compared with arguably the greatest all-around player of all time, Mark would have been judged on his own merits and accomplishments. But nobody has ever argued that life is fair, and so Mark Howe always will be measured against his Hall of Famer father and all the feats his dad accomplished over three decades of sparkling performances.

Having said this, it must be emphasized that Mark Howe not only suffered the comparisons nobly but also carved out a distinguished career that featured a run in Philadelphia (1982-92) that was as good as any Flyers fan ever could have asked.

Before Howe ever reached Broad Street, he had been spotlighted both because of his father and at times in spite of him. In fact, when Mark still was a teenager, he had been tabbed as a potential All-Star. At age 14, Mark was a leading member of the 1969-70 U.S. National Junior Champion Detroit Red

MARK STEVEN HOWE

Born: Detroit, Michigan, May 28, 1955

Position: Defense

NHL Teams: Hartford, 1979-82; Philadelphia, 1983-92; Detroit, 1992-95.

WHA Teams: Houston, 1973-77; New Engand, 1977-79

Awards/Honors: WHA Rookie of the Year, 1974; Played in WHA All-Star Game, WHA Second Team All-Star, 1974, 77, WHA First Team All-Star, 1979; NHL First Team All-Star 1983, 86, 87; Emery Edge Award, 1986; Voted Best Flyers Defenseman, 1983, 1986-88; Voted Flyers MVP, 1986

Gordie Howe's son, Mark Howe, emerged as one of the best Flyer defensemen of all time.

championship team, he did help the Flyers to the finals in both 1985 and 1987. (He did likewise with the Detroit Red Wings in 1995.) Unlike other offensive-minded defensemen, Howe also did a laudable job behind the blue line. His best season, numerically, was 1985-86, when he totalled 24 goals and 58 assists for 82 points. It was an impressive season, but as Howe has often stated, any year he played after December 27, 1980 was pure gravy to him.

The reason was quite simple: Howe was nearly killed during a game at the Hartford Civic Center while playing against the New York Islanders. Crosschecked by defenseman Bob Lorimer, Howe crashed into the sidepost of the net and then fell into the cage itself. In those days the nets were constructed in a more dangerous manner than the contemporary cages. The earlier goals featured a steel protrusion which extended from the back of the net, along the ice, toward the crease. It was meant to contain the puck, preventing shots from rebounding quickly out of the goal area. Few regarded this bayonet-like device as dangerous since it was flat to the ice and rarely was moved from this position.

But on this night the net rose off its mounting and tilted back, leaving its spear-like center prong sticking up as Howe—sliding uncontrollably—pitched into it back-first. Six inches of steel plunged into Mark's lower back and buttock, slicing through fat, touching the wall of the rectum and grazing the sphincter muscle—which controls continence and elimination—and then twisted toward his hip. It couldn't have been worse had he been bayoneted on the battlefield.

What followed was a combination of nightmare and miracle. As Howe pulled himself from the prong, he began to bleed heavily. He didn't know whether the makeshift spear had touched his spine or sliced through the organs. All he could tell those crowded around him was

Wings. At 16, he was a member of the 1972 silver medal-winning U.S. Olympic Team, one of the most underrated squads Uncle Sam ever produced. At 17, he starred for the Toronto Marlboros, winners of the 1973 Memorial Cup, emblematic of Canada's junior championship. At 18 and 19, Mark starred alongside his father and brother Marty as a member of the Avco-World trophy-winning Houston Aeros of the World Hockey Association.

Before he became a Flyer, Mark was making history. He was the first NHL defenseman to score two short-handed goals in a single period (October 9, 1980 at St. Louis) and the second defenseman in the NHL to score three goals in one period (Ian Turnbull was the first in 1976-77). Mark also holds the Hartford Whalers' (now Carolina Hurricanes) record of points in 21 straight games, set in 1978-79.

Although Mark never played for a Stanley Cup

that he had been stabbed. The full extent of the injury was masked by his equipment. There was no ambulance at the Civic Center and no first-aid equipment with which to deal with the shock and heavy bleeding.

Once an ambulance finally arrived, Howe was rushed to the hospital where he was treated in the emergency room. The bleeding was stopped, but it was an hour before Dr. John DeMaio, the family's physician-surgeon arrived. He had only been told that Howe had suffered a "laceration." Later he confessed to Mark's mother, Colleen Howe, that had he known the gravity of the injury, he would have insisted that treatment begin immediately.

"God had Mark in His arms at that moment," said Colleen, "but our blessing is that He went in there with

Mark was the first NHL defenseman to score two short-handed goals in a single period and the second defenseman in the NHL to score three goals in one period.

Leaning into the Rangers' Tomas Sandstrom, Mark Howe fights for puck control.

Mark and Mark survived with his career and his body."

Mark's recuperative powers were so strong that he only missed 17 games that season and finished with 19 goals and 46 assists, an accomplishment for any backliner.

Significantly, the injury inspired a major design change in the traditional Art Ross-type net. The steel centerpiece was removed and the net sat first on magnets and later a rubber piping to give it flexibility in case of collision.

Having fully recovered from the injury, Howe eventually was traded to the Flyers in August 1982. The deal was one of the biggest of the decade. Philadelphia not only received Mark but also the Whalers' third-round draft choice in exchange for Ken Linseman, Greg Adams and Philadelphia's first- and third-round draft choices in the 1983 entry draft.

In no time at all, Howe emerged as a dominant member of the Broad Street sextet although his dominance had more to do with finesse and less with belligerence. To some observers, Mark's style suggested a modified Bobby Orr. Howe skated as effortlessly as the immortal Bruin defenseman. Mark had the same offensive tendencies and a similar body style, and each was fearless in his own way.

That he quickly became the most significant two-way defenseman in Flyers history was not a total surprise. Howe's significant skating and passing abilities had previously helped him to a six-season World Hockey Association career that resulted in 208 goals and 296 assists for a total of 504 points. After moving to the NHL with the Whalers—part of the NHL-WHA merger— Howe played 16 more seasons during which he racked up 197 goals, 545 assists and 742 points. Thus, Mark played a total of 22 major-league seasons and totalled 405 goals, 841 assists and 1,246 points, outstanding numbers for any professional and enough to qualify him for the Hockey Hall of Fame at some point in the future. As a Flyer, he was voted a First Team NHL All-Star in 1983, 1986 and 1987. He also won the NHL's Emery Edge award in 1986 and was voted the best Flyers defenseman in 1983 as well as 1986-88. In 1986 he was named Philadelphia's most valuable player.

Taciturn and always underplaying his accomplishments, Mark proved as graceful in the locker room as he was on the ice. He clearly established himself as one of the most impressive all-around backliners in the decade of the 1980s and one of the best advertisements the Flyers ever had.

After the 1991-92 season he was traded to the Detroit Red Wings, the team for which his father had toiled so long. He remained an active NHL player until the conclusion of the 1995 Red Wings-Devils finals, after which he retired.

Mark's credentials have earned him praise from some of the NHL's most notable personalities, but perhaps the greatest endorsement came from his father.

"I'm very proud of Mark," Gordie Howe concluded. "He had a wonderful career."

And much of that wonderful career was spent in Philadelphia during one of the most glorious periods in Flyers history. If there was a classier player ever to wear the orange and black than Mark Howe, it would be difficult to find him.

Eric Lindros

No player ever created a bigger stir in the hockey world before becoming a Philadelphia Flyer than Eric Lindros. The hulking son of Carl and Bonnie Lindros, brother of Brett, Eric was the most publicized Canadian junior hockey player in history, more than Wayne Gretzky, more than Mario Lemieux. During his last season of amateur hockey with the Oshawa Generals in 1991-92, Eric was followed by the media more closely than most National Hockey League aces and interviewed as often as rock stars. Based on his size and consummate ability for his age, Lindros suggested all the potential of a Lemieux and Gretzky rolled into one handsome stick handler.

"The media would keep asking Eric, 'Are you a Gretzky? Are you a Lemieux? Or are you more like Mark Messier?'" said Andy Weidenbach, coach of the Junior Compuware team. "Eric always would reply, 'I'm a Lindros.'"

Lindros was a complicated youngster, not given to easy interpretation. His parents closely monitored his progress, and the result was seemingly endless controversy over where he would play and when. Or if he would play at all.

ERIC LINDROS

BORN: London, Ontario, February 28, 1973

Position: Center

NHL Teams: Phildelphia 1992-2001, New York Rangers 2001-present. Captain, Philadelphia, 1994-2000.

Awards/Honors: NHL/Upper Deck All-Rookie Team, 1993; Played in 1994, 95, 96, 97 All-Star Game; First Team All-Star, 1995; Second Team All-Star, 1996; Bobby Clarke Trophy, 1994, 95, 96; *Sporting News* Player of the Year, 1995; *Sporting News* First Team All Star, 1995; Hart Trophy, 1995; *The Hockey News/* Mennen NHL Most Valuable Player, 1995; *The Hockey News/* Louisville Player of the Year, 1995; *The Hockey News* First All-Star Team, 1995; Lester B. Pearson Award, 1995; *The Hockey News* Second All-Star Team, 1996; Flyers 100-point Club, 1995-96; Bobby Clarke Trophy, 1999; Canadian Olympian, 1998, 2002; 1998, 1999, 2000 All-Star Game.

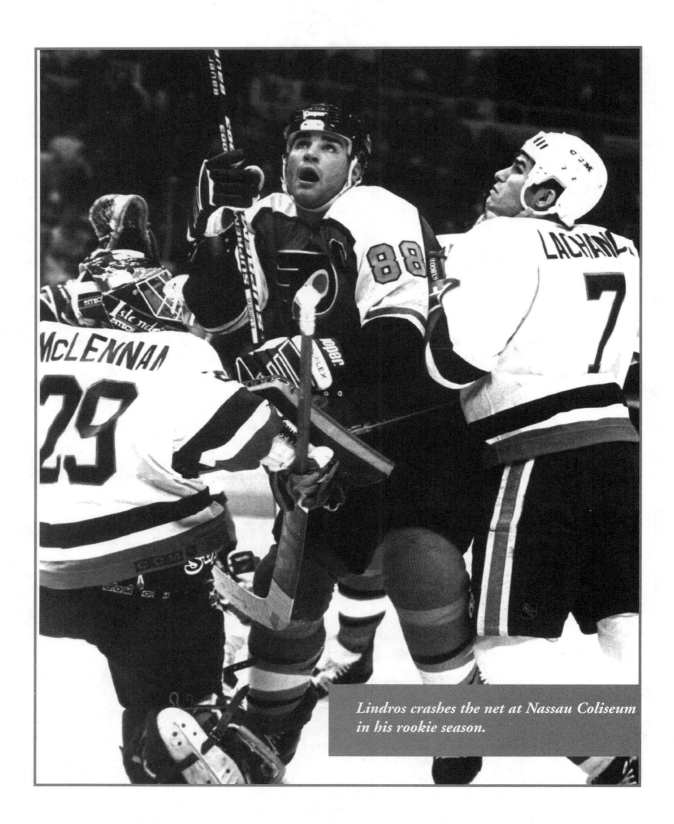

Lindros crashes the net at Nassau Coliseum in his rookie season.

King of the new Flyers era—Eric Lindros after signing with Philadelphia.

able the situation might become."

Rather than play for Quebec, Eric showed up for 13 games with Oshawa during the 1991-92 season. He also skated for the Canadian National Team and Canadian Olympic Team, not to mention in the Canada Cup.

Meanwhile, several National Hockey League teams, including the Rangers and Flyers, spent considerable time devising ways and means to obtain the Lindros signature. The showdown occurred during the league entry draft meetings in Montreal on June 20, 1992. Playing both the Rangers and Flyers against each other, Aubut finally concluded a controversial deal whose validity was immediately challenged. Philadelphia offered goalie Ron Hextall, defensemen Steve Duchesne, Kerry Huffman, centers Mike Ricci and Peter Forsberg as well as left wing Chris Simon and number-one draft picks in 1993 and 1994 plus $15 million for Lindros.

No matter how it was shaken, the exchange ranked as the most spectacular in hockey history, if not the most disputed. The Rangers had offered goalie John Vanbiesbrouck, defenseman James Patrick, forwards Darren Turcotte and Tony Amonte as well as an estimated $15 million cash for Lindros.

The Sault Ste. Marie Greyhounds were among the first to be dismissed by the Lindros Family. That was in May, 1989. For one thing, Eric did not want to be far from his Toronto home, and for another, he preferred being close to a university in order to take college courses while playing hockey.

By far the most notorious rejection was dealt to the Quebec Nordiques, who had drafted Lindros first overall in June, 1991. Although he went through the motions of adorning himself with a blue Quebec jersey, Eric had made it clear that he wanted no part of the team run by Marcel Aubut. Both his parents and his agent, Rick Curran, believed that predominantly francophone Quebec City would not be the most hospitable setting for the prodigy to thrive.

"Some people suggested Eric should give the Nordiques a try," said Curran, "and if things didn't work, then move on elsewhere. But it was not that simple. How do you get out once you're in? Eric realized that the system would never let him leave, no matter how intoler-

The Machiavellian moves notwithstanding, a settlement had to be made. To settle the Lindros tug of war, the league appointed a special abritrator, Larry Bertuzzi, who eventually approved the Flyers transaction. On July 15, 1992, the Flyers completed the biggest transaction in team history by signing Lindros to an unprecedented six-year contract.

No rookie ever was placed under a more sensitive microscope than the young behemoth. GREAT EXPECTATIONS ARE A TOUGH ORDER TO FILL shouted a headline that typified the outlook for Lindros.

Associated Press writer Barry Wilner summed it up thusly: "Superstars have a hard enough time living up to their billing. For a superstar-in-waiting, it's a virtually impossible task."

Lindros opened the 1992-93 campaign in the manner anticipated. One play symbolized the hopes and dreams of Philadelphia fans more than any other. It was an early-season game against the New Jersey Devils at

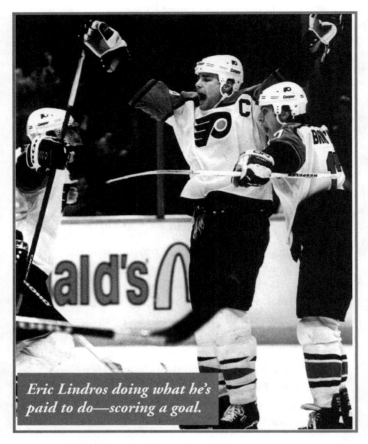

Eric Lindros doing what he's paid to do—scoring a goal.

"*The media would keep asking Eric, 'Are you a Gretzky? Are you a Lemieux? Or are you more like Mark Messier?'" said Andy Weidenbach, coach of the Junior Compuware team. "Eric always would reply, 'I'm a Lindros.'*"

The Spectrum. The contest was tied late in the third period when Eric stole the puck along the left boards near the center red line. As he gathered speed, Devils defenseman Scott Niedermayer sped toward the boards to block any passage. It appeared that Lindros was boxed into a no-move situation when he simply bowled over the enemy and swerved sharply to his right for a goalward thrust. Approximately two seconds later the red light had flashed and a capacity crowd rose in unison to toast the new hero.

At that point in time Lindros appeared hellbent for the Calder Trophy as NHL Rookie of the Year. Everything he did—and said—seemed just right.

"I'm not looking to be the guy who turns things around," Eric protested. "My role is to be a part of this team and we're basically a young team trying to develop something."

He centered a line with Brent Fedyk and Mark Recchi. The scouting report on Lindros read as follows: "He gets up to speed in a few strides and overpowers the opposition. He can dominate a game without scoring."

Recchi: "When we played together, he was only 19 but it was clear that he would get better as the years went

Jay and Ed Snider are delighted at having just signed the imposing young phenom, Eric Lindros.

on. I didn't think he would reach his peak until he was 24 or 25 years old."

The assumption, of course, was that Eric would achieve that superior level by avoiding injury. His overbearing image suggested a heavy tank that could crush the opposition but would be virtually invulnerable to counterattack.

"I am not some little freelancer who can wheel and deal and not hit anyone," said Lindros, bolstering the point.

This, however, would not be the case. From the beginning, he hit people, but they hit back. Some, such as rugged defensemen Darius Kasparaitis, Scott Stevens and Rich Pilon, hit back so hard that Lindros played in only 61 out of 84 games, missing 23 because of injuries. What's more, the Flyers missed the playoffs.

"I didn't expect it to come right away or overnight," Lindros explained. "It takes time."

Lindros finished his rookie season averaging more than a point a game (61-41-34-75), but he was a distant third in the Calder Trophy race for Rookie of the Year. Teemu Selanne was the clear-cut winner (132 points), followed by Joey Juneau (102). Lindros had 75. The Flyers high command had no choice but to be patient.

The 6'5" 240-pounder had a lot to commend. He was personable, attractive and just about everything the Philadelphians had hoped he would be, if not a leading scorer. And he was imposing. One day Bob Clarke put on his skates and played alongside Lindros in a scrimmage. When it was over, Clarke remarked, "When you stand there watching him, it looks like an apartment building coming at you."

Lindros knew from the get-go that his size would be a strategic asset and sometimes an intimidating one. Opponents have claimed that he's so big, he even sounds different when he churns across the ice.

"Listen for me," he once warned a foe, "you'll hear me coming."

Nevertheless, the skating high-rise missed 19 games in his sophomore year, 1993-94, but his production significantly increased (65-44-53-97). Despite playing four more games than the previous season, his penalty minutes dropped from 147 as a rookie to 103. He still was a marked man and he often was referred to as an opponent who rode into town "on the black horse." Some of

Welcome to Philadelphia, Eric.

his clashes, particularly with Scott Stevens, had already become classic.

"What goes around, comes around," Lindros explained. "That's true in all walks of life. There's always opportunities through the course of your career for someone you did something to that might have been cheap, for him to get you back—and it might be tenfold.

"My old teammate, Dave Brown, always talked about his little black book and you don't want to be in his little black book. I don't want to be in a black book."

But he still wasn't on a playoff team. In 1993-94 the Flyers missed again, and there were murmurs about whether he was capable of lifting the team to a higher level. Those questions finally were put to rest in 1994-95, the lockout-shortened season.

Shortly after play began in February 1995, the Flyers acquired John LeClair from Montreal and lined him up with Lindros and Mikael Renberg. The Legion of Doom trio was born, and Eric was off and flying. Because of the lockout-shortened year, he played only 46 games but still managed 29 goals and 41 assists for 70 points.

In his first NHL playoff, Lindros showed to advantage, particularly in the second round where he outplayed Mark Messier to lift Philadelphia to a series win over the defending champion Rangers. For a time it appeared as if the Flyers—and Lindros—could go all the way, but Stevens and the Devils intervened and they were out in six games. Nevertheless, Lindros seemed more relaxed, more open and ready for more prime-time starring roles.

"I didn't have my back up as much as I had before because [people are] not down my throat every time I turn a corner," he said. "I'm in a great organization. I play for a great team. I've got great linemates."

He also was developing a worrisome series of knee problems, usually occurring in the month of November. In 1992 it was his left knee. A year later it was his right knee. Then the left knee again in 1995. Still he played 73 games in 1995-96 and scored personal highs in all departments: 47 goals; 68 assists; 115 points. If ever a Philly team seemed primed to take a third Stanley Cup back to Broad Street, this club was it, and Lindros looked like the man who could pilot the cruise.

But once Philadelphia took on underdog Florida in the second round, Lindros became distracted and less effective. Targeted by rugged Panthers such as Ed Jovanovski, Lindros unraveled along with his teammates. They were knocked out in six games, leaving both Eric and the Flyers as a work in progress.

"People talk about defining greatness," said Lindros. "My ultimate goal is to be at the top of the stick, to succeed, to win championships and gold medals. Why else do you play? On the other hand, I don't think that because you don't win certain things it means you haven't been successful either.

"Look at Ray Bourque. He's played 19 seasons for the Bruins and doesn't have a Stanley Cup ring. Yet look at his career. He's one of the best defensemen ever in the league. It's hard to say that he hasn't been successful."

The closest Lindros came to earning a Stanley Cup ring was in the 1997 playoffs. As usual, his regular season was marred by mishap. He played only 52 games (32-47-79), but that was a mere prelude for a playoff run that looked oh-so-promising. Lindros would pump a dozen playoff goals in 19 postseason games. He would outduel Messier and hurtle Philadelphia over New York into the Stanley Cup finals against Detroit. Eric was only four wins away from Hockey's Holy Grail.

But it was not to be. The Red Wings threw a blanket over Philly's offense and swept the Flyers out of the tourney in four games. Not only was Lindros humbled, but his name became enmeshed in controversy. Reports had circulated that the big fellow was less than enchanted with coach Terry Murray and that something had to give.

There have been times when Eric Lindros simply leaped through the opposition.

After Murray was fired during the off season, like it or not, Lindros had the label "coach-killer" added to his dossier by critics who still found the captain wanting in key areas.

His supporters demanded patience. They pointed out that he would have an opportunity to demonstrate his leadership as well as artistry during the 1998 Olympic Winter Games at Nagano. With Mario Lemieux's retirement and Wayne Gretzky approaching his twilight years, Lindros was primed for a giant step forward in 1997-98. What he delivered was considerably less than that. At Nagano, Team Canada—captained by Lindros—didn't even qualify for a bronze medal, let alone a gold. His season in Philadelphia was pockmarked with problems. Once again, he was at least tangentially involved in clubhouse politics. Head coach Wayne Cashman—supposedly imported to soothe Lindros—was fired before season's end and replaced by Roger Neilson.

Meanwhile, Lindros was felled legitimately by a Kasparaitis check that limited his number of games played to 62. He still managed 30 goals and 42 assists for 72 points, but the 1998 playoffs would be his salvation, if there was to be any salvation at all.

There would be none. Skating against Dominik Hasek and the Buffalo Sabres, Lindros was virtually a non-factor. In five games he scored one goal, produced two assists and was minus-three in the plus-minus department. Philadelphia exited in five games, which was about as humiliating as any NHL defeat Lindros experienced.

Canadian author Allan Turowetz summed up the anti-Eric feeling thusly: "The big guy is more mythology than reality."

When the Flyers paid a fortune in players and cash for him, Lindros was expected to deliver a Stanley Cup either to The Spectrum or CoreStates Center. At the time, owner Ed Snider predicted that Lindros would bring Lord Stanley to Philadelphia in three years. Six years later, he still had not come through.

"Losing the Stanley Cup was disappointing," Lindros concluded, "but we'll get another chance. I just want to win. I don't care what it is or where it is."

Instead of getting better, the Lindros Saga in Philadelphia got worse by the month.

One of the most devastating blows was a body check thrown by New Jersey Devils defenseman Scott Stevens during Game 7 of the Flyers-Devils playoff at Philadelphia. Carrying the puck over the enemy blue line, Lindros was nailed with a crushing shoulder check that knocked him unconscious and out of the game. The Flyers were defeated and Lindros never was the same in Philadelphia after that—neither physically nor emotionally.

Where once Eric and general manager Bob Clarke had an avuncular relationship, it had turned sour to a point where general manager and player traded insults like tennis players exchanging volleys. Eventually the rift became irreparable. Lindros followed tradition, demanding a trade.

Once again, Lindros got his way. He was traded to the New York Rangers on August 20, 2001 for forwards Jan Hlavac, Pavel Brendl, defenseman Kim Johnsson and a third-round draft choice in the 2003 NHL entry draft.

As a Ranger, Lindros had a curious season. While he let the team in scoring with 73 points in 72 games—he also had a team-leading plus/minus rating of +19—the Rangers nevertheless missed the playoffs.

Eric, due to injuries, was sidelined for ten games, and coincidentally, the Broadway Blueshirts nose-dived when he was out. Concussions continue to plague him, and there was no certainty how much longer he could sustain a high level of play after absorbing another solid hit.

Pelle Lindbergh and the Vezina Trophy.

Pelle Lindbergh

Nobody will ever know precisely how great a goaltender Pelle Lindbergh ultimately would have been had he fulfilled his full potential in a complete National Hockey League career. The Swedish-born goaltender was killed instantly on November 10, 1986 in an automobile accident at the age of 26. At the time of his death, Lindbergh ranked among the league's premier puck stoppers and, according to many experts, seemed assured of another decade of Grade A goaltending.

Until that fatal moment on a dark road near the Flyers' practice rink in Voorhees, New Jersey, Lindbergh had been at the very top of his game. A season earlier he had not only played in the NHL All-Star Game but was named to the league's First All-Star Team. He also was the Vezina Trophy winner and the man who helped Philadelphia to the Stanley Cup finals against Edmonton. In that season, Lindbergh won 40 games, lost only 17 and tied seven. What's more, it signalled a great leap forward for the likeable Swede.

In 1983-84 he played only 34 games and posted a mediocre 4.05 goals-against average. It was clear that he required more acclimatization to the North American brand of hockey, and with that in mind, the Flyers dispatched him to their American Hockey League farm team in Maine. But the Broad Street high command knew that he had all the makings of a star. That was apparent in 1982-83 when he won 23 games, lost 13 and tied three. He not only was named to the NHL's All-Rookie Team but also played in the All-Star Game.

PE-ERIK "PELLE" LINDBERGH

Born: Stockholm, Sweden, May 24, 1959

Position: Goal

NHL Teams: Philadelphia, 1981-1986

Awards/Honors: Bronze Medal, 1980 Olympics; NHL All-Rookie Team, 1983; played in NHL All-Star Game, 1983; First Team NHL All-Star, 1985; Vezina Trophy, 1985; Bobby Clarke Trophy, 1985

At the time of his death in an automobile crash, Pelle Lindbergh was en route to the top of the heap among NHL goalies.

He made good on his word, becoming the first full-time European starting goaltender on any NHL team. He had developed a maturity beyond his years and displayed a resilience after a bad goal—or a bad game—that he never had before. And he was unsparing in his appreciation.

"Bernie Parent helped me a lot," he said. "He knew all about goaltending pressure. Whenever I had to discuss something—style or mood—I knew Bernie would be there for me.

"As for Mike Keenan, I knew that even if I had a bad game, he would come back and put me in the next one. That helped a lot, knowing that I wouldn't get benched every time I gave up a bad goal or two."

Lindbergh's newfound confidence carried over to the 1985 playoffs when the Flyers defeated the Rangers, Islanders and Nordiques on their way to the finals. He couldn't stop the powerhouse Oilers, who defeated Philadelphia in five games, but his overall playoff average, 2.50, was remarkable under the circumstances, plus he had a dozen wins in 18 games.

The Scandinavian star occasionally had to pinch himself to realize how far he had come and how lucky he was.

"I always thought back to my first years on the ice back home," he said. "I was only four years old when I started playing hockey in Sweden. I used to watch the World Championships on television. I remembered a Canadian goalie named Seth Martin and especially liked his mask. After watching him play, I said to myself, 'That's what I want to do.'

"From the age of ten on, it was my goal to become a professional goaltender. By the time I was 14, my idol was Bernie Parent. Believe it or not, I always dreamed of someday playing for the Flyers. They were my favorite

The fact that he slipped the following year was not surprising. Young players who emigrate from Europe often find it difficult to make a complete adjustment to the new surroundings and Lindbergh was no different than many others. Fortunately, Pelle had a friend and a counselor in Bernie Parent, the Flyers' Stanley Cup hero of the 1970s who had become the club's goaltending coach. Parent counseled Lindbergh, and Pelle became a willing pupil.

"When Pelle had a bad game in his early years it would take him five, six or maybe more games to get back in the groove," said Parent.

Some believed that Lindbergh's confidence took a near-fatal hit during the 1983 All-Star Game when he was victimized by Wayne Gretzky for four goals in the last 14 minutes of the game. But that overlooks the fact that Pelle always had been a fighter and the kind of character who could rebound from such a deflation. After the disastrous season, he vowed to return stronger than ever.

"I cleared my mind during the following summer," Lindbergh said. "I said I was going to forget about the bad year and concentrate on being the hockey player that I know I can be in this league."

team. So you can imagine what a dream come true it was to actually make the club."

Secure in the knowledge that he had become the number-one goalie on Broad Street, Lindbergh launched the 1985-86 season in fine form. After eight games, he already had a shutout and there were many more to anticipate. But then it happened. The dream ended abruptly on a road in New Jersey. Driving friends home in his Porsche, Lindbergh lost control of the sports car and crashed into a wall at high speed. Pelle was killed instantly.

In his eulogy, team captain Dave Poulin said: "I always told Pelle that I was personal friends with the winningest goalie in the National Hockey League and was darn proud of it."

> *"Believe it or not, I always dreamed of someday playing for the Flyers. They were my favorite team. So you can imagine what a dream come true it was to actually make the club."*

Goaltender Pelle Lindbergh does the splits as Louis Sleigher of Quebec tries to outflank him.

Dave (Hammer) Schultz gets a rude reception at the Nassau Coliseum.

Dave Schultz

To hockey purists, it would be sinful to include Dave Schultz on any list of top dozen—or even two dozen, for that matter—Flyers. The Nervous Nellies of hockey-watching and reporting considered The Hammer more of a detriment than an asset to The Game. However, none of those critics ever played for Philadelphia during the golden years of the early 1970s.

Schultz was as much a part of the Flyers' championship seasons in 1974 and 1975 as Bobby Clarke and Bernie Parent. In terms of his influence on The Game, Schultz ranked with Hall of Famers.

Gene Hart, the longtime voice of the Flyers, summed up the Schultz influence in his book, *Score!* As Hart viewed it, Schultz may have lacked the consummate ability of superstars against whom he skated, but his impact came in other ways.

"Looking back at the seventies," wrote Hart, "the most significant players of that decade were Bobby Orr, Phil Esposito, Guy Lafleur, Ken Dryden, Bobby Clarke and Bernie Parent. Some people may be surprised, or even laugh, but I add Schultz to that list.

"He was unique because, more than anyone else in that decade, he changed the face of The Game, while changing the faces of many of the game's players. He changed not only the record book but the rule book, and he changed the thinking of most of the teams in the league."

More than anything, he infused the Flyers with a sense of courage that had been lacking ever since they were physically licked by St. Louis in the 1968 play-

DAVID WILLIAM "THE HAMMER" SCHULTZ

BORN: Waldheim, Saskatchewan, October 14, 1949

Position: Left Wing

NHL Teams: Philadelphia, 1971-76; Los Angeles, 1976-77; Pittsburgh, 1977-79; Buffalo, 1979-80

Dave Schultz shows his displeasure with linesman Neil Armstrong after being given a misconduct penalty.

got my hand on his shirt, though, I would take over."

With such able support from the likes of Bob Kelly and Moose Dupont, Schultz became a holy terror wherever he skated. Meanwhile, the Flyers became branded The Broad Street Bullies, a nickname they wore with affection and pride under coach Fred Shero's leadership.

"It was a personality akin to that of the Big, Bad Bruins," noted Gene Hart, "but it was also uniquely the Flyers' own."

More importantly, the Flyers began winning big after Schultz arrived in Philadelphia to stay for the 1972-73 season. They became a four-way threat: 1. Bernie Parent's goaltending was impeccable; 2. Their star-lacking defense nevertheless played well as an entity; 3. Their well-balanced forward lines, led by Bobby Clarke, Bill Barber and Rick MacLeish provided top scoring; and 4. Schultz and his vigilantes intimidated the enemy the way no other team did before or since.

Overlooked by many who have evaluated The Schultz Legend over the years was one salient point: The Hammer could play hockey. And given the opportunity, he could play the game fairly well. During the 1973-74 season—the Flyers' best until then—he proved that point. Despite 348 penalty minutes, Schultz managed to score 20 goals and add 16 assists. Not so coincidentally, it marked the year that Philadelphia won its first Stanley Cup. During the postseason, he continued to play well, scoring twice and adding four assists in 17 playoff games.

Schultz, himself, later came to believe that his full potential as a stick handler and scorer never were realized at The Spectrum because of the accent on violence.

"I was fortunate to be on championship teams," said Schultz, "but there were things I would have done differently if I had had the chance. For instance, I could have been a better hockey player. But by the time I left the Flyers (1976), I had played that style for three years.

"I began to lose my confidence as a hockey player. Because I had taken on that role and was so into it, lots

offs. By the early 1970s, the Flyers general staff had acknowledged the need for robust performers who would give before they received. One by one, they added the likes of Bob Kelly, Andre Dupont and Don Saleski to the squad. But the slugger who provided the biggest boost was Schultz.

"Everybody knew why I was there," said The Hammer. "Before I arrived, the Flyers were a team that got the hell kicked out of them. I wouldn't let that happen to any team I played on. I would take a punch in the mouth in exchange for a win any time."

Schultz took punches and usually gave back more in return; at least when he was a Flyer, he did. Later on, it was a different story. As a Flyer, he liked to say that he signed his name with his knuckles. Usually, it was signed on the head of the toughest player who skated against him on the opposition. It didn't matter whether it was Wayne Cashman of the Bruins or Pierre Bouchard of the Canadiens. Schultz would take them on with a particular hockey fighting style that worked.

"I would give the other guy those first couple of shots," said Schultz, "while I got a grip on him. Once I

of people didn't think I could play the game. And I didn't have confidence in my other ability."

The Hammer had established himself as a fighter playing for the Flyers' American League farm teams in Quebec and Richmond at the start of the 1970s. In 1972 Dave was to be the beneficiary of a onetime event.

> *"Before I arrived, the Flyers were a team that got the hell kicked out of them. I wouldn't let that happen to any team I played on. I would take a punch in the mouth in exchange for a win any time."*

A new league, the World Hockey Association, had been formed and was attempting to compete with the National Hockey League. WHA teams such as the New York Raiders actively recruited NHL stars as well as potential aces. Schultz caught the eye of Raiders scouts and appeared ready to sign a contract with the new team in the new league. In fact, Schultz showed up at a Manhattan press conference during which he supposedly would accept a Raiders pact. Sitting in the last row of the room was Flyers general counsel Gil Stein who reported back to owner Ed Snider. Before the Raiders ever got Schultz's name on the dotted line, he showed up in Philadelphia and signed with the Flyers.

It was one of the best moves the Broad Street high command ever made. Schultz registered 259 penalty minutes in his rookie NHL season and also tallied nine goals and a dozen assists over 76 games. His belligerence appealed to Shero, who melded Dave into the destructive lineup.

City by city, the Flyers managed to cause a furor wherever they travelled. In a matter of months, they had become the most fascinating team in the league and certainly the most combative.

"The more I kept fighting," Schultz recalled, "the more I was rewarded. What really put the icing on the cake was we had become successful as a team. The more we kept winning, the more I felt I had to fight. The more publicity, the more I felt I had to live up to the reputation."

In no time at all, he had become a big-league hockey celebrity. He was sought out for radio and television interviews as well as magazine features. Writing in *Philadelphia Magazine*, Maury Levy noted, "Fighting has become a science with Dave Schultz . . . They don't call him 'The Hammer' for nothing."

Just in 1974-75, Schultz got into 30 major fights, winning most of them and busting the league's all-time penalty record, both in the regular season and the playoffs. He was such a celebrity in the (ahem) City of Brotherly Love that a group of fans organized into a group called Schultz's Army. They would show up at The Spectrum wearing helmets and other signs of endearment.

By contrast, he was hated in every other NHL rink. When he played at Nassau Coliseum against the Islanders, he was booed every time he came on the ice. Several uncomplimentary banners hung from the rafters and a young fan carried an effigy.

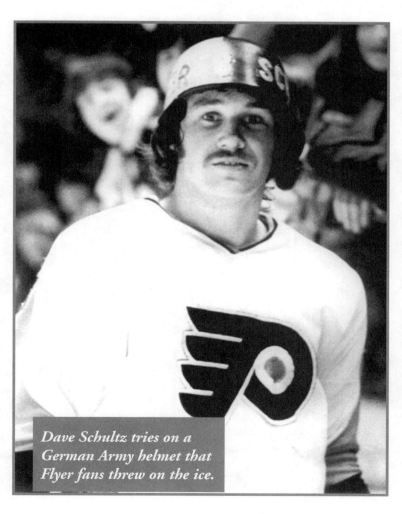

Dave Schultz tries on a German Army helmet that Flyer fans threw on the ice.

"Most fans in the other cities hated me," said Schultz, "but once I got away from the rink it was different. People would recognize me and wish me good luck."

His luck remained good in Philadelphia through the 1975-76 season. The Flyers, after winning two consecutive championships, had reached the finals for the third time in three years. The Hammer had another good season (71 games, 13 goals, 19 assists, 32 points), only four points off his personal record. But when Philly reached the finals against Montreal, Schultz's powers of intimidation were somewhat neutralized by big Canadiens such as Larry Robinson. Philadelphia was eliminated in four straight, and although he didn't know it at the time, Dave would soon be eliminated from the Flyers roster. Paul Holmgren, who could play as well as Schultz—and fight, too—was ready to step into the lineup.

Holmgren's presence enabled the Flyers to deal Schultz to Los Angeles in the fall of 1976. When he returned to The Spectrum in a Kings uniform, Schultz was momentarily hailed by his Faithful, but soon after Holmgren decisioned him in a fight, The Hammer heard the catcalls.

Schultz's remaining NHL seasons were disappointing. He hardly distinguished himself in Los Angeles and moved on to Pittsburgh and eventually Buffalo before calling it a big-league career. He later became a minor-league coach and most recently was working in the East Coast Hockey League.

Wherever he would go, Schultz would be remembered as the point man for the Philadelphia pugilists.

"When I played," he said, "there were so many new teams. The fastest way for them to get accepted was to play rough."

No team was rougher than the Flyers. And no player —when he was in his prime—was tougher than Dave Schultz. There are some who believe that because of his fists, The Hammer remains the most popular Flyer of all time.

Rick Tocchet

When the term "power forward" is mentioned by National Hockey League scouts, they use Clark Gillies and Terry O'Reilly as the quintessential examples of that desirable type of shooter. Left wing on the New York Islanders' top line with Mike Bossy and Bryan Trottier, Gillies helped the Nassau skaters to four consecutive Stanley Cups with a mixture of hard skating, accurate shooting and ready fists when necessary. O'Reilly, who played for some of the Boston Bruins' best clubs in the 1980s, was another big man who could intimidate the opposition with or without fighting.

It was the Flyers' good fortune to obtain a right wing who included the best of Gillies and O'Reilly in his repertoire. Rick Tocchet was rough around the edges, to be sure, but he learned quickly and well and in no time at all became one of Philadelphia's favorite athletes.

The Scarborough, Ontario native came to Philadelphia in 1984 when the Broad Street skaters were being reshaped into a dynamic outfit with many of the belligerent qualities of the Stanley Cup-winning squad of a decade earlier. They hit hard and often and blended skill with their bombast. That made Tocchet feel right at home, and his stats were commensurate with his hitting.

"For me to be a consistent scorer in the NHL," Tocchet once explained, "I've got to play aggressively."

Along with Peter Zezel and Scott Mellanby, Tocchet provided vim, vigor and vitality as well as a zest for fighting. While never a goon, Tocchet was never

RICHARD "RICK" TOCCHET

BORN: Scarborough, Ontario, April 9, 1964

Position: Right Wing

NHL Teams: Philadelphia, 1984-1992, 2000-present; Pittsburgh, 1992-1994; Los Angeles, 1994-1996; Boston, 1996; Washington, 1996-1997; Phoenix, 1997-2000

Awards/Honors: Flyers Class Guy Award, 1988; played in NHL All-Star Game, 1989, 1990, 1991, 1993; Bobby Clarke Trophy, 1990

Philadelphia never had a more versatile power forward than Rick Tocchet, here beating the Islanders' Kelly Hrudey.

choosy about his opponents and battled some of the NHL's best fighters while he skated for Philadelphia.

"When the name Rick Tocchet is mentioned," said Brian Burke, the former NHL vice president and now president of the Vancouver Canucks, "you think of 'complete game.' He has been a consistent player who performs night after night."

He played eight seasons at The Spectrum and in that time amassed 1,683 penalty minutes, tops on the Flyers' PIM list. That he could score also was evident, and, over the years, he developed into one of Philadelphia's most feared shooters. He stands in an impressive seventh place in all-time Flyers goals scored.

Tocchet arrived on Broad Street as a 20-year-old with no car, no friends and with only the most modest expectations from the general staff. After all, he had been selected 125th overall by the Flyers in 1983, not exactly a lofty position.

But in his last junior season after being plucked by Philly, Tocchet raised eyebrows in Sault Ste. Marie, scoring 41 goals and 64 assists for the Greyhounds. It was enough to win an invitation to the 1984 training camp presided over by coach Mike Keenan.

It was no secret that Keenan favored robust skaters, and Rick responded in kind. "Right from the beginning," Keenan remembered, "Tocchet showed me poise and maturity."

Rick made the big club and was teamed with the twins Ron and Rich Sutter, giving the Flyers a trio with virtually the same disturbing (to the opposition) qualities. They were used primarily in a defensive role, which meant that Tocchet's scoring was limited. His 14 goals in two seasons were not exactly what he had anticipated.

"It was difficult at first," Rick admitted. "I figured I would score more. But Mike made me more of a role player, and I adjusted to it. There are role players on every team, and when I was made one, I knew I had to do my job to help the team win."

One of his roles was to fight when necessary. He didn't need urging from Keenan. A player such as Tocchet

"For me to be a consistent scorer in the NHL," Tocchet once explained, *"I've got to play aggressively."*

knew precisely when to drop the gloves and when not to, and he was well aware of the consequences.

"You can use it as a tool to win a hockey game," he said. "Whatever's allowed in the rule book, I'll do to win. I know it sounds stupid, but if you're allowed to slash a guy in the neck, I'll do it to win."

This was reflected by his time in the sin bin. During the 1985-86 season he reached a total of 284 penalty minutes and went up to 288 a year later. That, in turn,

was followed by 301 PIM.

The Flyers prospered as Tocchet's penalty minutes multiplied. They reached the Stanley Cup Finals in 1985 and did it again in 1987. Meanwhile, Tocchet began scoring as never before. In 1987-88, he scored 31 goals despite the 301 penalty minutes, not an easy accomplishment.

"Fighting takes a lot out of your hands," Rick explained. "When you fight, you risk breaking a hand or a knuckle. And when you're in the penalty box, you're not on the ice. Look at it this way: I had 300-odd minutes; that's five full games I missed."

Flyers management realized that Tocchet was being overused as a fighter and decided to limit his strategic usefulness. Yes, he could still play his belligerent game, but it was not necessary to drop the gloves every game.

The results were positive. He reached the 45-goal mark—his highest total with the Flyers—and trimmed his penalty minutes to 183 in 1988-89.

Rick had achieved the perfect balance and continued with some of the same delightful digits in the next two campaigns.

Rick Tocchet took many routes to the net, some of them unorthodox.

In 1989-90 he scored 37 goals with 196 penalty minutes and a year later went up to 40 goals with a mere 150 PIM. His value as a power forward had been clearly established, and, it would have seemed, so had his tenure on Broad Street.

He had been named captain of the Flyers, had also won the team Class Guy Award and was the club's most valuable player in 1990. But there are no guarantees in the hockey business, and on February 19, 1992, Tocchet was dealt to Pittsburgh in a blockbuster deal that included teammates Kjell Samuelsson and goalie Ken Wregget. The Flyers received Mark Recchi, Brian Benning and a draft choice.

The deal was a shocker for many Philadelphians who had come to know and love Rick's rambunctious style, but it turned out to be a bonanza for Tocchet. Joining a Penguins team with Mario Lemieux and Jaromir Jagr, he helped them defeat Chicago in the 1992 Stanley Cup finals to earn his first Cup ring. In 14 playoff games for Pittsburgh, Rick racked up six goals and 13 assists for 19 points.

Rick has since played for Los Angeles, Boston, Washington and more recently the Phoenix Coyotes. After more than a decade and a half of major-league hockey, he remained a force and a desirable commodity for any team.

"I have the respect around the league," he said. "I like that feeling, going on the ice when I have that kind of respect."

Despite his many NHL stops, Tocchet always will be known first as a Flyer. He was a four-time participant in the NHL All-Star Game and gave Philadelphia the brand of respect its fans cherished. Likewise, the respect was returned to Rick.

Former teammate Brad Marsh summed up Rick's eight years on Broad Street as well as anyone. "Rick Tocchet was what the Philadelphia Flyers were all about!"

Translated: He was a fighter and a winner.

It seemed inevitable that Tocchet eventually would return to the City of Brotherly Love if there was any mileage left on his wheels.

Finally on March 8, 2000 general manager Bob Clarke reacquired the veteran in exchange for Mikael Renberg.

To the delight of Philadelphia fans, the spark remained.

After scoring goal number 400 as a player for Phoenix in the Flyers building (January 28, 1999), Rick became one of only two players (Pat Verbeek) in NHL history to collect 400 goals and 2,000 penalty minutes during his career.

Bedeviled by ailments, Tocchet began playing less and less.

He spent most of the 2001-02 season doing rehabilitation. Rick appeared in only 14 regular season games, collecting two assists and 28 penalty minutes. When he missed the first round of the playoffs, it was questioned whether or not the man who skated for almost two decades in the majors would be able to return again.

John LeClair

Every so often a team is fortunate enough to make a trade that proves to be a high-octane catalyst, a deal that galvanizes a club from the realm of mediocre to superior.

For the Flyers just such a deal was made on February 9, 1995, when general manager Bob Clarke exchanged top scorer Mark Recchi for John LeClair, Eric Desjardins and Gilbert Dionne.

At the time, LeClair was better known for his potential than his production. He had been a member of the Montreal Canadiens from 1991 to 1995 and had been looked upon as a future power forward from the Cam Neely-Clark Gillies genre of run-'em-over-and-score stick handlers.

Somehow, the 6'3", 225-pound left wing never fulfilled his press notices in Montreal. In plain English, he suffered a build-up to a letdown although the Habs high command kept hoping for the big breakout from the big guy.

Perhaps the Montreal brass gave up too soon. From the moment LeClair donned the black, orange and white of the Flyers he became a literal goal machine. In his very first game for Philadelphia against the New Jersey Devils at The Meadowlands, the massive forward scored his 50th career goal and gave every indication that he had found his niche. Instantly!

JOHN LeCLAIR

BORN: St. Albans, Vermont, July 5, 1969

Position: Left Wing

NHL Teams: Montreal, 1991-1995; Philadelphia, 1995-present

Awards/Honors: Pelle Lindbergh Memorial Trophy, 1995; NHL All-Star, 1995, 1996, 1997, 1998; *The Hockey News* First Team All-Star, 1995; *The Sporting News* First Team All-Star, 1995; Flyers 50-goal Club, 1996, 1997, 1998; *The Hockey News* Second Team All-Star, 1996; Bobby Clarke Trophy, 1997; 2000 All-Star Game; 1999 NHL Second Team All-Star

In John LeClair's first game for the Flyers he scored his 50th career goal.

An anomaly—how many NHL players come from St. Albans, Vermont?—LeClair was drafted by Montreal at the conclusion of his senior year of high school. He was the 33rd pick overall but opted for the University of Vermont.

His propensity for red lights was there for all to see as he amassed 56 goals and 60 assists in 92 collegiate games. Nearly half of them came in his senior year.

Following graduation in 1991 he joined the Habs for ten games at season's end and collected a pair of goals—one of them was a game-winner—and five assists. He managed three playoff games with a point.

His first full NHL season, 1991-92, hardly was a bonanza, although the Canadiens went 41-28-11 in 80 games. He collected eight goals and 11 assists in 59 games but also spent eight games with Fredericton in the American Hockey League.

In 1992-93, the Habs won 48 of 84 regular season games and went on to defeat Los Angeles for the Stanley Cup. John's point totals—19-25-44—were less than anticipated. Again.

"What happened in Montreal," explained LeClair, "is that the style we played was so defensive. I didn't get that many open chances. I'm not saying that that's bad. Look at it this way—we won a Stanley Cup with that style, so how could we complain?"

The Habs high command didn't complain—at least not publicly—about LeClair, although his numbers a year later were no more impressive. At times, he appeared to suffer a crisis of confidence.

LeClair: "A lot of my difficulties came from on the ice. I would get intimidated. I would say, 'Hey, there's Rick Tocchet.' Or, 'There's Luc Robitaille.' They were 50-goal scorers. I had to realize that I belonged with those guys."

The lockout 1994-95 season was John's last with the Montreal Canadiens. He played in nine games, scored one goal and helped on four others.

In a few words, he was militantly unimpressive. Meanwhile, the phone lines between Montreal and Philadelphia were buzzing. Finally, on February 9, 1995, Clarke pulled the trigger on a deal that would move LeClair to The Spectrum.

"Actually," Clarke admitted, "Eric Desjardins was the guy we wanted very badly. On the other hand, there was no way we would have made that deal without LeClair. We envisioned him playing on a line with Eric Lindros. We knew there was great upside potential for John.

"Our thinking was that in a more free-flowing, more offensive system, he would be a better scorer. And

we knew for sure he was the sort of big player who would help Eric. But who could tell how good he would be?"

LeClair's impact was immediate and potent. In 37 games as a Flyer, he scored 25 goals and tallied 24 assists. He and Lindros worked together like perfectly meshed gears. With Mikael Renberg as third man on the unit, the Legion of Doom was born—and boomed.

John was named a First Team NHL All-Star in the 1994-95 season. He finished ninth in league scoring; Lindros was second and Renberg eighth. LeClair also garnered the Pelle Lindbergh Memorial Trophy awarded to the Flyer who showed the most improvement since the previous season.

"People ask me over and over again to explain how I could all of a sudden score so many goals," said LeClair. "I'm playing with Eric and that was a big part of it."

Lindros was just as quick to attribute a good portion of his success to LeClair. "With Johnny on that side, things were getting cleared out. Overall, we were able to play a more physical game," said Lindros. "Since John came to Philly, I was able to become a better playmaker.

> *"A lot of my difficulties came from on the ice. I would get intimidated. I would say, 'Hey, there's Rick Tocchet.' Or, 'There's Luc Robitaille.' They were 50-goal scorers. I had to realize that I belonged with those guys."*

I would get the puck to him in the right spot. He certainly could hammer that thing."

In 1994-95 the Flyers reached the third playoff round before being eliminated by the eventual Stanley Cup-winning Devils. LeClair scored five goals and assisted on seven others in 15 games. Nevertheless, The Legion of Doom had become a presence and LeClair's star continued climbing.

A year later he entered the prestigious 50-goal club—he scored 51—being only the sixth Flyer to ever do so. He added 46 assists and a career-high 64 penalty minutes. Philadelphia finished first in the Eastern Conference, one point ahead of Pittsburgh, and for the second straight year, LeClair was named an NHL All-Star.

LeClair averaged a point a game in 11 playoff contests (6-5), but the Flyers were upset by the Florida Panthers in six postseason games.

Defusing the big man's weaponry had become a colossal challenge for enemy checkers and coaches. LeClair employed his abundant physique to shake off the opposition and reached 50 goals in 1996-97. His 97 points put him fourth in the scoring race, and he was named a Second Team All-Star. He led the Flyers in points, goals and also paced the entire NHL with a plus-44 plus-minus rating. As an extra added attraction, he took the Bobby Clarke Trophy as the Flyers' most valuable player.

Were there any doubt that LeClair had reached his highest level, it was dispelled when he was named to Team USA for the World Cup of Hockey. He led Uncle Sam's skaters in an upset over the favored Canadians. John totalled six goals and four assists to go with a plus-nine rating. He also was named to the All-Tournament Team.

His playoff performance in 1997 again was above average. In 19 games he came away with 21 points (9-12) and skated into the finals where Philadelphia was wiped out in four games by Detroit. The trauma of defeat inspired major changes, including a new coach.

LeClair excelled under the new regime in 1997-98, although the Legion of Doom was disassembled and Renberg traded to Tampa Bay. Undaunted, LeClair poured in 51 goals—only one fewer than NHL leader Teemu Selanne—and 35 assists. He finished sixth overall in scoring and his 32 penalty minutes gave him Lady Byng Trophy consideration.

Unquestionably, John LeClair closed the decade of the 1990s as one of the most productive Flyers ever to grace Broad Street. He became only the second Philadelphia forward in history to record three consecutive 50-goal seasons—Tim Kerr had four—and managed to limit his penalty minutes in the process.

In retrospect, the acquisition of the Vermonter ranks among the finest deals ever made by Bob Clarke. And one of the best things to happen to Philadelphia hockey.

He also gave more credibility to the legion of Americans playing in the NHL.

By the end of the 2000-01 season, following his tenth full year in the majors, LeClair found himself in select company. He has continued to rise up the all-time goals scored by an American-born player list, and entering the 2002-03 season, he was fifth on that list, only trailing names like Joe Mullen, Pat LaFontaine, Jeremy Roenick and Mike Modano.

Back problems continued to afflict LeClair. In 2000-2001 he played in only 16 games after he underwent disc surgery in October 2000.

He rebounded in the following campaign, finished second on the team in scoring (25-25-51), and he played in all 82 games as well as appearing in the Winter Olympics for Team USA and was perhaps one of their best players in the tournament.

LeClair underwent corrective surgery during the summer of 2002 in the hopes of regaining his high-scoring form. The prognosis was bright for the left wing and, therefore, the Flyers.

Rod Brind'Amour

I f one were asked to select the best trade the Philadelphia Flyers ever made, there would be several choices from which to pick, but among the less obvious—yet most meaningful—was one that evolved on September 22, 1991.

The St. Louis Blues fixed covetous eyes on Ron Sutter—he of the tenacious Alberta clan—and defenseman Murray Baron, a fixture on the Flyers' blue line. Each was desirable on Broad Street yet tradeable in the eyes of the general staff.

And so the trade was made. Sutter and Baron to the Mound City for a muscular forward of uncertain potential and an erratic scorer who played golf better than he played hockey.

Thus the Flyers had acquired Rod Brind'Amour—he of the sinewy physique—and the sharpshooting putter, Dan Quinn.

In retrospect it was a no-brainer for the Flyers, but at the time there were concerns the Broad Street brain trust had been duped. The Sutter reputation was solid throughout the league, and Baron had been reliable, if not Norris Trophy material.

There are no longer any questions.

Brind'Amour over a period of seven years has revealed himself as one of the most durable and dependable skaters ever to wear the Philadelphia colors.

ROD BRIND'AMOUR

Born: Ottawa, Ontario, August 9, 1970

Position: Center/Left Wing

NHL Teams: St. Louis, 1988-1991; Philadelphia, 1991-2000; Carolina 2000-present

Awards/Honors: NHL All-Rookie Team, 1990; Played in 1992 NHL All-Star Game; Bobby Clarke Trophy, 1992

A typical Rod Brind'Amour battle for the puck.

"From the start he had all the skills," said former teammate Peter Zezel. "Even in St. Louis he was a good up-and-down winger, a solid two-way player."

Yet he tallied only 49 points in 78 games as a Blue before he was dealt to Philadelphia. Was that as much as one could expect from him?

The reply was offered in 1991-92, Rod's first in Philly. His 33 goals almost doubled his figure for St. Louis, and 44 assists totalled 77 points along with 100 penalty minutes.

Poof! Just like that, Brind'Amour had become the Flyers' premier center and easily the most tenacious forward on the club. Perhaps more arresting was the fact that his stats continued to climb: 86 points in his second year at The Spectrum and 97 points in his third.

"He was like a machine," said former teammate Karl Dykhuis. "He would just keep going. Penalty-killing, power plays, five-on-five. Whenever the club needed an important faceoff in the last minute of a game, he was out there."

Although he was born in Ottawa, Brind'Amour moved with his family to Campbell River, British Columbia when he was a youth. As a teenager, he enrolled at the revered Notre Dame College (actually a high school) in Wilcox, Saskatchewan. A longtime feeder for pro players, Notre Dame won a Canadian Midget level title when Brind'Amour was a hound. That, plus some starry moments with Canada's Spengler Cup (world university) team in Europe inspired the Blues to make him the ninth overall draft choice in 1988.

His reaction was to enroll at Michigan State University, where he played in 1988-89. A season later he

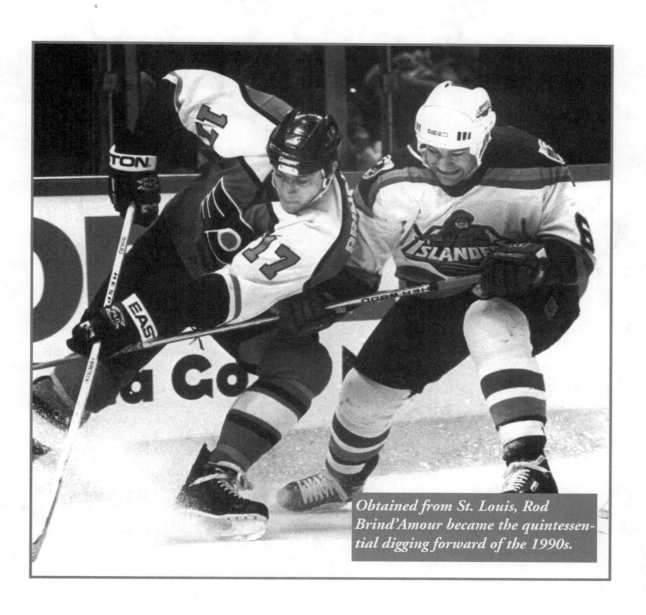

Obtained from St. Louis, Rod Brind'Amour became the quintessential digging forward of the 1990s.

Rod Brind'Amour's acreage—right in front of the enemy goal.

"He was like a machine," said former teammate Karl Dykhuis. "He would just keep going. Penalty-killing, power plays, five-on-five. Whenever the club needed an important faceoff in the last minute of a game, he was out there."

was in Missouri scoring 26 goals alongside some distinguished linemates.

"Playing with Adam Oates and Paul MacLean," Brind'Amour remembered, "you could put my mother there and she could score some points."

Even though he was the Blues' fifth leading scorer, his plus-minus total was a handsome plus-23. He combined offense and defense better than Oates, MacLean, Zezel and Brett Hull.

"In a way," said former Blues general manager Ron Caron, "Rod reminded me of that great Canadiens center, Henri Richard. He had leadership qualities and was all business on the ice."

He was all business off the ice as well, pumping iron and more iron and more iron after that. To say that Rod had muscles on top of his muscles would be gilding the rose and painting the lily.

Center Rod Brind'Amour has been an excellent all-around player for the Flyers in his seven seasons, picking up over 500 points including more than 15 short-handed tallies.

What he didn't have for his first three years in Philly was a playoff experience to discuss. When a club misses the postseason in three straight years, its high command talks trade. And whenever the Flyers were consulted about deals, the other general manager asked for Brind'Amour.

After a few years, the Brind'Amour trade talk took on charade-like proportions, but what really mattered was that Bob Clarke rejected each and every offer. By 1994-95 the Flyers were back in the playoff hunt, and Rod responded with 15 points (6-9) in 15 games.

When he signed a new Flyers contract, Brind'Amour did not ask for bonuses for individual points. "I don't want to worry about stuff like that," he said. "If the team wins, I'll sleep at night."

Some NHL observers have compared Brind'Amour's power forward style to Cam Neely, the former Bruins icon, and Rick Tocchet, who spent sev-

eral robust years on Broad Street. "Rod," said Ron Sutter, "is as good along the boards as any player I've seen."

His playoff ability never was more apparent than in the 1997 postseason when Philadelphia reached the finals before being swept by Detroit. Rod stuffed a career-high 13 goals in 19 games and added eight assists.

By 1997-98 he had reached the prime of his career. His 36 goals were one short of his career high, but it was the all-round game that impressed both friend and foe. The 38 assists merely emphasized the perfect balance of his offensive repertoire.

Nevertheless on January 23, 2000 the Flyers traded Brind'Amour to Carolina along with Jean-Marc Pelletier and a second-round pick in the 2000 NHL entry draft for Keith Primeau and a fifth-round pick in the 2000 NHL entry draft.

Brian Propp scores again!

Brian Propp

Unobtrusively, Brian Propp carved out a notable career in Philadelphia, although he certainly was noticed by enemy goaltenders. For 11 seasons on Broad Street, Propp quietly went about the business of being one of The Game's best left wingers.

His powerful wrist shot spoke eloquently and effectively during the decade of the 1980s when the Flyers iced some of their finest teams. A native of Lanigan, Saskatchewan, Propp was a Canadian prairie boy who preferred quiet leadership to high decibel antics.

It may come as a surprise to followers of the orange and black, but Propp can be found directly behind Bobby Clarke—in second place—on the Flyers' all-time playoff scoring list. He is third in all-time regular season scoring, which again is an arresting footnote, considering all the talent against which he competed.

Propp was as team-oriented as any Flyer. Had he not been, the likelihood is that he would have surpassed the 100-point mark. That he did not is as much a tribute to his attention to defense as well as offense.

"As long as our team is winning," he would say, "it's good. I personally get a better feeling playing on a club that wins most of its games than I would playing for a loser, even if I got 100 points or more for the loser."

Propp's attitude was appreciated by the high command, as were his more tangible accomplishments. Few Flyers could boast—as Brian could—that they helped the team reach the Stanley Cup finals on three different occasions. Propp

BRIAN PHILLIP PROPP

BORN: Lanigan, Saskatchewan, February 15, 1959

Position: Left Wing

NHL Teams: Philadelphia, 1979-1990; Boston, 1989-1990; Minnesota, 1990-1993; Hartford, 1993-1994

Awards/Honors: Played in NHL All-Star Game, 1980, 1982, 1984, 1986, 1990

skated for the clubs that did so in 1980, 1985 and 1987.

That he did so also is attributable to the tutoring he received. Upon becoming a Flyer in 1979, he skated alongside the nucleus that delivered Stanley Cups in 1974 and 1975 to The Spectrum.

"When I first got to Philly," Propp remembered, "guys like Reggie Leach, Bob Kelly, Bill Barber and Rick MacLeish helped me out a lot. Adjusting to a big city wasn't each for a kid like me then, but the vets made a big difference in a very positive way."

He came to the National Hockey League by way of Brandon (Manitoba) of the Western (Junior) Hockey League and made a relatively easy adjustment to the professional ranks. Despite his inexperience, Brian became

Pound for pound, and inch for inch, Brian Propp was one of the Flyers' most skilled scorers.

an instant scorer on a powerful club coached by Pat Quinn.

"Propp gave us a big lift," Quinn recalled. "Considering the jump from junior being so steep, we didn't even expect him to make our team."

In the normal scheme of things, Brian would have been dispatched to the Flyers' Maine farm team in the American Hockey League for seasoning. But despite a month-long goal slump, his work ethic enabled him to thrive. "His head was screwed on right," said Quinn. "Even in the midst of his slump, he worked and worked. For his age, that was impressive."

His numbers were impressive enough for Propp to qualify for the Calder Trophy as NHL Rookie of the Year. With 34 goals and 41 assists, his 75 points might

have done the trick in any other season, but Raymond Bourque, freshman sensation for the Boston Bruins, took the prize.

Propp's sophomore slump, in 1980-81, dropped him nine points under his freshman totals but hardly was cause for concern. By now even the harshest of his Philadelphia critics conceded that Brian had all the equipment for stardom and that the big numbers would come.

Sure enough, in 1981-82 he scored 44 goals and achieved 47 assists. With 91 points and a career-high 117 penalty minutes, he had become a true NHL presence and would remain so for years. Once Bobby Clarke and Bill Barber retired, a leadership void had to be filled, and Propp stepped forward, front and center. At age 25, he took over one of the youngest yet most competent

"As long as our team is winning," he would say, "it's good. I personally get a better feeling playing on a club that wins most of its games than I would playing for a loser, even if I got 100 points or more for the loser."

clubs on the continent.

"It was quite a change for me, considering what I was when I arrived in Philly," Propp said. "When I arrived there were players such as Clarke, Barber, Parent and MacLeish. They all had a lot of experience and I was a kid. All I wanted to do then was go out and play. I was too worried about making the team to even think about leading it.

"But as the veterans left and younger players came in, I tried to help them as much as I could. It became a conscious effort on my part."

At age 25, the preacher's son had taken the pulpit —while still remaining soft-spoken and relaxed. "I never was a screamer or a shouter," said Brian. "It wasn't my style to jump up and down over something."

As he matured, Propp delivered a more comprehensive game. "He played at a higher level," explained ex-teammate and captain Dave Poulin. "It wasn't a dras-

tic change but it was significant. What was so remarkable about Brian was that he had so few peaks and valleys."

Four times in his career he scored 90 or more points and was a winner in every way except for the gnawing fact that he never sipped champagne from the Stanley Cup. "When you lose—even in the finals—it's a disappointment. But you can't keep looking back; you've got to look ahead. I always tried to keep that philosophy in mind."

Some of Propp's best hockey was exhibited during the Mike Keenan regime. The moustached coach stressed the group over the individual and found a willing listener in Brian.

"We had such a team emphasis in Philadelphia as opposed to the star system elsewhere," Keenan recalled. "We were always more interested in promoting team goals rather than individual achievement. In that type of system, it's more difficult to get personal recognition.

"Brian had the ability to lead on the ice through his consistent level of performance. Game in and game out, he was always prepared to play."

Propp's career in Philadelphia ended in 1990 when he was dealt to the Boston Bruins. He was then moved on to the Minnesota North Stars, where he played with the 1991 Stanley Cup finalists, ultimately beaten by the Pittsburgh Penguins. He completed his NHL career with Hartford in 1993-94.

Brian Propp left major-league hockey as quietly as he had entered. But in between, he made plenty of noise with a sharpshooting stick and a creative mind.

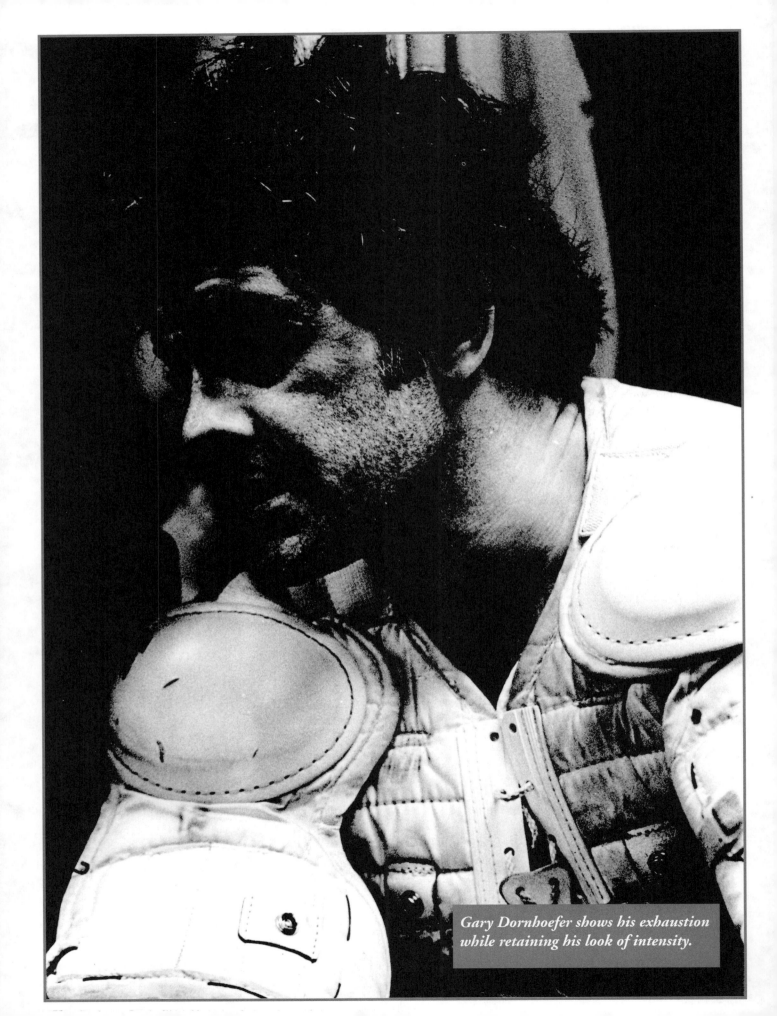

Gary Dornhoefer shows his exhaustion while retaining his look of intensity.

Gary Dornhoefer

I f ever there was a self-made star of the Flyers it was the long, lean native of Kitchener, Ontario—Gary Dornhoefer.

Studying him carefully, a hockey critic would not expect to find a man who would become as vital to his club as a Bobby Clarke, Rick MacLeish or Bernie Parent.

Dornhoefer did not skate with the lyrical grace of a Guy Lafleur.

His shot hardly had the potency one associates with an Eric Lindros.

Nor did he seem especially intimidating in spite of a relatively strong physique.

Vim, vigor and vitality were the trademarks that most endeared the gangly forward to Spectrum fans after Dornhoefer was obtained by Philadelphia as an original Broad Street skater in 1967 when the Flyers were born.

Previously, he had been with the Boston Bruins, having broken into the National Hockey League in 1963. His experience in Beantown hardly was superlative on a noncontending team whose only hope was the anticipated arrival of a wunderkind named Bobby Orr.

But in 1967 Orr was just a teenager and Dornhoefer—for reasons best known to the Bruins general staff—was regarded as expendable when the NHL expanded from six to a dozen teams.

GERNARD OTTO "GARY" DORNHOEFER

Born: Kitchener, Ontario, February 2, 1943

Position: Right Wing

NHL Teams: Boston, 1963-67; Philadelphia 1967-78

Awards/Honors: Played in 1973 All-Star Game; Flyers Class Guy Award, 1977; Flyers Hall of Fame, 1991

At the time of expansion, the Flyers were allowed to select 20 players. Some were terribly young and inexperienced. Others were aging and obviously over the hill, and a few were of major-league calibre.

All had one thing in common: they were castoffs, so it is not surprising that most of the players selected in that original expansion draft were not around a few years later.

One who did survive was Dornhoefer. Inexorably, he developed into one of the West Division's steadiest two-way players. By the time he had finished his sixth year as a Flyer, it was clear that Gary was one of the smartest picks made in the original draft.

In a half-dozen years on Broad Street he had 290 points and was, at the time, Philadelphia's all-time scoring leader. In 1972-73 he scored 30 goals and added 49 assists, which were season highs for him in both departments.

More importantly, he had become a dependable leader to whom the youngsters such as Bobby Clarke went to seek for advice and guidance, both on and off the ice.

"Gary was somebody to look up to," said Clarke. "He worked hard all the time, rarely drank or swore and was a good family man. He had all the qualities you look for in a person."

Those qualities were imparted to a Philadelphia team just beginning to flex its muscles in the early 1970s. By the 1973-74 season that club was ready for a run for the top, and Gary was there to give them a push.

"Winning helped," Dornhoefer recalled, "but believing in the guys I was with was very important. We had 20 guys who believed we could win. Everybody believed in everyone else."

Coach Fred Shero was also a believer, especially when it came to Dornhoefer. "Gary became a leader," said Shero. "He encouraged the other guys. They looked up to him and they liked him. When we needed a lift he'd go in and work twice as hard."

Dornhoefer and Shero had been through some lean times together. Shero once confessed that he felt more like a camp counselor than a major-league hockey coach. Fred, for example, liked to tell about some of the excuses he would hear when one of his players had not performed up to Shero's expectations, which were never that high anyway.

"One guy told me the reason he was not skating well was because he didn't have a pair of skates," Shero recalled. "I couldn't believe my ears. The guy could go out and buy any pair he wanted, made to measure, and have the bill sent to the Flyers. Instead, he borrowed a left skate from one player and a right skate from another. I only found out by accident. I swear, there were many times you could have cried."

Dornhoefer endured those years of adversity with Shero. "I went through it all with the club. Before we won the two Stanley Cups there was one team that lost the playoffs in four straight and another time we lost in seven games and another when we missed the playoffs in the last four seconds of the regular season."

There is no question that Dornhoefer paid his hockey dues. After two years of junior hockey and a half-season in the minors, he played part-time with the Bruins with minimum success. He bounced between Boston and the minors until rescued from hockey oblivion by expansion and the Flyers.

Not that he was gang busters. Far from it. In his premiere season with the Flyers (1967-68), he scored 13 goals but managed just eight in the following campaign. His performance was so unimpressive that the Flyers left him unprotected in the 1969 draft, but no other team claimed him.

Whether the shock of being unclaimed motivated Dornhoefer or not, he responded to the challenge with 26 goals and 29 assists during the 1969-70 campaign. "Gary came a long way," said former Flyers defenseman Larry Zeidel. "He polished his game and developed a more accurate shot. One of his problems had been frustration that led him to take bad shots. He became a smarter hockey player and a good competitor."

Checking never was a problem for Dornhoefer. "He enjoyed the physical part of the game more than the finesse part," said Clarke. "He really paid the price physically to play the game. He received more satisfaction from a good body check than from scoring a goal."

Leg injuries forced Dornhoefer to miss 19 games during the 1970-71 season, and consequently, his scoring output was down from the previous year—just 20 goals and 20 assists. To Shero's eyes, he was not shooting enough, but the coach was more than happy with his hitting. So was general manager Keith Allen.

"Gary was a character guy," said Allen. "He paid the price to play the game. He took a lot of punishment and never backed off. I knew he would succeed because of his determination and drive. Anyone who played with him had a lot of respect for him."

Dornhoefer's aggressiveness accounted for 183 penalty minutes in 1971-72 and 168 minutes the next season. Shero used him on power plays and for penalty-killing as well as his regular turn.

His first true season in the sun was 1972-73 when he was named to the West Team for the annual All-Star

When the Flyers were building toward their first Stanley Cup, Gary Dornhoefer provided them with grit and goals.

Game and came close to equaling what then was the NHL mark for scoring goals in consecutive games.

The record—which was held jointly by Andy Bathgate, who did it for the Rangers, and Bobby Hull, who did it for the Blackhawks—was ten. Gary came within three games of joining that select company. His string, in fact, was broken on a controversial scoring play against the Bruins at The Spectrum.

"He enjoyed the physical part of the game more than the finesse part," said Clarke. "He really paid the price physically to play the game. He received more satisfaction from a good body check than from scoring a goal."

Defenseman Joe Watson had fired a long shot that appeared to deflect off Dornhoefer's pads and into the net. Were that the case, it would have been Gary's goal and his scoring skein would have continued.

"I couldn't say for sure because, quite honestly, I didn't feel a thing," Dornhoefer said in retrospect. "If we were able to look at films, maybe it would show that I did touch it last. But no movies—or videotape—were taken so I guess we'll never know for sure."

Then, a pause: "Aw, heck, I wouldn't want the goal that way, anyway. I want to work for it."

During the 1972-73 season Dornhoefer was accorded one of the greatest ovations ever bestowed upon an athlete at The Spectrum. It happened in a Stanley Cup playoff game against the Minnesota North Stars. Jack Chevalier of the *Philadelphia Bulletin* described it this way:

"In the pressure of Stanley Cup sudden death, Dorny blasted through the Minnesota defense and backhanded a shot past Cesare Maniago to beat the North Stars, 3-2, after eight minutes and 35 seconds of overtime. The Spectrum crowd of 16,600 reacted with a leaping, arm-waving 'from the heart' ovation. It was probably the most exciting individual play by a Philly athlete since Dick Sisler beat the Dodgers in Brooklyn with that home run in 1950 and gave the Phillies the pennant."

Dornhoefer: "Yeah, they were yelling big. It was the loudest cheer I've heard in Philadelphia."

The Flyers went on to defeat the North Stars in that opening-round series and then gave the Canadiens fits before being ousted in five games. After the Montreal series, Shero called Dornhoefer "the best, most competitive player on ice."

While saddened by the loss, Gary was far from discouraged. "Everybody worked as hard as they could," he observed. "Montreal had a great club. They put the puck in the net when it counted, and we couldn't get it past Ken Dryden."

The Canadiens series was merely the prelude to better things to come. Dornhoefer was a member of the Stanley Cup-winning teams of 1974 and 1975 as well as the club that reached the finals in 1976 before losing to Les Canadiens.

If he had any misgivings they were over a shoulder separation he suffered in Game 3 of the 1974 Stanley Cup finals against Boston. It put him out for the re-mainder of the series and left him a spectator when the Flyers actually won the title.

"I was sitting in the press box," he remembered, "and as the seconds were counting down, assuring us victory, I felt left behind. I didn't feel I was part of the team since I wasn't on the ice at the end of the game."

Nevertheless, the intangibles—not to mention the tangibles—contributed by Dornhoefer had enabled them to reach that point, and everyone connected with the team praised him for that.

When he retired after the 1977-78 season, he had amassed an impressive dossier and was acknowledged with a Gary Dornhoefer Night at The Spectrum on April 9, 1978. His career totals included 787 games played. He finished with 214 goals and 328 assists for 542 points and 1,291 penalty minutes.

His assets were many, but Gary always saw things clearly and saw them whole. "I enjoyed the team concept where you and your teammates together could be successful," he once said. "When I played with the Flyers, the team concept was very evident."

Nobody articulated that concept better than Gary Dornhoefer.

Barry Ashbee

Barry Ashbee had become a forgotten man among hockey players long before he became a much-remembered player on the Flyers.

His name is so indelibly imprinted on the minds of Philadelphia hockey fans that it is difficult to believe that he only played four full seasons on Broad Street.

Then again, just about everything about the Weston, Ontario native's career was unusual, particularly since his major-league career didn't amount to much until after his 30th birthday.

In simple terms, Ashbee was a throwback to a simpler hockey era when it was customary for a player to graduate from junior ranks to low minor pros—as in the Eastern Professional Hockey League—and then to the upper pro ranks such as the American Hockey League.

That was during the six-team National Hockey League years when some splendid players never even reached the bigs for an assortment of reasons. Ashbee was one of those players.

His pro career was launched in 1959-60 with Kingston of the EPHL, and then he graduated to Hershey of the AHL in 1963. At the time Hershey was a farm team of the Bruins, and in 1965-66, the Boston brass thought enough of Ashbee to elevate him to Beantown for 14 games.

WILLIAM BARRY ASHBEE

Born: Weston, Ontario, July 28, 1939

Position: Defense

NHL Teams: Boston, 1965-1966; Philadelphia, 1970-1974

Awards/Honors: NHL Second Team All-Star, 1973-1974; Number 4 retired by Philadelphia, April 3, 1975; Elected to Flyers Hall of Fame, 1991

"He was not a great scorer nor a great shooter," said Fred Shero, the Flyers coach who himself had paid the price with years in the minors as a defenseman. "But Barry worked harder than anybody."

The experience was excellent, but the longevity was not. He played three more seasons in the AHL and seemed destined to complete his career riding the AHL buses when the Flyers decided to take a gamble in June 1970. Philadelphia traded Darryl Edestrand and Larry McKillop to Hershey for the big defenseman.

Ashbee was 31 years old at the time, apparently on the downside of his career. A casual observer would say that his wheels were worn and the Flyers would gain little from his presence.

It would be a mistaken appraisal. In 1970 the boys from Broad Street were seeking respect behind the blue line, and Ashbee would provide it in more ways than one.

Nobody summed up Ashbee's value to the Flyers more than legendary broadcaster Gene Hart, who handled play-by-play for Philadelphia when Barry was at his best. Writing in *Score! My Twenty-Five Years With The Broad Street Bullies*, Hart concluded:

"On paper, Barry Ashbee's career statistics look like those of a thousand other journeyman defensemen, and perhaps that is why he remained buried in the minor leagues for so long. When he finally made it to the Flyers at the age of thirty-one, my first impression of him was that he was a loner, an unhappy man, even an angry man. That may have been because of all those years in the minors, including seven years at Hershey during which he was given only one brief trial by the Boston Bruins, and that had been five years before. Or it may have been because of the pain that was always his companion, the pain that made it necessary for him to wear a padded 'horse collar' around his neck when he played to prevent further damage."

As Hart pointed out, Ashbee "learned to relax" and in time would become one of the NHL's steadiest defenseman. His style was not unlike that of Rod Langway, a Norris Trophy winner with the Washington Capitals. Ashbee was unspectacular but conspicuous to his teammates and goaltender because he always got the job done, neatly and without any fuss or fanfare.

"He was not a great scorer nor a great shooter," said Fred Shero, the Flyers coach who himself had paid the price with years in the minors as a defenseman. "But Barry worked harder than anybody."

It was, of course, a product of his minor-league apprenticeship. Few players ever appreciated being in the bigs more than Ashbee. It was as if he was determined to make up for the so-called "lost" years during which he toiled in Hershey.

He was nicknamed "Ashcan" by his fellow Philadelphians, and it diminished the respect he received from friend and foe alike on the ice. In 1974 he was voted to the NHL Second All-Star Team. His plus-minus rating that season was an astonishing plus-52, which is testimony to his effectiveness.

After watching Ashbee perform one night, Montreal Canadiens immortal Jean Beliveau succinctly noted, "I haven't seen a guy play a better game of defense all year."

Ashbee was the linchpin of Philadelphia's solid defense during the 1973-74 campaign, when the Flyers finished first in the West Division and guided Philadelphia to an opening-round triumph over Atlanta in the 1974 playoffs.

But on April 28, 1974, at Madison Square Garden during the semifinal playoff round series against the Rangers, Barry was struck flush in the eye by a blazing Dale Rolfe slap shot. It ended a major-league career that was just beginning to blossom. "I'm not bitter," insisted Ashbee. "Some people strive for sixty years and they can't make it. I got what I wanted when I was thirty-four—a Stanley Cup win with the Flyers. I had thought about being on a Cup winner since I was seven."

Barry became an assistant head coach and scout for the Flyers but suddenly, in 1977, discovered he had developed leukemia and died within a matter of just a few weeks.

The Flyers' management did not forget Barry Ashbee. The team retired his number—4—and annually awards a trophy in his name to the outstanding defenseman on the team. Each year, too, the Flyers' wives keep Barry's memory alive by conducting a fundraising event to fight cancer.

Perhaps the best and most vivid depiction of Ashbee was delivered by Father John Casey, the team chaplain, at an emotional memorial service shortly after the defenseman's death.

"I hope the Lord has prepared the greatest for him," said Father Casey. "A place where there's nothing but the greatest defensemen ... the ice is always smooth. And if they have a Stanley Cup there, I hope he wins it every year.

"Barry Ashbee will walk with the Flyers for a long, long time. His spirit will be with the Flyers forever. They will walk together forever."

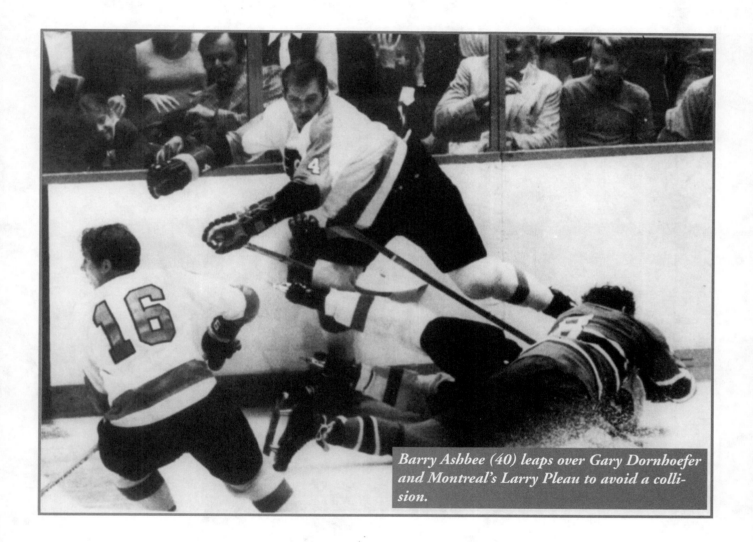

Barry Ashbee (40) leaps over Gary Dornhoefer and Montreal's Larry Pleau to avoid a collision.

Joe Watson's kid brother, Jimmy, ranked among the top young defensemen of the 1970s.

Jimmy Watson

Champions are made of one part talent, one part creativity, one part luck and one part pizzazz.

If one element is lacking, a hockey club is not likely to win a Stanley Cup.

In that sense, the Flyers were fortunate. When the championship clubs of 1974 and 1975 were being assembled, a bubbly defenseman from Smithers, British Columbia had arrived in town to join his older brother in making Philadelphia hockey history.

Jimmy Watson—not unlike his sibling, Joe—oozed excitement and all the good things that come with ice exuberance.

At first it was difficult to define his special qualities except in the most general terms, but the more he performed—starting in 1972-73—the more Spectrum fans realized that they had a jewel in their midst.

Watson could do it both ways. He played his end of the rink exquisitely but also could launch the counterattack and create goal-scoring opportunities. Jimmy did it so well that he often was overlooked, although never by his coach Fred Shero.

JAMES CHARLES "JIMMY" WATSON

BORN: Smithers, British Colombia, August 19, 1952

Position: Defense

NHL Teams: Philadelphia, 1972-1982

Awards/Honors: played in NHL All-Star Game, 1974, 1875, 1976, 1977, 1978; Barry Ashbee Trophy, 1976, 1978

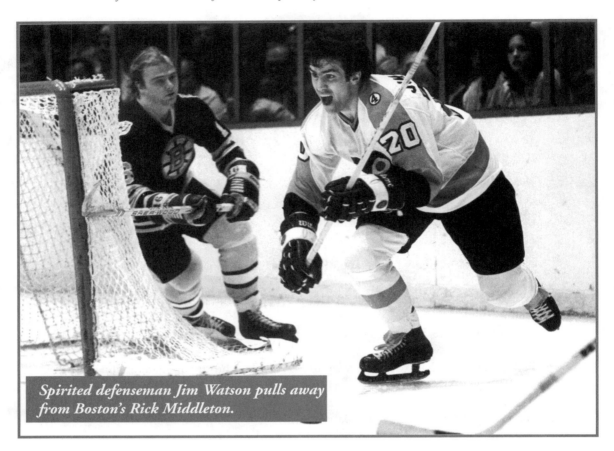

Spirited defenseman Jim Watson pulls away from Boston's Rick Middleton.

"Watson," said Shero, "was one of the best and most underrated defenseman in the NHL."

Like his older brother, Jimmy learned his hockey skills in Smithers and had a distant hope of reaching the major league. When Joe returned from his first season with the Bruins, Jimmy greeted him with the wide-eyed enthusiasm one would expect. "Boy," he said to Joe, "I'd love to be in your shoes."

Joe shot back, "Jimmy, you know I only made it because of hard work and commitment. You can do the same thing."

Remarkably, Watson played four seasons of junior hockey with Calgary of the Western Canada League, was regarded as one of the WCHL's best defensemen and yet was overlooked by every team in the NHL draft. The Rangers passed on Jimmy no less than four times until finally the Flyers plucked him in the third round. A total of 13 defensemen had been drafted before Watson.

At the time Jimmy didn't have a player agent, so he consulted with his older brother, Joe, who replied, "I'll negotiate your contract."

The elder Watson was as good as his word. He signed Jimmy for $45,000, which was $10,000 more than the team's second-round pick. Ironically, when it came time to announce the signing at a press conference in Philadelphia, Joe was AWOL. He had been stranded in British Columbia because of an airline strike.

"I got a better deal for Jimmy than I did for myself," laughed Joe.

For learning purposes, he was dispatched to Richmond of the American Hockey League in 1972-73 but did manage four National Hockey League games and two more in the playoffs. The sum total was one assist and a five-minute major penalty for fighting.

The front office had watched him closely and concluded that he was ready for The Show.

He was. In spades.

Despite precious little NHL experience, Watson played in 78 regular season games and totalled two goals and 18 assists. For the successful Stanley Cup run he was used in 17 games and grabbed a goal and two assists, not to mention 41 penalty minutes.

It was the start of something big. Jimmy's consistency was displayed on the board. After 68 games in 1974-75, Jimmy had chimed in with seven goals and 18 assists for 25 points, along with 72 penalty minutes. In

"Watson," said Shero, "was one of the best and most underrated defenseman in the NHL."

the playoffs—and the Flyers' second Cup run—he added a goal and eight assists in 17 games. The following seasons read like virtual clones of each other: 36 points, 66 penalty minutes in 1975-76; 26 points, 35 penalty minutes in 1976-77; 17 points, 62 penalty minutes in 1977-78. In each playoff, Jimmy contributed at least a goal and two assists.

Watson's undaunting steadiness got him into five NHL All-Star games, and no one could dispute his place as a major component in the Flyers' machine.

"Jimmy was the kind of player who gave you all his assets and nothing was held back," said Paul Holmgren, who became a teammate in the mid-1970s. "He was a true leader."

Having Joe as a teammate was a significant asset. The elder Watson had been an original Flyer, knew the ins and outs of the NHL and never was shy about imparting information.

"We helped each other," said Joe. "When Jimmy came to the Flyers, he may have looked up to me, but after seeing him play a few years, I had nothing but admiration for him."

Jimmy was a two-time winner of the Barry Ashbee Trophy for the outstanding Flyers defensemen. He won the award in 1976 and 1978.

"Jimmy was a very good defensive player," said brother Joe, "but he also had offensive skills."

Watson remained a Flyer to the end. His final season was 1981-82 during which he played in 76 games and tallied three goals and nine assists as well as 99 points.

His overall major-league totals—613 games, 38-148-186—may not be the stuff of which Hall of Fame nominations are made, but the intangibles lifted Jimmy Watson to a special level at The Spectrum, a level shared by Barry Ashbee and other superlative Philadelphia defensemen.

Joe Watson (14) and Ed Van Impe (2) attempt to stop a goal.

Joe Watson

Were it possible to measure energy generated for a hockey club over a ten-year period, Joe Watson would be rated the most galvanic Flyer—per minute played—of them all.

If his spirit could have been bottled, it would have made an awfully successful tonic, because this son of a meat-cutter and waitress in Smithers, British Columbia oozed with enthusiasm.

It should also be noted that he could play defense.

Proof of that is a 15-year-long National Hockey League portfolio that began with the Boston Bruins in 1964 and concluded with the Colorado Rockies in 1979. But the years 1967-1978 were the most relevant because in that period, Watson helped a brand new franchise earn respectability and then a pair of championships.

Joe's years as a Flyer encompassed every facet of the organization's development into a powerhouse as well as one that became a model for others in the NHL. It is to his credit that the Watson image and reputation enhanced the Flyers logo.

JOSEPH JOHN "THUNDERMOUTH" WATSON

Born: Smithers, British Colombia, July 6, 1943

Position: Defense

NHL Teams: Boston, 1964-1967; Philadelphia, 1967-1978; Colorado, 1978-1979

Awards/Honors: NHL All-Star, 1974; Barry Ashbee Trophy, 1975; Flyers Class Guy Award, 1978; inducted, Flyers Hall of Fame, 1996

The Watson saga began on Broad Street in 1967 when he became a cornerstone of an expansion franchise that joined Oakland, Pittsburgh, Minnesota, Los Angeles and St.Louis in the NHL's West Division.

"We weren't loaded with a lot of talent," said Watson's defensemate, Larry Zeidel, "but there was plenty of heart. And nobody—but nobody—had more heart than Joe."

The first year Flyers team distinguished itself by finishing in first place while winning over skeptical Philadelphians whose view of NHL hockey was not exactly enthusiastic at first. But a couple of looks at electric personalities like Watson, Zeidel and Ed Van Impe changed that. Blue-collar fans appreciated a blue-collar effort.

"I was a hard-working defenseman and I had to be," said Watson. "I wasn't as talented as a lot of players, so I had to work hard for what I achieved. I've always felt that the three biggest words of my life are 'Desire,' 'Discipline,' and 'Dedication.' I followed those words if I wanted to be a success."

Watson had begun employing those three Ds as a youngster, learning hockey in Smithers, where it was not uncommon for the thermometer to register 39 below zero in winter. "I certainly didn't want to spend the rest of my life there," said Joe. "I wanted to do whatever possible to get out of the cold. For me, that was hockey."

That would not be easy. Watson was realistic enough to realize that he had significant shortcomings as a player. Fortunately, he had a surplus of energy and was determined to make his dream come true, or at least give it his best shot.

"I wanted to be in the NHL since I was eight years old," he recalled. "Once, I told one of my teachers about it and he just smiled sympathetically. He knew that I wasn't loaded with natural talent. I wasn't a great skater or a shooter. I could pass pretty well and I wasn't afraid to hit or be hit. But the game, at every stage, meant hard work for me."

His first stop was Estevan, Saskatchewan. It was not exactly the tropics, but there was a hockey team in the Saskatchewan Junior League that welcomed Watson to its defense corps. A farm team of the Boston Bruins, Estevan was closely eyed by Hub scouts during the early 1960s when the big club was suffering terribly in the standings.

After two years in Western Canada, Watson got the signal to come to Beantown. Little was known about him other than that he was an exuberant blueliner who had come with a positive recommendation. As luck would have it, Watson arrived in Boston almost simultaneously with the long-sought wunderkind, Bobby Orr.

"This may seem strange," Watson chuckled, "but Bobby Orr and I broke in together, and I scored my first NHL goal before he scored his. Of course, he went on to score 900 more and I had less than 50 for my career."

Nevertheless, Watson played a full season for Boston in 1966-67 alongside Orr, producing a reasonable two goals and 13 assists, not to mention 38 penalty minutes. Not bad for the kid with the big grin. But it was not good enough for the Bruins brass to protect him in the expansion draft.

The Flyers plucked him on June 6, 1967 and he easily made the big club. Not for one year or two, but through the next decade. "I was a survivor," said Watson. "And the reason I was a survivor was because I played within my limitations.

"I always took a lot of pride in preventing someone from scoring goals, because I always thought defensemen were the backbone of a team. Hockey, when I broke into the NHL, was all defense. And there was always room for good defensive defensemen. There were lots of good hip checks and open-ice checks."

Many were delivered by Watson and his sidekick Ed Van Impe. Later, Joe's kid brother, Jimmy, became a Flyer and the club entered the mid-1970s as the most powerful of the expansion teams. Nobody expected Philly to actually win a Stanley Cup, but when they defeated Boston in a six-game final in 1974, it marked a huge triumph of spirit over skill. Watson is remembered as the last Flyer to touch the puck during the first championship game, and it should have qualified him to nab the rubber as a lifetime memento.

"Terry Crisp didn't play too much during the fi-

"I was a hard-working defenseman and I had to be," said Watson. "I wasn't as talented as a lot of players, so I had to work hard for what I achieved. I've always felt that the three biggest words of my life are 'Desire,' 'Discipline,' and 'Dedication.'"

nals," Watson remembered, "but he jumped on the ice and grabbed the puck before I could even reach down. I'll never forget that!"

Another puck he should have saved was used in the classic 1976 match between the Flyers and the powerhouse Soviet touring team at The Spectrum. Prior to the contest, the Russians had enjoyed unusual success against the NHL squads, but in this game, the visitors were beaten, 4-1. The game-winner—a short-handed score—was delivered by Watson in the second period.

"Our coach was Fred Shero," said Joe, "and after the game, he came up to me and said, 'Well, Joe, by scoring that goal, you just set the Russian program back 20 years.'

"Actually, that game really had a big impact on hockey, not only in America but in Russia as well. The Soviets realized that if they wanted to have the best teams in the world, they were going to have to change their style of play. After that, they became more aggressive."

As a Flyer, Watson played against his old buddy, Orr, for a decade. He regards the Bruin immortal as the greatest of all players. "The amazing thing about Orr was that even if you knew exactly what he was going to do, you couldn't stop him because he was so fast and strong.

"The only way to beat him was by exhausting him. Let him have the puck, but get a piece of him each time. That's what we did when we beat the Bruins for our first Cup. In the end, Orr was so tired, he had to take a penalty to stop Bob Clarke on a breakaway. That did it."

Nothing could top the double Stanley Cup parlay in terms of Watson's personal thrills, but overall, his years as a Flyer were a total joy. It was one of those rare mutual admiration society situations which ended, in a sense, when he was traded to Colorado in 1978.

"The Flyers were very fair about it," Watson said. "They told me I could play maybe 30 or 40 games for Philly. The other option was to play regularly for the Rockies. I preferred full ice time, so I went."

He had planned on at least a few more years of NHL hockey, but the fickle finger of fate intervened. Watson was playing his 16th game as a Rockie in St. Louis when Wayne Babych of the Blues slammed him into the boards.

Watson: "My leg bent 90 degrees. I tried to get up but couldn't. I didn't feel much of anything because of the shock. They shot me full of morphine, and I thought I was in hillbilly heaven. The doctors found that the right leg was broken in 13 places. I spent nine months in and out of hospitals and had six operations."

The injury marked the end of Watson's career, and as expected, it was a traumatic period. "I was only 35 and could have played another few years. But then you pick yourself off the floor. The key is keeping busy."

Watson did just that. He went to work for the Flyers and as recently as 1998 was listed as a "senior account executive" with the club.

"The Flyers," he noted, "have always put a great deal of importance on how they deal with the public, and that goes right along with my way of looking at things."

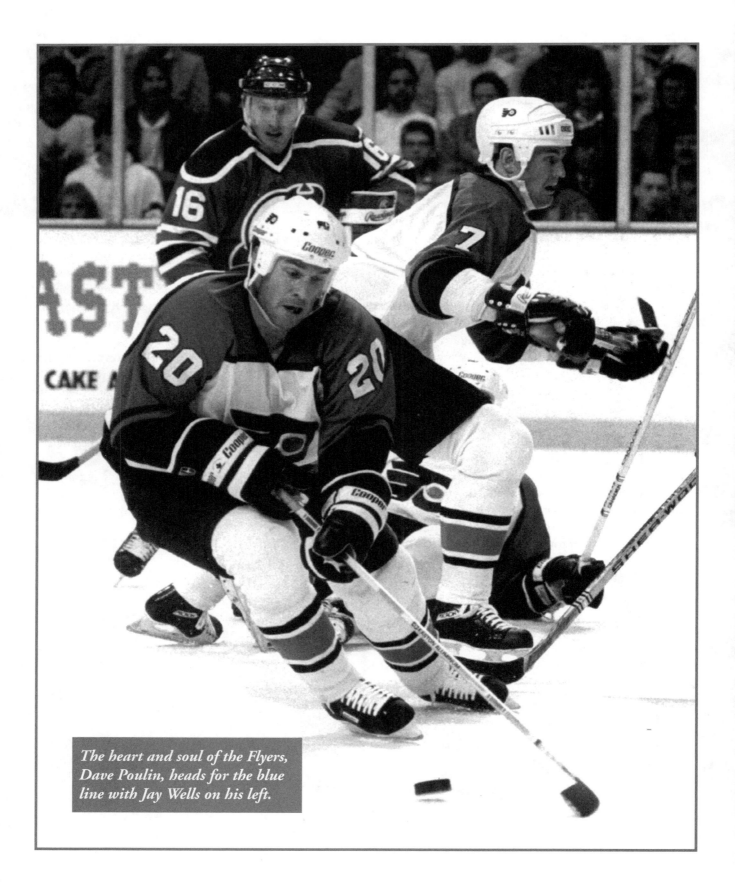

The heart and soul of the Flyers, Dave Poulin, heads for the blue line with Jay Wells on his left.

Dave Poulin

I t would have been absurd to suggest that the Flyers ever could find a captain who would equal Bobby Clarke when it came to intensity, ability and overall leadership qualities. Clarke was the sine qua non in terms of the "C."

He helped orchestrate the double Stanley Cup championships, and his hold on players, fans—and, yes, even management—was such that his subtitle, Mister Hockey, feels perfectly appropriate to this day, long after he hung up his skates.

Nevertheless, there was a personality who did follow Clarke's act and did so not so much as an understudy but virtually as an equal. Dave Poulin, it could be said without fear of contradiction, was a latter-day Bobby Clarke.

Poulin arrived on Broad Street in 1982 at a time when Clarke was winding down his illustrious career. On an afternoon during the 1982-83 season, Clarke was a special guest on a sports program hosted by Dick Schaap. The Flyers were visiting Manhattan for a game against the Rangers and were enjoying a day off in the Big Apple.

As if knowing that Poulin would someday replace him as team leader, Clarke had invited Poulin to tag along and enjoy the television show. Before

DAVID "DAVE" POULIN

BORN: Timmins, Ontario, December 17, 1958

Position: Center

NHL Teams: Philadelphia, 1982-1990; Boston, 1990-1993; Washington, 1993-1995

Awards/Honors: Flyers Class Guy Award, 1984; Captain, Philadelphia, 1984-1990; Played in1986, 1987, 1988 All-Star Games; Frank J. Selke Trophy, 1987

moving before the camera, Clarke turned to a sportswriter friend and pointed at Poulin.

"Keep an eye on that young man," Clarke noted. "You're going to see a lot of him in the NHL. And in a couple of years you will see one of the best players the Flyers ever had."

It was a prophetic statement. Poulin enjoyed one of those rare metamorphoses from unknown to star in a rather short space of time. He was a one-man portrait in courage and displayed that fortitude on many occasions, but one is particularly memorable.

The date was May 2, 1987. Philadelphia was engaged in a bitter playoff with the Islanders, one that had reached a seventh and final game. New York had rallied to tie the series at three games apiece and appeared on the brink of a major upset.

Poulin had missed the six previous games because of cracked ribs and was not expected to be available for the seventh match. But when the Flyers skated onto the Spectrum ice for the showdown, the captain was there, wearing a flak jacket underneath his jersey.

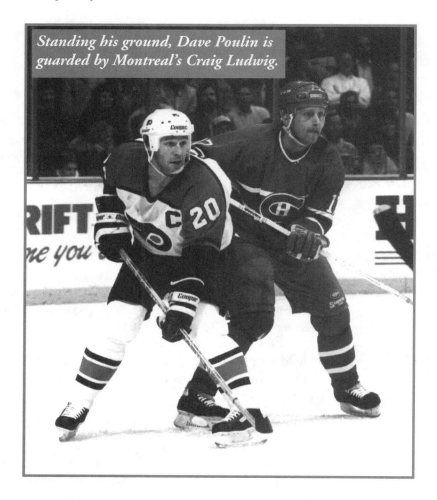

Standing his ground, Dave Poulin is guarded by Montreal's Craig Ludwig.

Sometimes such heroic returns fall flat. The player attempts to make an impact, but the injury is too severe and limits his ability to perform. On rare occasions, the comeback kid delivers. Which is precisely what happened after the opening faceoff.

It was as if each and every Flyer was ignited by the sight of Poulin. They charged at the Islanders like a team possessed and so thoroughly dominated the first period as to leave no doubt about the game's outcome. More importantly, it was Poulin who led the charge that decided the game. He powered his way to the net—in the finest Bobby Clarke tradition—fired a shot and then watched as the rebound was tucked behind beleaguered goalie Kelly Hrudey.

Before the Islanders could regroup, Philadelphia sent formation after formation over the blue line. The final score was 5-1 for the Flyers. It could be said that it also was 5-1 for Dave Poulin.

Considering his first games at The Spectrum, one should have expected something like this outburst. In his rookie year, Poulin played 73 games and racked up 76 points. It was a Philadelphia record for a freshman and a forecast of the man's consistency.

A season later there was no concern about the sophomore slump. He played 73 games and scored 74 points. Someone who averages a point a game after two years in the National Hockey League would figure to have been a top draft choice, but this hardly was the case with Poulin.

A native of Timmins, Ontario, he had no thoughts about playing in the NHL but rather wanted to concen-

"Keep an eye on that young man [Poulin]," Clarke noted. "You're going to see a lot of him in the NHL. And in a couple of years you will see one of the best players the Flyers ever had."

trate on a college education.

"While I was playing Tier II hockey, we had a hotshot defenseman who everybody wanted," Poulin recalled. "All the schools started coming to see him and he decided to go to Michigan State. But he also had a letter from Notre Dame, which he ignored.

"I picked up the letter and filled out an application and sent it back to the college. And that's how I wound up at Notre Dame. I had six recruiting trips but decided that it was for me and cancelled the other five."

Poulin still wasn't thinking seriously about a hockey career. He wanted to concentrate on academics—and did.

NHL scouts were not especially interested in him. He was considered too small at the time, although he had begun to fill out after his teens.

He graduated from Notre Dame with a business degree after playing four years of college hockey.

Few players ever played more heroically through pain than Dave Poulin, a protege of Flyers leader Bob Clarke.

Clearly, he was getting the ice bug, so he jetted to Sweden and played for Vaxco H.C., coached by Ted Sator, who would figure prominently in Dave's future.

As soon as Sator took over as Flyers coach, he invited Poulin to training camp, and in no time at all Dave made the same kind of impression he continued to make throughout his playing career.

"He was our best forward," said Bob McCammon, alluding to the 1983 playoffs when McCammon was general manager on Broad Street. "Dave took the body and never stopped working. He always was a selfless, dedicated, hard-working player.

"We didn't have two stronger players on the team. Dave was strong on his skates and very mature because of his college experience."

Poulin was in the right place at the right time. The early 1980s was a period of transition at The Spectrum.

The Old Guard—led by Clarke—was leaving and a new administration was taking over. When Mike Keenan moved behind the Flyers bench in 1984, Poulin had an ideal leader.

"Timing is everything," said Dave. "When Mike moved in as coach and Clarke moved upstairs, we were a young team and they were looking for a young captain; someone to grow with the team in that role."

Poulin was the man. Clarke knew it. The fans knew it, and, one supposes, Dave knew it as well, although the ascent to the captaincy was not without its concerns.

"The 'C' seemed to weigh a lot at the start," Poulin said. "But my personality was such that I would not shy away from the responsibility. I was the type of player who wanted to be on the ice the last minute of a tie game."

Such dedication was favorably reflected in the statistics. Never a three-digit scorer, Poulin played all ends of the ice. In 1984-85 he finished with a plus-43 in the plus-minus ratings and two years later was plus-47. His appreciation of hockey's nuances often approached professorial levels.

Poulin: "This is a game that can never be perfected. But there are certain variables over which you have some control. Those are the areas in which you must focus your concentration. It is a humbling game, such a team-oriented game. It's a lot of guys depending on each other."

And if they depended on Poulin, well they should have because of his personal and pronounced touch as captain. He always was there for his teammates and always dependable when the chips were down.

"He brought intensity and dedication to the game," said McCammon, "along with good hockey sense. He knew when the team needed a lift, and like Clarke, he made things happen. Dave didn't have too many bad games."

The Poulin years in Philadelphia never produced a Stanley Cup, but there were a couple of trips to the finals. During the 1989 playoffs he scored six goals and five assists in 19 games, but that would be Dave's last major hurrah as a Flyer.

Midway through the 1989-90 season—January 16, 1990 to be exact—he was traded to Boston for Ken Linseman. During the 1990 playoffs, as a Bruin, he played in 18 postseason games and went 8-5-13. He remained a Bruin until the conclusion of the 1992-93 season and signed as a free agent with Washington on August 3, 1993.

It was a disappointing conclusion to a distinguished NHL life. Dave managed only 29 games with the Capitals and put only nine points—including four goals—on the board. After that he called it a career.

Rather appropriately, he went from the NHL back to the collegiate ranks and eventually emerged as head coach of Notre Dame.

"I was no different than anyone else who had played The Game," Poulin concluded. "I knew that I wouldn't be able to play it forever."

But when he did play it, he played it with a passion and precision that left him as one of the most memorable of Flyers.

Ed Van Impe

At a glance, Ed Van Impe seemed too awkward to be a successful big-leaguer.

His skating reminded one of a snowshoer crossing the frozen tundra. His shot had a popgun consistency and his physique hardly suggested a Mister America.

In a hockey sense, however, the sum was not a total of its parts.

Van Impe was all hockey player, through and through a nonpareil competitor and a defenseman who staked out his portion of ice and defied any foe to cross his imaginary border.

Those who did paid the price in welts, lacerations, bruises and, occasionally, sutures. No doubt due to his Western Canadian roots, Van Impe had a frontier quality that was a throwback to an earlier era.

The husky, heavily bearded veteran preferred preventing a score rather than flashing the red light himself—not that he could do the latter very easily.

He also was appreciated for his long stewardship in the minors before ever reaching the National Hockey League in 1966 with the Chicago

ED VAN IMPE

BORN: Saskatoon, Saskatchewan, May 27, 1940

Position: Defense

NHL Teams: Chicago, 1966-1967, Philadelphia, 1967-1976; Pittsburgh, 1976-1977

Awards/Honors: Captain, Philadelphia, 1968-1969, 1972-1973; played in NHL All-Star Game, 1969, 1974, 1975; Inducted to Flyers Hall of Fame, 1993

Defenseman Ed Van Impe was an "original" Flyer.

Blackhawks. But hockey was in his blood and had been since he first laced on a pair of skates at an outdoor rink back home.

A native of Saskatoon, Saskatchewan, Van Impe began playing organized hockey at the age of six. His idol was Doug Harvey, who starred on defense for the Montreal Canadiens. As a Hab, Harvey skated on the club that won an unprecedented five straight Stanley Cups between 1956 and 1960.

"Harvey's style really impressed me," said Van Impe. "He always seemed to know what to do with the puck when he got it."

After three years of junior hockey in Saskatoon, Ed was invited to the St. Catherines, Ontario training camp of the Blackhawks. "I didn't know what to expect from the pros," Van Impe said. "It was pretty strange to be in the middle of stars like Glenn Hall, Bobby Hull and Stan Mikita."

His reward was a ticket to the Blackhawks' farm team in Calgary, Alberta, where he enjoyed a successful, albeit penalty-filled, season. Still, he had hoped to play for Chicago in his second pro season and was dismayed when he got his railway ticket to Buffalo.

"I didn't realize it at the time," he said, "but I was going to be with Buffalo for five long years. Getting to the top was a slow, agonizing process, but I learned along the way."

He eventually graduated to the NHL at the age of 25, teaming on the blue line with Pat Stapleton. Surprisingly, his first NHL game resulted in his first goal, the game-winner in a contest with Les Canadiens. To top off the season, he finished second to Bobby Orr of the Bruins in the voting for the Calder Trophy as Rookie of the Year.

That should have assured him of a long tenure in the Windy City. Instead, he was left unprotected in the expansion draft and claimed by Philadelphia before the 1967-68 season. Ed's response was remarkably mature and without rancor.

"I have no bad feelings about Chicago," said Van Impe. "I'm satisfied with the move to the Flyers."

General manager Bud Poile was more than satisfied with his acquisition. After helping the Flyers to the West Division title in their opening campaign, he was named captain the next year.

"It's been said before but I'll say it again," Van Impe asserted, "it's a big thrill just to play in the NHL, but being named captain of an NHL team is quite an honor. I'm not a holler guy. The best way I can lead this team is to go out on the ice and help win some games."

Ed's willingness to take the team's younger players aside and patiently instruct them contributed to his captaincy. His reputation around the league was another story. A horror story, if you listened to some opponents. Those who drifted to Van Impe's side of the rink were apt to feel the swing of lumber, as in cross check, high stick or butt end. He was not particular and his message was clear. Beware, brother, beware!

"I didn't want other teams to push us around," he said. "It was my belief that opposing forwards had to respect us. I had to keep them wondering what I might do."

They wondered, all right, because one never knew just what response might be delivered by Van Impe other than the fact that it would be with vigor.

Not that he wasn't well-wounded himself. Ed's face was the victim of an Alex Delvecchio shot in 1967 dur-

Ed Van Impe was one of goaltender Bernie Parent's (30) best protectors during the Flyers' Stanley Cup victories in 1974 and 1975.

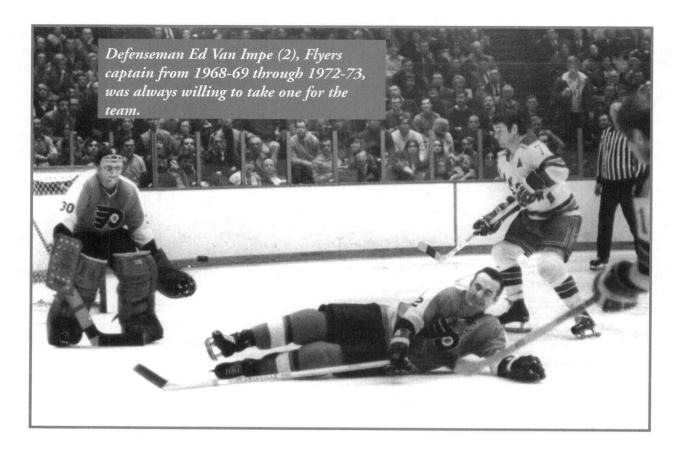

Defenseman Ed Van Impe (2), Flyers captain from 1968-69 through 1972-73, was always willing to take one for the team.

ing a game against Detroit and a blue line drive from Wayne Muloin of the California Golden Seals in 1970. The first injury required 16 stitches, and the second cost him six teeth and 35 stitches, although it did not prevent him from returning in the third period of that same contest.

Vic Stasiuk, coach of the Flyers at the time of the first incident, remarked, "Van Impe has a killer instinct. Not many hockey players would have taken the chance that he did. A guy who will make a move like that really comes to play the game."

Van Impe's lone setback in Philadelphia—if it could be called one—was his battle with the captaincy. Some players are made to wear the "C" and others find it an onerous part of their occupation. The latter was the case with Ed, and he voluntarily abdicated the position early in the 1971-72 season during the coaching reign of Fred Shero.

"Fred and I discussed it," Van Impe explained. "We decided that it would be in the best interests of the club if I just took care of myself and concentrated on doing my own job. If anyone needs advice, I'll be available."

His successor could not have been more appropriate—Bobby Clarke.

"It's been said before but I'll say it again," Van Impe asserted, "it's a big thrill just to play in the NHL, but being named captain of an NHL team is quite an honor. I'm not a holler guy. The best way I can lead this team is to go out on the ice and help win some games."

That the switch was successful for Van Impe was evident by his tenure on Broad Street. His play was jacked up a notch and he became a force on the two Stanley Cup-winning teams in 1974 and 1975.

"His defense was never better after he gave up the captain's role," added Shero. "He was right up there with the most valuable players on the team."

Van Impe remained a Flyer until 1976 when he was dealt to Pittsburgh. He concluded his NHL career a year later. He had played a full decade of big-league hockey, although there are those who still argue that the Blackhawks could have employed him a lot sooner than they had.

But Ed never complained about the treatment. "I owe a lot of thanks to [Blackhawks coach] Billy Reay. He was soft-spoken, but when he spoke he had a point to make. He made a lot of sense."

As for his long years in the minors, "All that experience helped me. If I had come up to the NHL sooner, I might have been sent back down. Those six years in the minors were worth every minute of it."

And those seasons on Broad Street were worth every second Ed Van Impe was on the ice.

One of the original Flyers, Ed Van Impe (2) was a gritty, hard-hitting defenseman. But off the ice, Van Impe was a perfect gentleman.

The Flyers didn't win the Stanley Cup in 1987, but Ron Hextall annexed the Conn Smythe Trophy.

Ron Hextall

Ron Hextall never will be mistaken for the best goaltender in Flyers history, but he certainly ranks among the most vital, vociferous and—when all is said and done—the classiest.

And the fightingest.

In a sense it is sad that Hextall is more remembered for his temper than his talent. Prior to a landmark injury that forever altered his performance, Ron had been at the very top of the National Hockey League list of puck stoppers.

He won the Vezina Trophy in 1987, and following a heroic playoff runs, Hextall emerged in the spring of that year with the Conn Smythe Trophy as the playoffs' most valuable player. And this despite the fact that his Philadelphia team was downed by the Edmonton Oilers.

Another aspect of his game that also has gone underplayed in terms of its historic significance is his puck handling. Hextall not only advanced the art of goaltender participation in the action, he often became a "third defenseman" on the ice for Philadelphia.

Judging by his bloodlines, this was not surprising. Ron's grandfather, Bryan Hextall, Sr., played for the New York Rangers when they won the 1940

RON HEXTALL

Born: Winnipeg, Manitoba, May 3, 1964

Position: Goal

NHL Teams: Philadelphia, 1986-1992; Quebec, 1992-1993; New York Islanders, 1993-1994; Philadelphia, 1994-1999

Awards/Honors: Vezina Trophy, 1987; Conn Smythe Trophy, 1987; NHL First Team All-Star, 1987; NHL All-Rookie Team, 1987; played in NHL All-Star Game, 1987, 1988; Bobby Clarke Trophy, 1987, 1988, 1989

Stanley Cup and was notorious for his belligerent brand of hockey. His father, Bryan, Jr., and his uncle Dennis also took The Game very seriously. Thus, Ron grew up in a hockey-intense family circle that encouraged him to follow the path charted by his elders.

"My father actually wanted me to become a forward," Ron remembered. "He insisted that I learn to skate well and if I still wanted to become a goalie, I would have that skill. I took his advice and played forward until I was eight years old. Then our regular goalie got hurt, so I went between the pipes and never left."

He was good enough to play for the Brandon Wheat Kings of the Western Junior Hockey League. It was there that he began to incorporate the aggressive style into his repertoire.

"Even though I was in goal," he explained, "I loved to be involved in the play. When I saved a shot, I always looked to pass to a teammate. My puck-playing simply evolved from there. By the time I was playing for Brandon, I could shoot the puck with my goalie stick rather well."

He also became involved when the game turned nasty. If he could play the puck, Hextall figured he also could toss a few punches when the spirit moved him. Before he ever reached Philadelphia, he had become a fighting goalie.

Hextall: "There had been a mystique about goaltenders, that they're just supposed to stand in the net and stop the puck. And that was all there was to it. When I started to do things differently, people would say, 'Well, that's not the way it's supposed to be.' But that was the way I played and I said to myself, 'I'll be darned if I'm going to change.'"

He didn't, and his game suffered not a bit. During his stint with Brandon, he was drafted by the Flyers. It was in June 1982, and you had to look carefully to determine where he was. Hextall's name was not called until after the 118th pick in the sixth round.

Following his last season as a junior, 1983-84, Ron turned pro with Kalamazoo of the International League and then moved on to Hershey in the American League. It was a short drive from Philadelphia to Chocolatetown, USA, and the Flyers' scouts watched Hextall's evolution carefully. By the fall of 1986, they had decided he was ready. He was invited to the Flyers' training camp in September 1986, hoping he could crack the majors.

"At first," he recalled, "I was very optimistic. I thought I had a decent shot at making the club. Then I had a bad day and heard whispers that I was going back to Hershey. All I could do was try my best—and I did."

He played 66 games as an NHL rookie, posting a 3.00 goals-against average as well as 37 wins, 21 losses

and six ties. To say that Hextall was exuberant would be the understatement of the half-century.

"I never expected things to go as well as they did," he noted. "Here I was in the league I always wanted to be in with the guys behind me all the way. I was thriving."

His opponents would have chosen another word. Hextall seemed as anxious to stir a fracas as stop a puck. One night at the Meadowlands in New Jersey, he assaulted Devils goalie Alain Chevrier at the end of a game. Another time he would bolt from his crease in a playoff game and throw his blocker at Montreal Canadiens defenseman Chris Chelios. The latter episode—in 1989—earned him a 12-game suspension.

"Any player in the league, except for me, could have done that," said Hextall, "and got nothing. I should have gotten a two-minute minor penalty for roughing or maybe five minutes for leaving the crease. But because I did something out of the ordinary for a goalie —bang!— I get 12 games."

In retrospect, such episodes were small potatoes compared with the big games and big years. There was the 26-game playoff season and another in which he played 15. There was a spectacular run during the late 1980s during which his Flyers had become one of the NHL's elite, thanks in part to Hextall.

"When I had my first tour of duty in Philadelphia, we had Mark Howe and Brad McCrimmon on defense. That was the best defensive tandem at the time. Brad Marsh and Doug Crossman got the rest of the ice time. In those days the Flyers stuck with four guys, and it worked well."

As much as Hextall was beloved by teammates and Broad Streeters, he was loathed by the opposition. Fans in foreign rinks thought nothing of chanting HEX-TALL, HEX-TALL in the hopes of unnerving him. It rarely worked but the din did not go unnoticed.

"It was hard not to hear what was going on," he remembered. "Everybody was always telling me about it, whether they were feeling sorry or happy for me. My teammates would come up to me and say, 'Don't worry about the fans.' But after a while I became immune to it."

He was not, however, immune from being traded. Following a severe groin injury in 1989-90, his ice time became limited. "I was stretching a lot," he said, "and I think I got over-flexible. I wasn't strong enough. I would do the splits and they would just give out."

After seven high-profile years in Philadelphia, the Flyers decided that he was expendable. As part of the complicated deal that brought Eric Lindros to Broad Street, Hextall was moved to Quebec on June 20, 1992.

Hextall in action.

ing Tampa Bay at the ThunderDome in St. Petersburg, and the Islanders needed a win to clinch a playoff berth in their homestretch race with the Florida Panthers.

While most of his teammates performed dreadfully, Hextall outdid himself, keeping every puck out of his net until teammate Steve Thomas fired a pair to clinch the 2-0 victory. "It was Ronnie's best game of the year," said general manager Don Maloney.

It was Hextall's last moment of glory as an Islander. Facing the Rangers in the opening playoff round, he lost his groove, lost three out of the three games he started and finished with an horrendous 6.08 goals, against average. When the opportunity presented itself, Maloney dealt Hextall back to Philadelphia for Tommy Soderstrom on September 22, 1994.

"That was hard for me to swallow," he admitted, "that the Flyers didn't want me anymore."

He played competently in the strange French-Canadian surroundings, good enough to land a playoff berth for Les Nordiques. But they exited in a six-game opening round, and the next thing Ron knew he was moved to the Islanders.

"I wasn't crazy about being traded either time, but the second time around was easier because we didn't put down the same kind of roots in Quebec. Hockey is funny; you never know what's coming. It's just like the puck; you have to be ready for it."

His one year at Nassau Coliseum was bittersweet. At times Hextall was nothing short of sensational, and at other times, he was mediocre. His finest hour was in the next to last game of the season. New York was play-

Some seasoned Flyers-watchers could not believe that general manager Bob Clarke would gamble on Hextall returning to form, particularly after his debacle in the 1994 playoffs. But Clarke was a believer, and Hextall made a triumphant return. He may not have simmered with the old-time bluster, but he still was a solid net minder and a more mature one.

"We all mature as life goes on," he reflected. "I was a smarter goalie in my second time around with the Flyers than I was during the first run. I could handle situations better. I kept my emotions more intact on the ice than when I would let them get the best of me."

His numbers were better than they had been on Long Island or in Quebec: 2.89, then 2.17 and 2.56. But there were difficulties that could not be totally erased.

During the 1995 third playoff round against the

Ron Hextall stones Brian Bellows at point-blank range.

Devils, Philadelphia was favored, but Hextall allowed a couple of questionable goals that turned the series in New Jersey's favor. It would happen again in 1997, although his club reached the finals against Detroit. Word among the media was that Clarke had to deal for a more reliable goaltender in order to win a Stanley Cup.

Undaunted, the G.M. stayed with Hextall at the start of 1997-98, and Ron's game remained first-rate. He played in 46 games and posted a 2.17 goals-against average— fifth best in the NHL—with 21 wins, 17 losses and seven ties, not to mention four shutouts. Clarke did not trade him; however, late in the season, the G.M. moved second-string goalie Garth Snow to Vancouver for Sean Burke.

The Flyers chose to start Burke in the opening play-off round against Buffalo and lost in five games. Ron

Hockey is funny; you never know what's coming. It's just like the puck; you have to be ready for it."

saw action for only 20 minutes of the entire series but received no decision.

Hextall, who always faced the music when it came to discussing his assets or debits with the media, understood the situation. He had been around long enough to know that a goalie's life is not an easy one, not when you're a rookie and not when you're a veteran.

Mark Messier goes wide on a sprawling Ron Hextall.

"I learned over the years that the goalie is the guy everyone notices when he makes a mistake," said Hextall. "He's an easy target. The first time I was booed—probably in my fourth year in Philly—I'll admit it hurt. It was hard. But you step back and realize it's not a personal thing. They just thought I was not playing the way they expected me to play. There's really nothing wrong with that. Mike Schmidt—the best third baseman of all time—got booed in Philly. So did Bernie Parent, Pelle Lindbergh. Even Billy Smith—as great a goalie as the Islanders ever had—was booed at Nassau. It comes with the territory."

Surely, Ron Hextall had nothing for which to apologize.

"When I started my career," he concluded, "I said I'd like to play until I was 35. When I went through the tough injuries in Philadelphia, I said to myself, 'Please, just let me play until I'm 32.' I figured that anything after 32 would be great. I knew that there would be a time when the fun ran out. And that would be when I'd say I had enough."

By the fall of 1998, age and injuries had taken its toll. He managed to play only 23 games but still wound up above .500. His final stats were ten wins, seven losses and four ties. His goals-against average was 2.53.

Following that season, Hextall turned to scouting, a position he retained through the 2002-03 season.

While the fighting goalie never could claim that he was a Cup champion, he nevertheless will go down in history as one of the most dedicated and proud Flyers.

Paul Holmgren, one of the toughest Flyers ever, celebrates a goal.

Paul Holmgren

Paul Holmgren was as noble a Flyer as ever graced the Philadelphia ice lanes, both as a player and a coach.

He was a stand-up guy. Playing forward, he would back smaller players such as Ken Linseman who simply would be fodder for the bigger fighters.

"Kenny was too little to fight," Holmgren once said. "He looked to me to look after him."

That was okay with Holmgren. He knew why he was employed by the Flyers, and he took care of business in a dispassionate but dedicated manner.

He also was the centerpiece in one of the most significant changing of the guards ever experienced by the Flyers.

This followed Philadelphia's double Stanley Cup victories. The Broad Street Bullies had bulldozed their opposition, led by fist-throwing Dave (Hammer) Schultz. They carried their intimidation tactics into the 1976 Stanley Cup finals in the hopes of winning a third consecutive Cup, but forces militated against such a victory.

For one thing, crack goalie Bernie Parent no longer was guarding the cage. For another, Schultz had suffered decisive defeats to Clark Gillies of the New

PAUL HOWARD HOLMGREN

Born: St. Paul, Minnesota, December 2, 1955

Position: Right Wing

NHL Teams: Philadelphia, 1975-1984; Minnesota, 1984-1985

Awards/Honors: Played in 1981 NHL All-Star Game

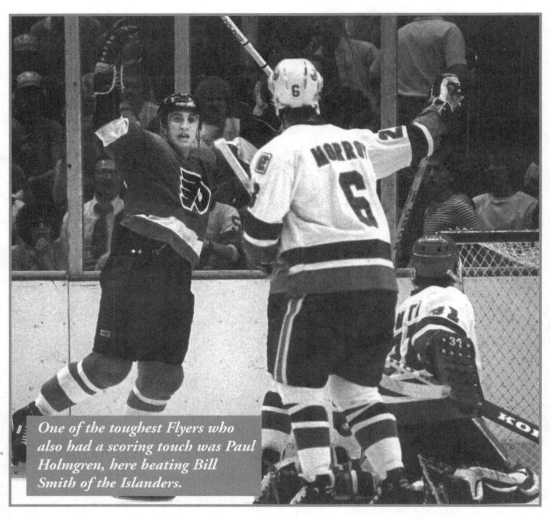

One of the toughest Flyers who also had a scoring touch was Paul Holmgren, here beating Bill Smith of the Islanders.

Schultz got the message.

"When I saw that big rookie, Holmgren, I didn't feel terribly secure," Schultz reflected.

His intuition was good. Before the season opened, Schultz had been dealt to Los Angeles. The Hammer, who had fought his butt off protecting the likes of Rick MacLeish, Bob Clarke and Orest Kindrachuk, to name a few, had been exchanged for a pair of draft choices.

That was secondary. Primary was the challenge of replacing the fighting void left by The Hammer. "I just hope we don't regret this," said Clarke, alluding to Schultz's departure.

Were there any regrets, they were dispelled once and for all by Holmgren on the night of October 19, 1976.

Los Angeles was scheduled to visit Philadelphia, and it meant homecoming for Schultz. It also meant that his fans would expect a battle. That came with The Hammer's territory, and he rarely failed to oblige.

Early in the first period hostilities erupted. It began with a fistfight between Bob Kelly and Dave Hutchison. Minutes later, Jack McIlhargey and Hutchison collided. Then Dupont stepped in to further inflame the conflagration.

Schultz looked around and noticed Holmgren.

"Let's go!" he suggested, offering the standard hockey player's invite to a fight.

At the time Holmgren had a mask attached to his helmet. It was designed to protect an injured eye. Before Schultz could organize his attack, Holmgren launched a series of rights and then hurled Schultz to the ice. Suddenly, the crowd roared.

Where once the packed Spectrum crowd had stood

York Islanders and Ken Houston of the Atlanta Flames. The Hammer's reputation began slipping, and management took due note of the dilemma.

To fortify the fighting brigade, the general staff had imported two imposing forwards. Mel Bridgman was a big, mean center. He was young, offered innumerable offensive options and carried a reputation as a better-than-decent fighter.

The other attack force was a native of Minnesota who had made his professional debut in the World Hockey Association. Playing for the Minnesota Fighting Saints in 1975-76, Holmgren established himself as a reasonable checking forward who also could double as an enforcer, if necessary.

"It was obvious that he could handle his dukes," said former WHA slugger Nick Fotiu.

The Flyers acquired him in 1975-76, but he played in only one NHL game—worth two minutes in penalties—and the rest in Richmond of the AHL. But in September 1976 he showed up at the Flyers training camp.

"It was obvious that he could handle his dukes," said former WHA slugger Nick Fotiu.

behind The Hammer, now it was Holmgren who won the cheers.

"Holmgren pummeled me around the right eye and nose," Schultz remembered. "Meanwhile, the Spectrum was going crazy. In Philadelphia, I was now a bum."

Conversely, Holmgren had become a hero. But he would establish himself as more than a fighter and a better all-round player than Schultz ever was. Whereas The Hammer's best season as a goal-scorer was 20 goals, Holmgren reached 30 in 1979-80—as well as 267 penalty minutes—before moving on to a sensational playoff.

Over a spread of 18 postseason contests, he scored ten goals and ten assists for 20 points. Holmgren had become a power forward par excellence and a member of the Flyers who reached the 1980 Stanley Cup finals against the Islanders.

The blend of brute force and artistry continued the following season. During the 1981 playoffs Holmgren averaged more than a point a game and maintained his intimidating qualities.

Holmgren continued as a Flyer through the middle of the 1983-84 season when he was sent to the Minnesota North Stars. The curtain was pulled on his NHL career in 1984-85, and he eventually moved into coaching. His Flyers employment behind

the bench began in 1988 when he succeeded Mike Keenan.

Holmgren had been a Keenan assistant, hired in 1985 after Ted Sator had left to coach the Rangers. When Keenan was fired in the spring of 1988, Holmgren's turn had come.

Paul was called a "players' coach." It was a tag that he wore with some uneasiness.

Holmgren: "I'm not sure what the term 'players' coach' means. What I expect is the same that Mike Keenan expected from his players when he was in Philadelphia. I expect them to work their hardest and do their best and do what they do best all the time. For example, a Craig Berube is expected to play tough and physical. On the other hand, a skill player like Pelle Eklund is

One of the best cornermen, Paul Holmgren is this time trapped by Islanders defenseman Dave Langevin.

expected to score goals. What fans don't see is what the coach does when they are not around. Nobody knows what I do behind closed doors with my team. Personally, I don't think anybody has to know.

"As far as ranting and raving on the bench, blasting players in public, I would never do that. What I say in the locker room is for the players' ears alone. What's said in the room is sacred."

Holmgren was behind the Flyers' bench as head coach from 1988-89 through 1991-92. Paul's best season was his first, when the Flyers finished at .500 but went to the Conference finals against Montreal. They were beaten in six games but fought hard and long and came close to an upset. After that it was downhill for Holmgren. The team missed the playoffs in the next two years, and consequently he was given his walking papers. His successor was Bill Dineen, but some players believed that Holmgren took a bum rap.

"Under Keenan, the team didn't change much," said Mark Howe. "Not for four years. I never saw a team stick with the same players for four years and win. We were going downhill for four years."

Holmgren resumed coaching in Hartford from 1992 to 1995. His motto remained the same as it had been on Broad Street: "Have pride in yourself, work hard and play for the sweater."

During training camp in 1994 he added the general manager's job to his portfolio. After 17 games, he gave up coaching and hired Pierre McGuire for the job. Nothing worked, and to compound the distress, a late afternoon car wreck resulted in a DWI offense against Holmgren. He later checked into a detoxification clinic in California to begin recovery. Following that, he publicly admitting that he suffered from a drinking problem and vowed to change his life.

Holmgren's coaching career ended on November 5, 1995 when he was replaced by Paul Maurice. Fortunately, Paul remained in hockey and took a new position as and NHL scout, a position he retained through the 1990s.

Ken Linseman

Wearing spectacles that topped off his slight frame, Ken Linseman looked very much like the antique collector he claimed to be. He stood in a group, conversing articulately on a variety of subjects, none of which had anything to do with a stick or puck.

"I've been attracted to antiques since I was growing up in Kingston, Ontario," he explained. "My grandmother owned things that were 100 years old. I have some Victorian items and a lot of German antiques—not gaudy, but classy.

"There's no comparison between the old and the modern in terms of quality of craftsmanship. I love old buildings with character. That's why I love cities like Philadelphia."

And Philadelphia, in turn, loved Ken Linseman for four years.

But not because he was an expert on the antiquities. The affection for Linseman was rooted in his effortless skating, his knack for ferreting a puck out of the corners and his ability to ignite the red light.

Those who favored a more volatile brand of hockey were lured to Linseman because of his penchant for troublemaking. After all, he was not nicknamed "The Rat" because he did imitations of Little Lord Fauntleroy.

His penalty minutes invariably were in triple digits and once—in 1981-82—Ken's PIM reached 275.

Despite his on-ice indiscretions, Linseman was admired for his tenacity

KEN LINSEMAN

Born: Kingston, Ontario, August 11, 1958

Position: Center

NHL Teams: Philadelphia, 1978-1982; Edmonton, 1982-1984; Boston, 1984-1989; Philadelphia, 1989-1990; Edmonton, 1990-1991; Toronoto, 1991-1992

Some speedy puck handling courtesy of Ken Linseman.

and willingness to sacrifice a relatively minuscule physique in order to corral the puck.

"I always had a lot of respect for the way he played the game," said Terry O'Reilly, the longtime Boston Bruins power forward. "He played it hard and he played it as tough as a lot of guys twice his size."

Linseman was Philadelphia's second choice—seventh overall—in the 1978 amateur draft. Prior to his National Hockey League debut, he played the 1977-78 season with Birmingham in the World Hockey Association. It was there that he attracted the Flyers' attention and admiration. Playing in what many considered a goon league, Linseman not only survived but tallied 76 points in 71 games.

The Flyers had intended for him to play the 1978-79 season in Maine of the American Hockey League, but Ken showed enough to get 30 big-league games under his belt and managed eight playoff games. That did it. He averaged a point a game (2-6-8) and won a berth on the 1979-80 squad that went all the way to the Stanley Cup finals before losing to the New York Islanders in six games.

"The more competitive and intense the situation," said Linseman, "the more I liked it."

He underlined his point in the 1980 playoffs. Over 17 postseason games, he scored four goals and had 18 assists and 22 points. Of all the Flyers, he was the most dangerous to the Islanders in Game 6, which went into sudden-death overtime before being decided by Bob Nystrom's goal.

"There's such a fine line between winning and losing that you can't let down," he opined. "From the time I started playing junior hockey, there was some kind of challenge for me to go for."

If Linseman wasn't looking for a fight, a challenge would do. When the WHA Bulls offered him a contract in Birmingham, the sport's establishment attempted to prevent him from signing because hockey's minimum draft age was 20. Linseman went to court.

At the time it was considered an unprecedented and even brassy move on the teenager's part. Undaunted, Linseman won a landmark case that paved the way for the draft age to be permanently lowered to 18.

When he set up shop at The Spectrum, Linseman maintained a rough-housing tradition that had its roots in the Dave Schultz-Andre Dupont-Bob Kelly years. In his first full season he totalled 107 penalty minutes.

"I was never sure whether I was supposed to be a goal-scorer or playmaker or just start trouble," Linseman explained. "I took some stupid penalties."

O'Reilly: "I used to think Ken had a bonus clause in his contract for penalty minutes."

Coincidentally—or maybe not so coincidentally— Linseman enjoyed his finest points season the year he reached 275 penalty minutes. In 1981-82, he scored 24 goals and 68 assists for 92 points.

"He came to play every night," said Bruins general manager Harry Sinden. "He played well almost every night. He seemed to respond pretty well when there was a challenge."

His critics charged that Linseman had a knack for committing mayhem but disappearing behind bigger teammates when retribution was sought. That modus operandi inspired Minnesota skating coach Dick Vraa to note, "As a baby, I bet Kenny threw Pablum at his mother."

He was an integral element during the Flyers' 35-game win streak during the 1979-80 season and played top-level hockey in Philadelphia through the 1981-82 season.

Ken Linseman takes on Rick Ley of Hartford.

Philadelphia acquired Ken Linseman as compensation for the New York Rangers' signing of Coach Fred Shero.

But on August 19, 1982 the Flyers traded Linseman, Greg Adams and their first- and third-round picks in the 1983 NHL entry draft to Hartford in exchange for Mark Howe and the Whalers' third-round pick (Derrick Smith) in the 1983 draft. The Whalers immediately dealt Linseman to the Edmonton Oilers along with Don Nachbaur in exchange for Risto Siltanen and Brent Loney.

"I had always felt that even though the Flyers reached the finals in 1980, I didn't feel that much satisfaction," said Linseman. "I wanted to win the whole damn thing. The Stanley Cup."

He got his wish with Edmonton.

Linseman played two seasons for the Oilers—1982-83 and 1983-84. In the first, he reached the finals, but

"The more competitive and intense the situation," said Linseman, "the more I liked it."

Edmonton was swept in four games by the New York Islanders. But the teams met again in the 1984 finals, and this time the Oilers won in five games. It was Linseman who scored the Cup-winner in Game 5.

Following the 1983-84 season, he was traded to Boston for Mike Krushelnyski. He spent five and a half seasons with the Bruins before being dealt back to Philadelphia for Dave Poulin.

"We needed more offense," said general manager Bob Clarke. "Ken Linseman can provide that."

Well, sort of.

In 29 games as a Flyer revisited, Linseman scored five goals and nine assists. For Clarke, it was too little and too late. Ken was moved back to Edmonton in 1990-91 and finished his NHL career with Toronto a season later.

Over more than a decade Ken Linseman made an impact. What kind would depend on whether he played for you or not. Nobody summed up the feeling better than Glen Sonmor, who coached him in Birmingham.

"When he was on your side," Sonmor concluded, "you loved him. But if he wasn't, Kenny was an S.O.B."

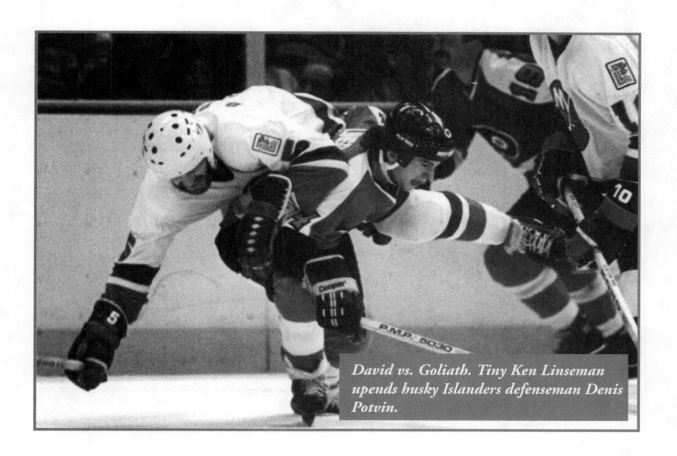

David vs. Goliath. Tiny Ken Linseman upends husky Islanders defenseman Denis Potvin.

Andre (Moose) Dupont lays the lumber on Pat Conacher of the Rangers.

Andre "Moose" Dupont

One of the more endearing qualities about the Broad Street Bullies when they were rampaging through the National Hockey League in the 1970s was the abundance of unadulterated characters on the team.

There was a Hammer, a Big Bird, and most of all, a Moose.

Andre Dupont, defenseman, oozed with humor and a zest for life out of every pore. On the ice, he also oozed with another form of enthusiasm, although his opposition was not as appreciative. When Moose met the opposition, it never was on the friendliest of terms.

He hit hard, he hit often, and when the spirit moved him, he fought. Dupont didn't win all of his fights, but he never, never backed down from one whether the foe was a heavyweight or a middleweight. No less a connoisseur of fisticuffs, Don (Grapes) Cherry remained one of Dupont's most ardent admirers through the defenseman's career.

"I remember one time when Moose had a beauty of a fight with Stan Jonathan of the Bruins," Cherry recalled. "Dupont was cut pretty good but hung in, throwing them at the end although Jonathan was one of the league's best fighters at the time.

ANDRE "MOOSE" DUPONT

Born: Trois-Rivieres, Quebec, July 27, 1949

Position: Defense

NHL Teams: New York Rangers, 1970-1971; St. Louis, 1971-1973; Philadelphia, 1973-1980; Quebec, 1980-1983

Awards/Honors: played in NHL All-Star Game, 1976; Barry Ashbee Trophy, 1977; Flyers Class Guy Award, 1980

"Later in the game there was another fight in the corner between two other guys. John Wensink was watching. Don Saleski came up behind Wensink—another top slugger—and pushed him but then skated away. Wensink turned around looking for trouble, and guess who had to take him on—none other than Moose Dupont! One thing about Moose, he always showed up."

Andre originally showed up with the Montreal Canadiens farm system. He played for the Habs' junior team in 1968-69 and seemed to be en route to a career in his native province of Quebec. But the New York Rangers drafted him in the first round of the 1969 amateur draft and assigned him to their Omaha team in the Central Hockey League.

Moose played most of the 1969-70 season in Nebraska and returned there the following year, but the Broadway Blueshirts elevated him for seven games. In that brief introduction to the bigs, he scored a goal, had two assists and 21 penalty minutes. All appearances suggested that he was made for the Big Apple, but in November 1971 the Rangers packaged Moose in a comprehensive deal and dispatched him to St. Louis, where he played two years for the Blues.

Precisely why he was traded again is a bit of a mystery, but the Flyers never complained. Philadelphia dealt Brent Hughes and Pierre Plante to St. Louis on December 14, 1972 and received the ebullient French-Canadian in return.

"When I was in St. Louis," Dupont remembered, "the team was not doing well. They were active on the trade market, trying to shake up the club. It was my good fortune to be dealt to Philly."

He was fortunate because the Flyers at the time were coached by Fred Shero, who just happened to have been Dupont's mentor in Omaha.

"Freddie had been a terrific coach for me in the minors," added Dupont, "so I considered myself lucky to wind up working for him again, only this time in the NHL."

If it was a marriage made in hockey heaven for Dupont, Shero and the Flyers shared the enthusiasm. "We had won a championship in Omaha," said Shero, "and Moose had a lot to do with it. We had been together through adversity and now he was going to be playing for a good team on the rise."

That it was.

Dupont made his Flyers debut at a most propitious time. The club was going up, up, UP, and with exhilarating skaters such as Bobby Clarke, Bill Barber and Joe Watson, the sky seemed the limit for the orange-and-black.

They would soon be nicknamed the Broad Street

"One thing about Moose, he always showed up."

Bullies, and Moose would be front and center among the brawlers; that is, when he wasn't playing strong, sensible defense.

"A lot of people accused us of playing 'goon hockey,'" said Dupont. "I don't think it was 'goon hockey.' Our game was that everybody had to hit. Nobody cheated. It was as simple as that. If some people were intimidated, I don't think we should be blamed."

Shero insisted that his skaters play the man and Dupont gladly took his coach literally. In fact, he took his coach's advice the way he would have taken his father's advice, because Fred Shero was accepted like a father to the defenseman.

"Everything I knew about hockey I learned from him," said Dupont. "When I made a mistake, he explained what I did wrong instead of getting on me about it."

One of Shero's most insightful decisions was pairing Dupont on defense with the veteran Barry Ashbee, who had spent considerable time learning the trade in the minor leagues. When Ashbee's career abruptly ended due to an eye injury, Barry became an assistant coach and worked assiduously with Dupont.

"Asher was quite a man," said Dupont. "I used to run around a lot on the ice, but he made me understand the guys have to come to me."

Dupont's rambunctiousness was reflected in the penalty minutes. He was always in the three digits and occasionally took some heat from the high command.

"His fault was taking penalties at the wrong time," said assistant coach Mike Nykoluk. "Like when we were on the power play. He would try to intimidate people when we had the extra man."

That Moose learned his lessons was proven by his tenure in Philadelphia. He played on both Stanley Cup championship teams and remained on Broad Street through the decade of the 1970s.

"There was no question of his value to the Flyers," said onetime coach Pat Quinn. "He was steady, fearless and strong. If he had been put on the trading block during his prime there were many teams looking to get him."

As much as his teammates enjoyed having Dupont

Moose Dupont takes Boston's Gary Doak out of the play at The Spectrum.

at their side during the games, they revelled in his humor off the ice. And since English was his second language, Moose was not exactly professorial in handling Uncle Sam's language.

Nor was he particular about the opponent's ethnic characteristics. Once during a match against the Toronto Maple Leafs, Dupont singled out Leaf' defenseman Borje Salming for needling. It should be noted that just about everyone in the NHL knew that Salming was the first outstanding Swede to make an imprint in North American hockey.

Nevertheless, Moose kept referring to him as "Swiss Cheese."

Flyers teammate Gary Dornhoefer was at a loss to figure out the object of Dupont's derision and finally questioned Moose. When Dupont noted that he was try-

ing to get Salming's goat, Dornhoefer explained that there was no Swiss blood in the Toronto backliner.

"Same t'ing," barked Dupont and once again shouted, "Hey, Swiss Cheese!"

The Moose lasted in Philadelphia long after The Hammer but did not finish his career as a Flyer. He was sold by the Flyers to the Quebec Nordiques during the summer of 1980 and played three more seasons of solid hockey in his native province.

"The Flyers were nice enough to tell me a year in advance that I probably would be leaving the team," said Dupont. "It hurt me to leave old friends, but it was good that I wound up in Quebec."

And speaking of old friends, Andre Dupont always will be remembered as one by any and all who watched him work the trenches for the Flyers.

Mel Bridgman was an effective captain in the post-Bob Clarke era.

Mel Bridgman

When you are your club's first choice in the entry draft and also happen to be the first overall selection, you are thrust so deep into the National Hockey League pressure cooker, only a stir-frying could be hotter.

Mel Bridgman knew all about it.

After a sensational 1974-75 season with Victoria in the Western (Junior) Hockey League, Bridgman was plucked ahead of everyone by the Flyers and absorbed the hullabaloo that goes with a phenom's territory.

What made it even more anxiety-provoking was the fact that to obtain him, the Flyers had paid a high price. Philadelphia sent Bill Clement, a center from both the 1974 and 1975 Cup teams, Don McLean, their first-round pick in 1975, and the Flyers' first-round pick of 1976 to the Washington Capitals.

When he attended the orange and black training camp, he immediately noticed that centers Bobby Clarke, Rick MacLeish, Orest Kindrachuk and Terry Crisp were ahead of him in the pecking order of pivots. Obviously it was not easy for Bridgman at first, and when the Trenton, Ontario native arrived on Broad Street he shied away from the spotlight like an introvert ducks a conversation.

"Mel was very shy and withdrawn," teammate Ross Lonsberry remem-

KEN JOHN BRIDGMAN

BORN: Trenton, Ontario, April 28, 1955

Position: Center

NHL Teams: Philadelphia, 1975-1982; Calgary, 1981-1983; New Jersey, 1983-1987; Detroit, 1987-1988; Vancouver, 1988-1989

Awards/Honors: Captain, Philadelphia, 1974-1981; Captain, New Jersey, 1984-1987

Mel Bridgman is virtually carried to the bench by a big goal.

When Philadelphia eliminated Toronto in the quarter-finals that year, Mel delivered a pair of goals and a steady two-way game for the clincher. It was a game that persuaded the pundits that the kid was here to stay.

"He showed us then and there that he was a super kid," said Terry Crisp, one of the Flyers' veterans at the time. "There he was, just 20 years old, playing in his first playoff and it hardly fazed him."

At the time Bridgman centered a line with Lonsberry on right wing and either Gary Dornhoefer or Bob Kelly on the left side. His linemates would vary over the years, but Mel's consistency was unwavering.

In 1979-80, playing under coach Pat Quinn, he was a major force in the Flyers' march to the Stanley Cup finals against the New York Islanders. "He had a special determination," recalled Quinn. "When Mel went after the puck, he was like a bulldog. He had his mind set. If you put a wall between him and his assignment, you would lose the wall."

Although his top point season at The Spectrum was 1978-79 when he produced 24 goals and 35 assists, his overall play was what gratified coaches such as Quinn and Fred Shero.

"Mel was worth what the Flyers gave up to get him," said Shero. "He could do so many things, but best of all, he was big and strong. He wasn't afraid to go after the puck and take a shot to get it, and he could give a shot to knock someone off the puck, too."

In the estimation of some critics, Bridgman could have—and, perhaps, should have—been an even better player for the Flyers. Conceivably, he was limited in scope when he came to the two-time Cup winners.

"In a way," Bridgman reflected, "I sometimes wished I had come up with a team that wasn't quite so good. I could have gotten more ice time and maybe moved my career ahead a little faster. But that's hindsight.

"The good thing about coming to the Flyers was that I learned about winning and to be a winner. That kind of development is as important as individual development."

bered. "He was pretty nervous and unsure of himself. The veterans on the team really kidded him a lot."

But there was no kidding about Bridgman's game. Blending offensive gifts with a rugged frame, he enjoyed a superior NHL rookie season in 1975-76, tallying 23 goals and 27 assists for 50 points over a full 80-game schedule.

"Bridgman did a lot of growing up between that rookie training camp and the playoffs," Lonsberry added. "He came out of his shell and became one of us."

Better still, he continued producing. Breaking into the lineup of a two-time Stanley Cup-winning team was difficult enough, but Mel continued to help the club in its quest for a third straight title. That the Flyers failed—although they did reach the finals—was not Bridgman's fault. Over 16 playoff games, he produced six goals and eight assists for 14 points.

To those who would quarrel with Bridgman's numbers, Mel's defense was simple enough; his role had been altered from scorer—which he did well in junior hockey—to checking forward. He played against the enemy's best lines and also killed penalties.

To his everlasting chagrin, in 1980 Bridgman was on the ice in the sudden-death overtime of Game 6 when Bob Nystrom beat goalie Pete Peeters for the Islanders' victory over the Flyers and New York's first Stanley Cup.

Mel Bridgman's thrust is foiled by Blues goalie Ed Staniowski.

"We came close, oh so close, to winning the Cup that year," he said.

Bridgman: "After losing the way we did, you stay awake nights thinking of things you might have done as an individual to change the outcome of just one game."

Bridgman need not have complained. In the spring of 1980 he enjoyed his secondbest point production with two goals and nine assists for 11 points in 19 games. His work ethic was so flawless that when Clarke became a player-coach in 1979, Mel was named Philadelphia captain.

"In order to be effective," Bridgman said, "I had to work as hard as I could. I had to go into the corners and not worry."

He never seemed to worry about his security as a longtime Flyer until the fall of 1981. Badly in need of defensive help, the think tank on Broad Street scoured NHL rosters and decided that Brad Marsh, a solid Calgary backliner, would be ideal in Philly. The problem was that the Flames wanted value in return.

On November 11, 1981 Bridgman was dealt to Calgary for Marsh. He played two seasons in Western Canada before being swapped for Steve Tambellini and Joel Quennville of the New Jersey Devils on June 21, 1983. Mel became Devils captain and starred at The Meadowlands until he was swapped to Detroit in 1986-87.

"In order to be effective," Bridgman said, "I had to work as hard as I could. I had to go into the corners and not worry."

His last season as a major-leaguer was spent in Vancouver in 1988-89 after which he retired and eventually moved into Ottawa Senators' front office before a stint at hockey agenting.

All things considered, Bridgman's 13-year big-league career was a commendable, if not stupendous, one which featured all the subtle aspects of hockey that are appreciated by coaches and teammates.

If Mel Bridgman was not the greatest of Flyers, it certainly was not for lack of trying.

Although not known for his scoring prowess, defenseman Brad Marsh was known to have scored big goals, including a huge Game 7 playoff shot against the Islanders.

Brad Marsh

Brad Marsh never wanted to wear a helmet in a National Hockey League game, and he had the legal small print to support his dream.

NHL bylaws required that players entering the league after June 1, 1979 wear helmets.

Marsh became an Atlanta Flame in 1978 and therefore was exempt.

"I wanted to be the last player in the league without a helmet," he said.

His wish was almost fulfilled over a career that spanned 15 years of the most dogged, efficient hockey that a cerebral—sometimes plodding—defenseman could display.

Because of his determination to play bareheaded, Marsh's career nearly was curtailed in 1968.

Skating for the orange and black, Marsh was playing against the Bruins at The Spectrum when he was hit by Boston defenseman Raymond Bourque and right wing Cam Neely near the Boston blue line.

Marsh's head was driven into a post that supports the glass near the end of the bench. He toppled backward and smacked his head violently on the ice.

"He could have died, right then and there," said then Bruins right wing Willi Plett. "He was unconscious for a short time, with blood pouring

BRAD MARSH

BORN: London, Ontario, March 31, 1958
Position: Defense

NHL Teams: Atlanta/Calgary, 1978-1981; Philadelphia, 1981-1988; Toronto, 1988-1991; Detroit, 1991-1992; Ottawa, 1992-1993

Awards/Honors: Captain, Calgary, 1980-1981; Flyers Class Guy Award, 1985

Glenn (Chico) Resch gets a victory hug from defenseman Brad Marsh.

ership qualities that one expected from a Bobby Clarke before him.

"Brad had that innate ability to lead that you don't always see with just the performance on the ice," said his former Flyers coach Ted Sator.

He came to the Flyers after two seasons in Atlanta and a season and a quarter with Calgary. Philadelphia gambled by sending top center Mel Bridgman to the Flames in exchange for Marsh. In retrospect, it was a no-brainer. Not that Bridgman was a flub in his new environs but rather that Marsh provided Philadelphians with seven sterling seasons on the blue line.

"He also was the master of the lost art of shot-blocking," added Sator. "And Brad did it so exceptionally well."

Marsh: "Shot-blocking was an individual thing. No coach ever demanded it of me. It was something that came naturally to me, but it wasn't always easy. Sometimes I would go down and make the block and it was great. But when I missed, I looked like a bum out there. I never had time to do much thinking about it. I had

from his head. He could have been killed. Absolutely stone-cold dead."

Ultimately, medics determined that he had suffered a severe concussion, and he was required to sit out four games before returning—with a helmet—against the Pittsburgh Penguins a week later.

"Something I've had all my life [hockey] was almost taken away from me," said Marsh. "If I had hurt my knee, I probably would have had a brace on it. It was as simple as that."

Well, not quite.

One could study the Marsh style and say that it was simple, basic, right to the point. But it was more than that. Brad worked long and hard to master the game's subtleties so that every move was as efficient as the one before. What's more, he displayed the rare lead-

to react right away."

His adjustment to Flyers hockey was swift and sure in 1981-82. His point totals were insignificant, because he was not imported to Philadelphia to light the red lamps.

"Brad's reliability was what made him so valuable," said Sator. "He was so smart and he rarely put himself in an awkward position even when he was rushing the puck."

At 6'3", 220 pounds, Marsh threw devastating body checks and occasionally scored big goals. During the 1987 playoff against the New York Islanders, Brad delivered one of the biggest tallies of his career in the seventh game of the series.

Trapping the puck along the left boards, Marsh sent a laser that baffled goalie Kelly Hrudey. It was the back-

"He also was the master of the lost art of shot-blocking," added Sator. "And Brad did it so exceptionally well."

breaker that settled the bitter series in Philadelphia's favor. By that time, he had matured into one of the league's foremost stay-at-home backliners.

"As I got older," he analyzed, "I adapted to my capabilities. Granted, if I could have skated as fast as Mark Howe and stick-handle and shoot like some of the other players, I might have been a more offensive-minded defenseman. But when all was said and done, I relied on being strong in front of the net."

He also was strong in the dressing room. It was his nature to take new players under his wing. When Czech defenseman Miro Dvorak arrived at The Spectrum unable to speak English, Marsh bought a Czech-English dictionary and helped him adapt to life in North America.

"I remember the first time I met Miro at the airport," said Marsh. "I shook his hand and he didn't know a word of English. That night we happened to room together after an exhibition game. I knew how to say 'beer' in Czech. So I ordered some beers from room service. With my dictionary, it was amazing what I could accomplish over a couple of beers.

"As it turned out, Dvorak lived close to me, so I got in the habit of picking him up on the way to practice. I did a lot of things for him, but I wouldn't have done them if I didn't like him. In time, he became one of my closest friends."

More than most players, Marsh appreciated every mo-

ment of his NHL life, especially his years on Broad Street. "I couldn't think of any job that was better than the one I had. That's why I wanted to play well into my 30s."

He accomplished that goal, although not with the Flyers. His final year at The Spectrum was 1987-88. It was a typical Marsh year, 70 games played, three goals, nine assists, 12 points and 57 penalty minutes. His durability was unquestioned, but the Flyers had doubts about whether his best days were behind him.

Left unprotected in the waiver draft on October 3, 1988, Marsh was claimed by the Toronto Maple Leafs and played three seasons in Canada's Queen City before being dealt to Detroit. One season with the Red Wings led to a move to the expansion Ottawa Senators where he once again found himself a fan favorite.

They loved him in Ottawa for the same reason they did in Philadelphia: he was an unvarnished workaholic.

"I had to work hard to be on any team that I played for, whether it was the Flyers or Senators," Marsh concluded. "People called me a 'throwback' because they said the old-time players gave so much every game. I felt that that was something that came natural to me."

So natural, in fact, that it's hard to imagine that Brad Marsh lacked the lyrical assets that endeared Philadelphia fans to marquee names like MacLeish, Barber and Brind'Amour.

The goalie's helper—Brad Marsh makes a save for Ron Hextall.

Pelle Eklund quietly emerged as one of the Flyers' top sharp shooting European imports.

Per-Erik Eklund

The press release distributed at The Spectrum hardly suggested big things ahead.

It was all of four paragraphs, headed FLYERS SIGN SWEDISH STAR PER-ERIK EKLUND.

Big deal.

Such signings are announced all the time, and when they really matter, the press releases usually run from two to three pages.

This one didn't even fill out one sheet of paper, but it did include a quote from Flyers general manager Bob Clarke.

"With Eklund's speed, skating ability and playmaking skills, he has all the necessary tools to become a great National Hockey League player."

Having prided themselves on their Broad Street Bully image, the Flyers had not been inclined to sprinkle their lineup with Scandinavians, but Eklund's European credentials were hard to ignore. When he came to training camp in the fall of 1985, Pelle revealed that he was every bit as good as his press clippings.

"The first thing that impressed us," recalled teammate Tim Kerr, "was how Pelle skated, found the open man and made the plays while skating, not gliding. That was impressive. He was terrific when it came to looking around and finding someone on our team who was free—and doing it while he was in full motion."

PER-ERIK "PELLE" EKLUND

BORN: Stockholm, Sweden, March 22, 1963

Position: Center

NHL Teams: Philadelphia, 1984-1994; Dallas, 1994

Awards/Honors: Bobby Clarke Trophy, 1991

Pelle Eklund looks for an open teammate.

"With Eklund's speed, skating ability and playmaking skills, he has all the necessary tools to become a great National Hockey League player."

Mike Keenan was less enthused. Uncertain about Eklund's ability to meld into the tougher NHL fabric, the coach spotted Pelle with specialty team duty early in the season. The Swede replied with his stick, constantly feeding Kerr for his many power play goals.

"After a while," said Dave Poulin, "everyone realized that Pelle was good enough to play in all situations. He had great lateral movement and gained the offensive zone almost at will. What's more, he attracted so much attention that he freed his wingers. That's one reason why Tim was free for those power play goals."

His rookie stats were commendable; not quite a point a game, but over 70 contests there were 15 goals and 51 assists for 66 points.

"From about our 50th game," Poulin remembered, "Eklund was our top offensive centerman. His talents just snowballed after that."

Concerns about Pelle withstanding the heavy hitting were unwarranted.

He became a regular in his second full season, 1986-87, and enjoyed the Flyers' ride to the Stanley Cup finals. Despite stiff playoff checking, he collected seven goals and added 20 assists in 26 games

"What you noticed," commented *Philadelphia In-*

Per-Erik Eklund celebrates a goal against Edmonton.

quirer columnist Bill Lyon, "were the wheels and the creativity."

And the easy adjustment to North American big league hockey.

Eklund: "The big change was in rink size. NHL rinks were smaller, so I had to know every time where my own players were before I got the puck. I found that the opposition was on me real quick and I had to adjust to that."

At first, Clarke believed that Eklund's problem—assuming that he had one—was his unselfishness. He passed instead of shooting, but the results nevertheless were positive.

In 1988-89 he reached a new point high (18-51-69). "I learned that the game in North America involves much more skating...up and down...much more so than in Sweden. Back home, we would set up the play, take it easy, let the play develop. In the NHL, you keep the puck and go right away; then you're coming back."

The 69-point level was reached once more in 1990-91, after which Eklund's star began to plummet. He played 51 and 55 games, respectively, in 1991-92 and 1992-93. A season later he was dealt to the Minnesota North Stars, playing only five games before calling it a career.

In a sense it was sad that Pelle concluded his NHL tenure with a short stint outside a Flyers uniform. His nine years on Broad Street are what really mattered—to himself and to Philadelphians.

As Tim Kerr succinctly noted, "Pelle Eklund was just one of the best on our team."

Among all-time Flyers snipers, Mark Recchi ranks near the top.

Mark Recchi

Mark Recchi did not wear the Flyers colors for very long. Two full seasons, to be exact, and part of two others. But in that relatively brief stint in Philadelphia he made a more positive impression than players who were at The Spectrum more than twice that time.

The pint-sized right wing from Kamloops, British Columbia won the hearts of Philadelphians because of his tenacity, teamsmanship and tendency to be in the right place at the right time when a big goal was required.

He surprised no one.

Before his arrival in The City of Brotherly Love, Recchi not only surpassed the 100-point level as a Pittsburgh Penguin (40-73-113) but also played a major role in the Pens' first Stanley Cup championship in 1991. En route to the silverware, Recchi registered ten goals and 24 assists for 34 points in 24 playoff games.

"For that to happen in only my second year in the league was unreal," said Recchi. "I know of guys who have played 15 to 20 years and never won a Cup. It's a shame because it's something I wish everyone could enjoy once in their life."

MARK RECCHI

BORN: Kamloops, British Colombia, February 1, 1968

Position: Right Wing

NHL Teams: Pittsburgh, 1988-1992; Montreal, 1995-1999; Philadelphia 1992-1995, 1999-present

Awards/Honors: Flyers' Flyers 50-goal Club, 1992-1993; Flyers' Flyers 100-point Club, 1992-1994; Flyers Class Guy Award, 1993; Bobby Clarke Trophy, 1993; NHL All-Star, 1991, 1993, 1994, 1997; NHL All-Star Game MVP, 1997; Molson Cup Player of the Year, 1997; Bobby Clarke Trophy, 2000; 1998, 1999, 2000 NHL All-Star Game

Mark had anticipated a long and fruitful career in Pittsburgh.

Certainly, 1991-92 was fruitful—for as long as it lasted. He was on target for another three-digit point season when his brief National Hockey League career exploded in his face. Just when he anticipated playing on another Cup-winning team, the Penguins announced that Recchi was the centerpiece of a three-team deal.

Pittsburgh shipped Mark, along with defenseman Brian Benning and Los Angeles' first-round draft choice (Jason Bowen) to Philadelphia for Rick Tocchet, Kjell Samuelsson, Ken Wregget and a conditional third-round draft choice.

In one fell swoop, Recchi moved from the champions to the last-place Flyers. "Hey," he said after recovering from the shock, "it's part of the business. Pittsburgh felt that I was expendable and they moved me."

Recchi didn't miss a beat. He continued to average more than a point per game and quickly endeared himself to the Spectrum crowd. "I got to love Philadelphia," he said. "The Flyers were a classy organization and let me play my game."

His game featured a doggedness that reminded Philadelphians of Bobby Clarke before him.

"I got that from my parents," Mark explained. "They would always say, 'If you want to play, go play hard, but don't ever go out there and not give one hundred percent.'"

> *"[My parents] would always say, 'If you want to play, go play hard, but don't ever go out there and not give one hundred percent.'"*

His first full season on Broad Street was 1992-93 when the 5'10", 185-pounder fulfilled his notices. With 123 points (53-70), he broke Clarke's team record of 119 points and also squeezed in a 17-game point scoring streak.

"Mark was unbelievable," said his coach of the time, Bill Dineen. "He did everything I asked of him and showed real leadership qualities. He had become a complete hockey player in Philadelphia."

Recchi skated alongside Eric Lindros at center and Brent Fedyk on the left side. They were called The Crazy 8s and for a time comprised the NHL's most explosive trio.

Recchi's consistency was emphasized in 1993-94 when he totalled 40 goals and 67 assists for 107 points, his third season over the century mark. But there was an asterisk; Philadelphia missed the playoffs yet again and demands for change—not necessarily trading Mark—were heard along the Schuykill River and thereabouts.

"We had acquired a lot of new guys, and that meant time was needed to let them get to know each other," Recchi asserted. "We had to try and keep an even keel until things straightened out."

They did straighten out at The Spectrum, but not until after Mark had been given his walking papers. Along with a 1995 third-round draft pick, Recchi was sent to the Montreal Canadiens for John LeClair, Gilbert Dionne and Eric Desjardins.

Recchi played four seasons for the Canadiens before Bob Clarke reacquired him on March 10, 1999 as the Flyers dealt Dainius Zubrus along with a second round pick in the 1999 NHL entry draft.

Bob Clarke never had to apologize for bringing Recchi back to Broad Street. In 1999-2000 Recchi appeared in all 82 games and scored 28 goals and 63 assists for a team high of 91 points. Mark also led the team in scoring in the 2001-02 season (22-42-64).

Before he was traded to the Canadiens, Mark summed up his days on Broad Street succinctly, "It was fun while it lasted."

For Flyers fans, it was even more fun after he returned.

It took a lot for the Flyers to lose Mark Recchi, mainly John LeClair.

Murray Craven

I f one were to select a "most underrated" Flyers forward of the past two decades, Murray Craven would be close to the top of the list if not the leader himself.

Rejected by the Red Wings after two "cups of coffee" in Detroit, Craven was traded to Philadelphia on October 10, 1984 along with Joe Paterson in exchange for a fading star named Darryl Sittler. During his pair of Motor City stints (1982-83, 1983-84), Murray had accumulated 46 games and a dozen points; hardly worth writing home about.

But the Flyers were looking to the future. The Spectrum high command had been quietly impressed with his junior career at Medicine Hat in the Western Hockey League, and when he was introduced to Broad Street at the start of the 1984-85 season, they believed he was ready for big things, although Murray had his doubts.

"I wasn't all that confident," Craven recalled, "nor was I relaxed. But after a while, I realized that the trade was the best thing that ever happened to me."

The Medicine Hat native played 80 games that first season with the orange and black. That he finished with 26 goals and 35 assists merely was the introductory statement. He played 19 playoff games in the spring of 1985, adding four goals and six assists.

MURRAY CRAVEN

BORN: Medicine Hat, Alberta, July 20, 1964

Position: Left Wing

NHL Teams: Detroit, 1982-1984; Philadelphia, 1984-1991; Hartford, 1991-1993; Vancouver, 1993-1994; Chicago, 1994-1997; San Jose, 1997-present

Awards/Honors: Flyers Class Guy Award, 1986

It was the start of a career that would extend seven seasons and change with the Flyers, featuring some delicious results. One of his favorites was in the 1985 Prince of Wales finals between Philadelphia and Quebec. The series was tied at two games apiece with the clubs locked in a 1-1 tie at Le Colisee.

Just as fans were settling back, anticipating overtime, Craven startled everyone with a sparkling rush and flashbulb-lighting goal.

Then there was the game with the Islanders on November 17, 1985. At the time, Philadelphia boasted a franchise record-tying 12 straight wins. The game went into overtime. Standing behind the goal line, Murray scored on a crazy deflection.

How about January 10, 1987? The score was tied between the Flyers and Bruins at Boston Garden. Six minutes remained on the clock when Tim Kerr passed behind Craven, but he whirled and whacked a blind backhander over the goal line.

"Murray skated well, shot the puck well and anticipated well," said Mike Keenan, who coached Craven in Philadelphia. "He also read the play well and had good overall skills. I also liked his attitude; he was a real good team man."

Playing either left wing or center, Craven was one of Keenan's most versatile performers, finishing his first year as a Flyer with the fourth best plus-minus on the club, plus-45. Better still, he accompanied Philadelphia to the Stanley Cup finals against Edmonton. "For me," Murray added, "that first year with the Flyers was like a Cinderella story."

The precise night when he figuratively put on the golden slipper occurred in the 2-1 victory over Quebec. It was one of the most meaningful goals of his career and a harbinger of things to come.

His most productive career as a Flyer was 1987-88 when he reached the 30-goal plateau and added 46 assists for 76 points. By this time he already had been recognized for his off-ice assets as well as his contributions to the attack.

For example, the Philadelphia Hockey Writers' Association presented him with its Class Guy Award, given

One of the most underrated Flyers, Murray Craven, downs Wayne Gretzky.

"Murray skated well, shot the puck well and anticipated well," said Mike Keenan. *"He also read the play well and had good overall skills. I also liked his attitude; he was a real good team man."*

to the player who distinguished himself in his relationship with the media. Those who have interviewed Murray over the years understand why he was the winner. Articulate, patient and ever-available, Craven has been a newsman's dream come true.

"I've always gotten along with the media," he explained, "and never had any bad encounters with any of them any place that I've played. It's not something I worked on, but rather good fortune."

His good fortune as a Flyer continued through 1989-90 when he fell one short of tying his previous point high (76). He appeared in 76 games, good for 25 goals and 50 assists. That was the good news. The bad news was that the Flyers missed the playoffs for the first time since the 1971-72 season.

Craven hardly was the culprit. He still was performing efficiently despite his supporting cast. In 1990-91 he scored 19 goals and 47 assists for 66 points in 77 games, but again the Flyers were out of playoff contention.

"The bottom line is this: if we don't make the

playoffs, it really doesn't matter what kind of numbers I put on the board," said Craven.

Craven's days were numbered. On November 13, 1991, he was traded from Philadelphia to Hartford with a draft pick for Kevin Dineen. To his credit, Craven retained his efficiency as a Whaler, although he lasted only two seasons in Connecticut.

He was traded to Vancouver for Robert Kron on March 22, 1993. Murray averaged a point a game over ten games. A year later he helped spark Vancouver to the Stanley Cup finals before losing to the Rangers in Game 7. Craven tallied a respectable four goals and nine assists over 22 playoff games.

From Vancouver, he moved on to Chicago—for Christian Ruuttu—and was a standby for the Blackhawks until July 1997 when he was dealt to San Jose for Petri Varis and a 1998 sixth-round pick. Craven had by now logged 15 NHL seasons, a remarkable achievement when one considers that he never has been a steady first-liner.

Once again, Craven established his value, although his mathematics were hardly Gretzkyesque. What mattered to Murray—and the Sharks—was that he was a playoff player once more. San Jose reached the postseason tournament and gave the favored Dallas Stars considerable trouble before bowing.

As always, Craven was the same player he was in Philadelphia—a class guy.

One of the true unsung heroes of the Flyers was forward Murray Craven, seen here taking out Mike Krushelnyski in the 1985 Stanley Cup Finals.

"The Hound," Bob Kelly, scored the 1975 Stanley Cup winner against Buffalo.

Bob "Hound" Kelly

While some Flyers aficionados might regard a description of Bob Kelly as the poor man's Bobby Clarke, it is in fact a high compliment.

For starters, there never could be another Clarke in the estimation of the Philly Faithful, and if there were to be an approximation, it would have to resemble a tenacious corner man without peer, a tireless checker and a skater oozing spirit from every corpuscle.

They called him Hound, which also may not sound like a compliment—but it was. Kelly sniffed out pucks like a bloodhound on the trail of an escaped convict. More often than not, he got to the rubber, usually in anger—the way coach Fred Shero preferred—and with unlimited gusto.

Overlooked in most Kelly analyses is his offensive production. Given the opportunity, the Oakville, Ontario native could score. In 1976-77 he tallied 22 goals along with 24 assists for 46 points. The additional 117 penalty minutes emphasized the ubiquitous muscular aspect of his game.

"In terms of pure toughness, Kelly was first on the Flyers," said Dave Schultz, the notorious Hammer. "I was second. But with all due respect, Kelly became the heavyweight champion of the Flyers."

By far the most meaningful goal ever scored by Kelly was delivered in the sixth game of the 1975 Stanley Cup finals against the Buffalo Sabres. Playing at a jam-packed Aud, the teams fought through two periods without a score. Judg-

BOB "HOUND" KELLY

BORN: Oakville, Ontario, November 25, 1950

Position: Left Wing

NHL Teams: Philadelphia, 1970-1980; Washington, 1980-1982

ing by the pace, observers believed—and rightly so, as it turned out—that the first goal scored would be the winner.

The Kelly score was the result of a play which coach Fred Shero had his players work over and over throughout the season. The idea was to score a goal by bulling your way out front from behind the net. Shero would hand over five dollars to the man who kept beating the goalie and who stayed out the longest.

Using Shero's plan right from the textbook, Kelly got the puck early in the third period with the score tied, 0-0. Hound moved from behind the Sabres' net out in front and jammed the puck into the goal. The score won the Stanley Cup for the second year in a row.

Kelly not only was a clutch performer for Philadelphia but a rib-tickling dressing room humorist as well. "We had an unusually colorful cast of characters on our club," said Schultz, "with Hound as our lead clown."

In his book, *The Hammer*, Schultz detailed a few choice Kelly stories. One of the more popular ones involved a gag usually played on rookies in the NHL. It was called a "snipe hunt" and, according to Schultz, went something like this when Hound was involved:

"According to the scenario, Kelly would be 'accidentally' lured into a search for snipes, which, he was told, are little birds that are hunted at night. The plot involved getting Kelly out in the woods then arrested on a trumped-up charge of illegal hunting and brought before a judge who demanded bail money. At that point the group, assured that Kelly was scared out of his pants, would suddenly appear to get the big laugh.

"Ed Van Impe directed the comedy with ample assistance from Bobby Taylor and Bobby Clarke. The first scene opened in the dressing room, after a practice. The guys were sitting around, gabbing about nothing in particular, when Van Impe turned to Taylor and Clarke and said, 'Are you ready for the snipe hunt?'

"They went into a whole business about getting flashlights, sneakers and all the other equipment that goes with catching birds at night. One by one, the

"In terms of pure toughness, Kelly was first on the Flyers," said Dave Schultz, the notorious Hammer. "I was second. But with all due respect, Kelly became the heavyweight champion of the Flyers."

Bob Kelly, in front of his own net, takes no chances with a relentless Mike Milbury.

players who said they would go on the hunt began practicing their snipe calls. The more they got into it, the more Kelly's curiosity piqued, until he could resist no longer and begged Van Impe to take him along. Van Impe said he would consider the request and then added, 'For starters, Bob, you have to practice your snipe call.' Kelly warbled a few calls and it was clear he was hooked.

"Now the plot thickened. Van Impe phoned some friends who were in a Delaware County police department and let them in on the gag. He got the cops

Bob Kelly attempts to wrist one over Ranger goaltender Eddie Giacomin.

and a magistrate to agree to play it straight when they were asked to apprehend Kelly. Even some of the wives became involved. Someone told Kelly that snipes make a delicious meal and that Diane Van Impe specialized in cooking them. Kelly approached Mrs. Van Impe and asked how she handled snipe. 'We like it best when the breasts are cooked in wine sauce,' she said. 'It's really quite delicious.' Kelly's mouth was watering.

"The night of the snipe hunt, everyone arrived at a hunting area called the Willows ready to go. The garb included old clothes, sneakers, beat-up hats and all manner of impromptu equipment—including Diane Van Impe's pantyhose, which were hooked onto a hockey stick. Kelly looked the stick over and asked Van Impe, 'But will it work?' To which Eddie replied, 'It worked before so it should work again.'

"Kelly was instructed to hide in the bushes with someone while the rest of the guys fanned out in different directions, alternately shouting, 'There goes one; there goes another.' Armed with a flashlight and a makeshift net, Kelly began uttering his ear-piercing snipe call while beating the bushes. Now all sounds were limited to Kelly and his partner, who was about ten yards away.

"Suddenly, a siren was heard and a red emergency light broke through the night. The police had arrived, and before Kelly knew what to do, a cop moved right in on him. The dialogue went like this:

"COP: What the hell are you doing here?
"KELLY: Snipe hunting.
"COP: Fine, but where's your license?
"KELLY: Hell, I don't have one.
"COP: Well, this is a snipe preserve, you have to have one.
"KELLY: (fumphing) Er...but...I had no idea...

"Meanwhile, one of the other Flyers (a stooge, of course) moved in on the cop's partner and pretended to assault him. A gunshot went through the air, whereupon the first cop shouted, 'What happened?' The other cop (who had been "attacked") answered, 'The guy ran away but I hit him!'

"Kelly was horrified, especially when he realized that one of his teammates was 'shot,' all because of a snipe hunt. Kelly was now alone with the two cops. They handcuffed him and hauled him off to the stationhouse. Like a common criminal, he was fingerprinted, photographed and placed behind bars until it was time for him to appear before the judge. Meanwhile, the rest of the guys took in the proceedings behind closed doors.

"With Kelly standing sheepishly in front of him, the judge charged him for lawbreaking and then, in mock sorrow, added 'I am beside myself that I have to miss *Monday Night Football* all because of you, Mister Kelly.'

"The judge told Kelly he could get out of jail if he could come up with twenty-five hundred dollars in cash or a certified check. Kelly said he didn't have the cash but he did have a certified check. The judge was amazed and asked, 'How'd you get a certified check from a bank at ten-thirty at night?'

"Kelly said he had gotten his bonus the other day, gone to the bank, and got ten checks with his name on them. The judge came back fast with a perfect squelch: 'Okay, do you have anyone here who can help you, who can act as a character witness?'

"Kelly's head dropped because he figured he was screwed again. Finally, he said, 'No, Your Honor,' and looked like he was about to burst into tears. At that moment, all the doors flew open and the rest of the guys burst into the courtroom, laughing their heads off. Kelly was in a state of shock.

"He took it beautifully. His resilience, in fact, is what enabled us to trap him again and again. Another time, several players were on a fishing trip in northern Saskatchwan with a friend of the team named Len Warren. The plan this time was for Warren to get to a telephone at the boathouse and call Kelly back at the cabin once the guys got back with the boat. Since we were way out in the woods where they used only old crank telephones, it would be easy for Warren to conceal his voice and slur over some of the words.

"Sure enough, as soon as the boat landed, someone ran out and paged Kelly. He ran to the cabin phone and the dialogue sounded like this:

"VOICE: (muffled) Long-distance for Mr. Bob Kelly.

"KELLY: This is Bob Kelly.

"VOICE: Just a moment for Mr. Keith Allen (The Flyers' general manager).

"There was a pause.

"VOICE: Bob . . . sorry . . . traded . . . poor connection . . . bye-bye.

"KELLY: Where? How?

"As the players walked into the cabin, Kelly was in a stupor, talking to himself. 'My wife...the house...leaving Philly...' For a half-hour he walked around in a daze.

When it looked like he might slit his throat, we told him it was a gag.

"One time Bob drove up to Rexy's, our postgame hangout. The rain was coming down in torrents, and as he walked toward the restaurant he noticed the window of Wayne Hillman's car was halfway open. When he got inside he said, 'Wayne, I just noticed it's raining in your car on account of your window being half open.' Hillman looked at him with a blank expression and replied, 'Bob, why the devil didn't you close it?'

"'I couldn't,' said Kelly. 'The door was locked.'"

The humor notwithstanding, Kelly played 741 games with the Flyers and they all were serious encounters for the Oakville, Ontario native. Apart from his heroics on the two Stanley Cup-winning teams, Hound continued to deliver high-octane performances through the 1970s.

In the 1978 playoffs, Kelly contributed three goals and five assists for eight points in a dozen games as well as 26 penalty minutes.

His final season on Broad Street was 1979-80, when he finished with 35 points (15-20) in 75 games. Hound continued as an integral member of the Flyers club that took the Islanders to six games in the Stanley Cup finals before losing in double overtime.

On August 21, 1980, Kelly was traded to the Washington Capitals for the Caps' third-round choice (Bill Campbell) in the 1982 entry draft.

In retrospect, it was a colossal blunder. Hound rebounded to a career season (26-36-62) with 157 penalty minutes. But it also was the beginning of a precipitous end. He concluded his major-league career a decade-plus-one after it had begun in 1981-82.

Playing only 16 games for the star-spangled Capitals, Hound never scored a goal and garnered but four assists and a dozen penalty minutes.

What will be remembered, however, were nine glorious playoff years on Broad Street, an unchallenged work ethic, a singular and often heroic toughness and, most of all, that Cup-winning goal in 1975.

Tom Bladon

To put Tom Bladon in the same category as Hall of Famer Bobby Orr would be a stretch.

But, then again, it would not be that much of a stretch if one category were stressed.

That would be teenagers who made the leap from junior (amateur) hockey to the NHL without missing a beat.

Orr hedgehopped from the Ontario Hockey Association to the Boston Bruins in 1966.

Bladon flew from Edmonton of the Western Canada Hockey League to the Flyers in 1972 and hit the ice skating as a member of the 1972-73 Philly sextet that was en route to quasi-dynasty status.

The Edmonton-born defenseman was 19 when he was thrust into the major-league cauldron and was the first to admit that it was a trying time for him.

"In junior," Bladon remembered, "you can make a mistake and get away with it. In the NHL you make a mistake and you'd better look in the net, because that's where the puck is going to be.

"For me the big change was making the proper adjustment for whatever player I was defending against. I found that I had to stay close to some opponents and others I could give more room."

THOMAS GEORGE "BOMBER" BLADON

Born: Edmonton, Alberta, December 29, 1952

Position: Defense

NHL Teams: Philadelphia, 1972-78; Pittsburgh, 1978-80; Edmonton, 1980; Winnipeg, 1980-81; Detroit, 1981

Awards/Honors: Played in 1977, 1978 All-Star Games

At 6'1", 190 pounds, Bladon appealed to the Flyers for several reasons, not the least of which was his size. He was a second-round pick behind Bill Barber and immediately clicked in his new NHL milieu.

As a rookie, Bladon tallied 11 goals and 31 assists for 42 points in 78 games. In his sophomore year, 1973-74, Tom was a prime member of the Stanley Cup-winning team and was the same on the 1975 championship team.

His 1975 playoff production—four goals, six assists, ten points in 16 games—was superior for a second-year man. It also heralded bigger and better regular season stats.

"We underrated Tom," recalled general manager Keith Allen. "We started off evaluating him as a teenager and he instantly showed he was more than that."

When all is said and done, Bladon permanently etched his name in the Flyers' honor roll with one remarkable effort during the 1977-78 season.

The Cleveland Barons came into The Spectrum one cold December night, and they saw one of the best performances in NHL history. Bladon had a four-goal, four-assist night, as the Flyers cruised 11-1.

Bladon mused, "Every time I touched the puck it turned into a goal," and when asked if he would send the stick to the Hall of Fame he replied, "Sure, but the people would probably say, 'Tom who?'"

Bladon wound up plus-10 that night as he broke Bobby Orr's record of points by a defenseman in one game (seven).

"That's the one that'll mean the most to him," said Matt DiPaolo, team physical therapist. "These guys love to be plus in any game, but plus-10—wow!"

That game turned the Philadelphia fans in Bladon's favor. After being booed for the larger part of his first six seasons in Philly, Bladon got a measure of satisfaction as many of the fans in the arena, including his harshest critics, gave him a rousing ovation.

The following year, Bladon was traded from Philadelphia with Ross Lonsberry and Orenst Kindrachuk for Pittsburgh's first-round choice (Behn Wilson) in the 1978 amateur draft. The trade signaled the decline of Bladon's career.

He played two seasons in Pittsburgh, and then the

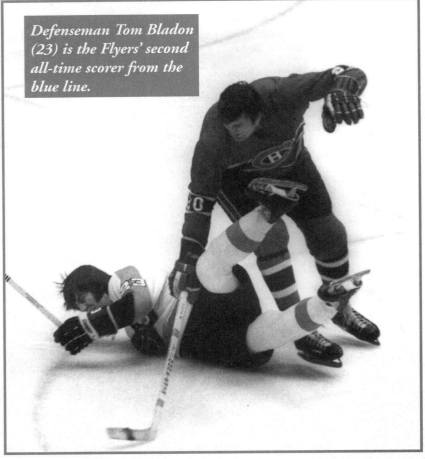

Defenseman Tom Bladon (23) is the Flyers' second all-time scorer from the blue line.

> *"We underrated Tom," recalled general manager Keith Allen. "We started off evaluating him as a teenager and he instantly showed he was more than that."*

Edmonton Oilers signed Bladon as a free agent on July 10, 1980. After appearing in one game, he signed a free agent contract with the Winnipeg Jets on December 13, 1980.

After playing nine games with the Jets, Bladon signed a free agent contract with the Detroit Red Wings in January of 1981. Bladon was never the same once he left the comfort of the Flyers locker room, but Philadelphia fans will never forget that record-setting night back on December 11, 1977.

Four goals. Four assists. All in one NHL game. Immortality of a sort never achieved by Bobby Orr.

Doug Favell

Doug Favell's most significant detour obstructing his entrance into Philadelphia sports immortality was Bernie Parent. The latter made it. The former did not.

It was the misfortune of Favell to follow Parent, first through the Boston Bruins' farm system and then to Broad Street when the NHL expanded from six to twelve teams in 1967. It is noteworthy that Parent was drafted first and Favell second.

Even being drafted second should have been a godsend to the peripatetic Favell. He had played splendidly for Boston's farm team in Oklahoma City and San Francisco in the mid-1960s. But then again, so did Parent, who had come from Oklahoma City as well but had the advantage of NHL experience with Boston before Favell set skate in a big-league rink.

When the two came to training camp in September 1967, Parent seemed to have the starting goaltending job in his pocket.

Perhaps, but not in the net.

Given an opportunity to show that he had the goods, Favell played long and strong through training camp, emerging with enough backing to get a few starting assignments. In no time at all Flyers coach Keith Allen realized he had two gems, not just one, and Favell got almost as much crease time as Parent.

DOUGLAS ROBERT "DOUG" FAVELL

BORN: St. Catherines, Ontario, April 5, 1945

Position: Goaltender

NHL Teams: Philadelphia, 1967-73; Toronto, 1973-76; Colorado, 1976-79

Doug Favell is third all time in games played by a Flyers goaltender, behind only Bernie Parent and Ron Hextall.

Santa Claus with Flyers goalies Bernie Parent (30) and Doug Favell (1).

Doug's response was emphatic. The St. Catherines, Ontario native played like a starter and worked 37 games. The stint featured four shutouts and a notably impressive 2.27 goals-against average. Parent's, by contrast, was 2.49. Doug's overall 15-15-6 won-loss-tie mark was more than the Flyers had expected from the freshman.

The Favell-Parent tandem spearheaded a Flyers drive to first place and virtually assured Philly of long-term security in goal. What made the duet even more intriguing was the point-counterpoint in style and personality.

Parent was a classic, stand-up, kick-save type of stopper. By contrast, Favell employed a flop-at-all-costs, whatever-works-will-do philosophy.

Whereas Parent was thoughtful to the point of being a worrier, Favell believed that life was just a bowl of cherries—with a few pucks thrown in for good measure.

But the smile on Favell's face diminished somewhat during the 1968 playoffs. The first sign of trouble developed at a scrimmage before the opening of the Philadelphia-St. Louis series. A grey-haired goalie with a middle-aged pot belly took his place in front of the net normally

guarded by Favell. It was Stu Nahan, Philadelphia's play-by-play announcer, who raised the question: what happened to Favell?

"We sent him to the hospital," replied coach Keith Allen. "He wasn't feeling well when he reported this morning; we sent him for an examination."

Favell's illness was not the Flyers' only problem. They encountered a tough Blues team that took a three-games-to-one advantage before the Flyers rebounded, 6-1. It was in Game 5 that Favell showed the moxie that has always marked his career.

A huge brawl erupted after Noel Picard of St. Louis flattened Claude Laforge of the Flyers. Players from both benches poured over the boards like infantrymen rushing over their trenches. "Some claimed it was the greatest fight in hockey history," said Hugh Brown of the *Philadelphia Bulletin.*

Whatever its ranking, the fight stirred the adrenaline of Favell who had been watching the action from the Flyers' bench. Suddenly, Doug leaped over the boards when he saw Picard put the slug on Laforge.

"I was going after Picard," Favell remembered, "but

In no time at all, Flyers coach Keith Allen realized he had two gems, not just one, and Favell got almost as much crease time as Parent.

on the way Dickie Moore [of the Blues] challenged me. I said I didn't want to have anything to do with him, but Moore came at me and we had it out."

The Flyers may have come out even in the fight, but they lost the series in the seventh game after a gallant comeback. Favell appeared in two games—discounting his one-round fight with Moore—and came away with a dismal 4.00 goals-against average. It proved to be the signal that Parent was taking over as king of the Broad Street goal.

Favell played only 20 games in his sophomore NHL season, 1968-69, and another three with Quebec of the American Hockey League. But no downer was deeper nor more depressing than an 8-0 loss to the Blues at The Spectrum. In that contest St. Louis center Red Berenson pumped six goals past Favell.

"Red was great and I was lousy," said Favell. "There's nothing more to say about it."

Actually there is—and was.

"The most amazing thing about Red's performance," explained St.Louis goalie Jacques Plante, "was that he didn't get one cheap goal. Every one was a good, clean shot at Favell."

But no amount of rationalizing could erase the image the six-goal effort had created for Favell. Unfortunately, it would not be his last encounter with the fickle finger of fate.

After Parent was dealt to Toronto in January 1971, all signs indicated that Favell would have another good shot at being numero uno. He was sharing the net minding with veteran Bruce Gamble as the 1971-72 season reached the homestretch.

Then tragedy struck. Gamble suffered a heart attack during a game in Vancouver. At the age of 33 he was told that he never could play hockey again. What's more, the Flyers had enjoyed a winning record with Gamble and now turned the reins over to Favell.

Still the Flyers remained in playoff contention right down to the final night of the season when they played the Sabres at Buffalo. A win or a tie would mean fourth place even if their pursuers, the Pittsburgh Penguins, won their home game against St. Louis.

The Buffalo scoreboard began revealing grim news for the Flyers from Pittsburgh, where the Penguins were skating to an easy 6-2 victory over the Blues. No matter. A tie would be just fine for Philadelphia, and the Flyers had the situation well in hand.

Bobby Clarke put them ahead at 19:51 of the first period, and Rick Foley made it 2-0 Philadelphia at 8:53 of the second. Favell, so far, had been impenetrable.

Buffalo, however, failed to play dead, and less than two minutes later Gil Perreault broke free of the Flyers' defense, put two big feints on Favell, and now the Flyers' lead was cut to one. "We knew what we had to do," said Shero. "We were watching the scoreboard and saw what was happening in Pittsburgh."

Philadelphia escaped the second period still leading 2-1. In the last period the Sabres were manacled throughout the first eight minutes, but Ed Van Impe was tagged with a hooking penalty and on came the Sabres' power play. At 8:47 Rene Robert tied the score. The Flyers were now one goal away from first place. "Even after Buffalo tied us," Shero explained, "we were going for the victory. But in the last three or four minutes we started playing for the tie. I decided it would be better to make sure of getting into the playoffs. I told the team only one man was to go in deep and that the wings should pick up their men. We were doing the job..."

Tenaciously, the Flyers checked every Buffalo attempt to move the puck toward Favell until there were less than 50 seconds remaining in the period. Sabres manager-coach Punch Imlach had two of his favorite skaters on the ice, Mike Byers and Gerry Meehan, both of whom had been with the Flyers.

"I looked up at the scoreboard," said Meehan, "and the message up there said I had once played 12 games with the Flyers. I kept thinking 'Wouldn't it be funny if I scored the goal that made it 3-2?'"

Now with less than ten seconds remaining, the Flyers were preparing to vault the boards and embrace goalie Favell for the start of the playoff-clinching celebration. But then Byers trapped the puck in his end of the rink and spotted Meehan near the center red line. His pass was true, and Meehan took it squarely on his stick in full flight toward the Philadelphia goal.

At the moment Meehan received the puck, defenseman Van Impe moved into position at the Flyers' blue line. "Van Impe was in front of me," Meehan recalled, "and he kept backing in. I think maybe he screened Favell a little. I just wound up and shot."

The puck orbited and sped on target toward the right side of the net as Meehan watched its dramatic flight about knee high. "I never saw it," said Favell, "until it was on top of me."

When he finally saw it, Favell frantically kicked out his left pad. "It went right past his knee," Meehan noted.

Favell collapsed to the ice, falling on his left buttock as the fateful puck stuck in the webbing of the net. "I couldn't believe it," said the goalie.

"Could you believe it?" groaned defenseman Jean Potvin. "We lost fourth place with four seconds to go."

Flyers goaltenders such as Doug Favell, pictured here, loved the defensive play of Andre Dupont (28).

Despite the traumatic ending, Favell remained a Flyer with mixed reviews. When Fred Shero took over as Flyers coach in 1971, he learned what others before him had discovered about Favell. Shero thus devised a philosophy for handling the goaltender.

"As long as Doug plays well," said Shero, "he stays in there."

Midway through the 1972-73 season Shero publicly criticized Favell for the goalie's uninspired behavior during practice sessions. At one point, Shero benched Favell in favor of the less-experienced Michel Belhumeur and Bob Taylor.

Favell's response was a one-liner: "What am I, a head of lettuce?"

Nevertheless, Philadelphia moved into the playoffs on the strength of Doug's first-rate goaltending and knocked off Minnesota in the opening round with Favell at the very top of his game. However, the second round was another story with Montreal eliminating Philly. Sadly, Doug lost a 3-2 third-period lead in the final match,

allowing a 65-foot shot by Frank Mahovlich to dip under his glove. After that goal, the Flyers were dead.

Ditto for Favell's NHL career on Broad Street.

On July 23, 1973 he was traded to Toronto to complete a deal in which Philadelphia traded its 1973 first-round amateur draft choice (Bob Neely) to Toronto for Toronto's second-round choice in the 1973 amateur draft (Larry Goodenough) and the rights to Bernie Parent.

Favell impressed with a 2.71 goals-against average in 32 games, but that marked the final golden season for the ebullient one in the bigs. He bounced from Toronto to Colorado in 1976-77 and ironically completed his pro career with the Flyers' American League team in 1978-79.

He did, however, distinguish himself one more time, but not as a puck stopper. The record book lists four assists for Doug alongside his 4.48 goals-against average.

A Bernie Parent he was not, but then again, who was beside Bernard?

The bottom line for Doug Favell is that he provided Philadelphia fans with some sparkling—and depressing—moments, good fun, 16 regular season shutouts and one in the playoffs.

He was a good one aspiring to be great but never quite made that big step to the top. Through it all, Doug Favell still emerges as a lifetime favorite in Philly.

North Star Danny Grant (21) gets set to blast a point-blank shot at Flyers goalie Doug Favell (1).

Illka Sinisalo

He was like a phantom. Now you see him, now you don't. He came directly to Pennsylvania from his native Finland in 1981 and set up home at The Spectrum for almost ten years.

Over that span he exhibited a brand of artistry and rhythm that was rarely equalled in a Flyers uniform, and still, hardly anyone knew him.

Illka Sinisalo was the semi-hidden star. A headline in the Flyers' own magazine said it all: HE'S MORE COMFORTABLE BEING A HOCKEY PLAYER THAN A CELEBRITY.

"I played game by game and tried to score every game," the flying Finn explained. "After the season, I would check to see how many I had."

He checked after his rookie year, 1981-82, and discovered that he had played in 66 games and scored 16 goals along with 22 assists. The 38 points would eventually be doubled as the slick right wing acclimatized himself to the NHL.

"The hitting in North America was something I had to adjust to more than anything," Sinisalo recalled. "After a while, I got used to it. I learned not to be afraid to take my man out of the play. You would get hit and then you would hit people yourself. I learned that it was all part of the NHL game."

As a sophomore, he boosted his points total by a dozen (21-29-50) although he played in only 61 games.

"At first," he remembered, "I didn't play that much, but gradually the management got more confidence in me and I got more and more ice time."

ILLKA SINISALO

BORN: Valeakaski, Finland July 10, 1958

Position: Right Wing

NHL Teams: Philadelphia, 1981-90; Minnesota, 1990-91; Los Angeles, 1991-92

Among those Flyers with whom he teamed, Peter Zezel and Dave Poulin were among the most admiring.

Zezel: "With Ilkka all I had to do was get him a lead pass or lay it out to him. I knew he would then beat his man and the puck would be in the back of the net."

Poulin: "I could understand the culture change he endured. I had lived and played in Europe for a year before I came to the NHL. I knew what it was like in a different culture. It took a couple of years to get fully comfortable. After a while, Ilkka was right at home in Philadelphia."

The most he ever played was in 1985-86. It was a robust season for Ilkka. He played in 74 games and hit a personal record 39 goals and 37 assists for 78 points.

"By this time," Sinisalo said, "I had the feel of the NHL. I trusted myself and the coaches trusted me. That was the biggest thing. They knew that I could deliver and it made it a lot easier for me all the way around."

Sinisalo played with smarts and speed. "He was explosive," said former Flyers captain Dave Poulin. "He was capable of scoring at any point. In his prime he was one of the fastest players in the league."

Also one of the most unique.

His first NHL goal fell into the historic category. It was a penalty shot against the Pittsburgh Penguins—and a goal. It marked Ilkka as only the second player in NHL annals to score his first big-league goal on a penalty shot. The other was Ralph Bowman of the St. Louis Eagles during the 1934-35 season.

Sinisalo would intimidate the foe with his speed. Enemy defensemen would look up, see the Finn and back up, allowing the other Flyers more room to maneuver.

Battling Ilkka Sinisalo and Kirk Muller reflect the growing Flyers-Devils rivalry.

Sinisalo played with smarts and speed. "He was explosive," said former Flyers captain Dave Poulin. "He was capable of scoring at any point. In his prime he was one of the fastest players in the league."

Flyers coaches of that era, such as E. J. McGuire, would marvel at his skills.

"Ilkka would win our practice shootouts all the time," said McGuire.

"I'd always put my money on him to win."

During his first three NHL seasons—while Bob McCammon was behind the bench—Sinisalo was a part-time player. The arrival of Mike Keenan as coach for the start of Ilkka's fourth year meant an expanded role. He took a regular turn, worked the power play and also was a penalty-killer.

"He showed improvement every year," said Keenan. "Once he started scoring all those goals, his confidence went sky-high."

Sinisalo's last solid season as a big-leaguer coincided with his final fling as a Flyer, 1989-90. Over 59 games, he scored 23 goals and 23 assists, but it marked the first time since coming to Philadelphia that the club missed the playoffs.

That did it for Illka. He was dealt to Minnesota for the 1990-91 season and then moved on to Los Angeles before calling it a career.

What kind of career?

Quiet and splendid, simultaneously.

The Flyers were blessed with one of Finland's finest forwards, Ilkka Sinisalo.

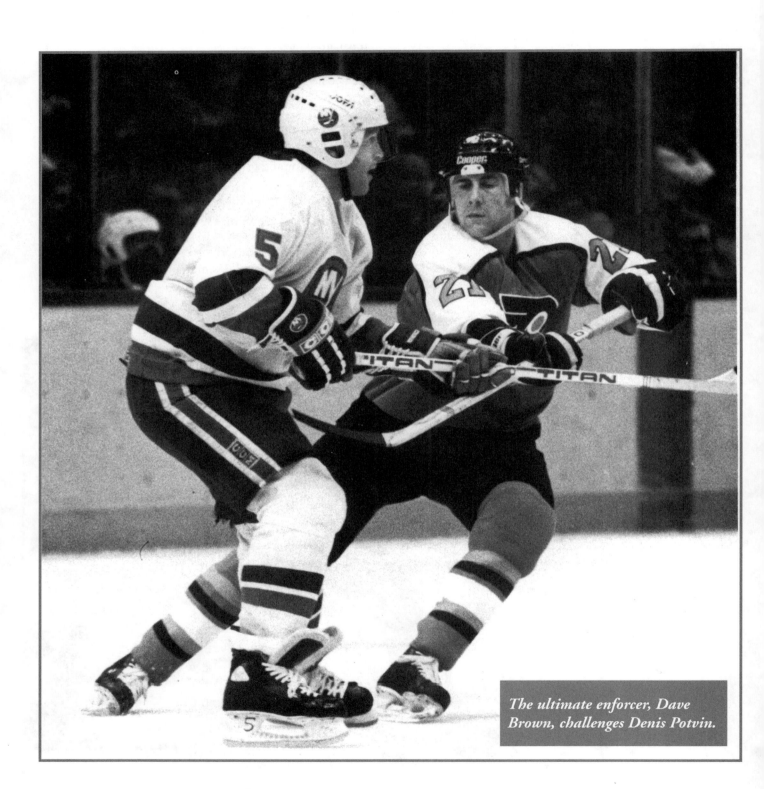

The ultimate enforcer, Dave Brown, challenges Denis Potvin.

Dave Brown

I f ever the Flyers dressed an enforcer who legitimately could be called the successor to Dave Schultz as both fighter and favorite, that man would be Dave Brown.

Over a period of five-plus years, starting in 1984, Brown terrorized the National Hockey League as The Hammer had a decade earlier. There was one key difference; Schultz has two Stanley Cup rings and Brown none.

But Brown won as many fights—if not more—and commanded respect wherever he skated. Schultz had the edge in one department. Hammer had a 20-goal season, whereas Brown never exceeded a dozen goals.

A native of Saskatoon, Brown was selected by Philadelphia in the 1982 entry draft. The seventh Flyers pick, he was 140th overall and attended his first NHL training camp in the fall of 1982.

When camp broke, he remained in Portland, having earned a spot on the American League Mariners, coached then by Tom McVie. "Dave," said McVie, "was always the first one out for practice and the last one off. I never coached a player who wanted to improve himself more than Dave Brown."

While he was learning, Dave set a new AHL record for penalty minutes with 418, while adding 97 more in the playoffs. Late in the 1983-84 season he made his big-league debut with the Flyers in a pair of mid-March road games against the Bruins and Rangers.

DAVID "DAVE" BROWN

Born: Saskatoon, Saskatchewan, October 12, 1962

Position: Right Wing

NHL Teams: Philadelphia, 1982-89, 1991-95; Edmonton, 1989-91; San Jose, 1995-96.

Dave Brown is intercepted by Jack O'Callahan of the Blackhawks.

He scored no points in the two games but did send Boston rookie defenseman Gord Kluzak to the hospital —on Brown's first shift. He also scored his first NHL goal during that 19-game stint and squeezed in a pair of playoff games.

Under Mike Keenan's tutelage in 1984-85, Brown became a Philadelphia regular because he deserved to be in the bigs. "He was a much better hockey player than he got credit for," said Keenan. "He developed into a good one. He could read the play well and played strong defensively."

Brown: "My skating wasn't good enough to keep up with everybody at first, so I had to play good positional hockey. I never liked getting scored on and I realized early on that if I wasn't going to score much, I had to make sure the other line wasn't scoring against us when I was on the ice."

More than anything, it was Brown the intimidator who made an impact on the opposition. His clashes with the Rangers—including the near destruction of Tomas Sandstrom—became legendary.

"The enforcer part kept me around the game," he recalled. "I did that while I worked on my hockey skills. I knew that there was a point where I had to fight, but there also was a point where I had to play some hockey."

One of his most productive years was 1985-86 when he tallied ten goals and seven assists as well as 277 penalty minutes. During a game against the Canadiens he scored a particularly big goal in a 6-3 Flyers win, but such events were more the exception than the rule.

"Any time I scored it was a big moment," Brown remembered. "I wish that I could do that more often."

"The enforcer part kept me around the game. I did that while I worked on my hockey skills. I knew that there was a point where I had to fight, but there also was a point where I had to play some hockey."

He did in 1987-88 when Philly—and Brown—skated to the Stanley Cup finals. He accumulated twelve goals and five assists during the regular season—he was limited to only 47 games—and added a goal and two assists in 26 playoff games.

Brown's first romance with Philly soon would end. D (as in Dealt) Day was February 7, 1989. The Flyers traded Brown to Edmonton for Keith Acton and the Oilers' sixth-round draft choice in the 1991 entry draft (Dimitri Yushkevich).

Dave remained an Oiler—he played on Edmonton's Stanley Cup-winning team in 1990—until May 1991 when he was returned to Broad Street along with Corey Foster and the rights to Jari Kurri for Scott Mellanby, Craig Berube and Craig Fisher.

Interestingly, he played 70 games for three consecutive seasons beginning with 1991-92. Brown's playing career ended after the 1995-96 season. On June 18, 1996 he was named a Flyers assistant coach.

Brown played a total of 729 career regular season games for the Flyers and scored 45 goals and 52 assists in that span.

Small potatoes, of course, when you match those numbers with his 1,789 penalty minutes. The man was a fitting successor to The Hammer.

And, arguably, just as beloved.

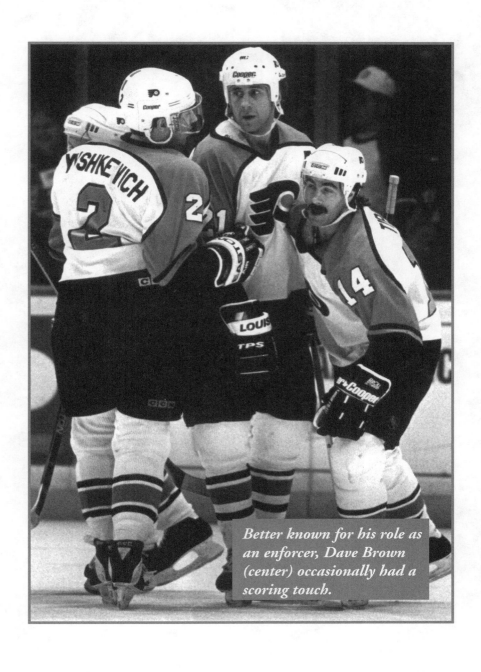

Better known for his role as an enforcer, Dave Brown (center) occasionally had a scoring touch.

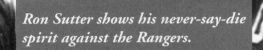

Ron Sutter shows his never-say-die spirit against the Rangers.

Ron Sutter

Disturb should have been his middle name.
If not that, then Hustle.
Ron Sutter did both very well.

In between he scored a fair amount of goals, set up many more and for nearly a decade gave the Flyers a brand of center ice pizzazz that only one of the Sutter clan can bestow upon a team.

That Ron was a special breed was as obvious as his surname. Each of the big-league Sutters was special.

Brian was the first, captaining the St. Louis Blues like none other before or since. Darryl did likewise with the Chicago Blackhawks. Duane was a member of four New York Islanders Stanley Cup-winning teams. Brent followed Duane on the Island.

Then came twin brothers Ron and Rich.

They starred together for Lethbridge in the Western Hockey League and each was drafted in 1982. Ron was drafted in the first round, fourth overall by the Flyers. Selected six picks later, Rich went to the Pittsburgh Penguins and played a combined nine games before being traded to Philly on October 23, 1983.

RONALD "RON" SUTTER

Born: Viking, Alberta, December 2, 1963

Position: Center

NHL Teams: Philadelphia, 1982-91; St. Louis, 1991-94; Quebec, 1994; N.Y. Islanders, 1994-96; Boston, 1996; San Jose, 1996-present.

Awards/Honors: Captain, Philadelphia 1989-91, Flyers Class Guy Award, 1989

Ron Sutter, one of several illustrious Sutter brothers, starred for the Flyers in the 1980s.

Ron had made his NHL debut—albeit temporary—in 1982-83 when he was summoned from the junior ranks. He scored his first major-league goal against Quebec Nordiques goalie John Garrett. Sutter, who was nineteen at the time, made hockey history when the red light went on.

Never before had five brothers scored an NHL goal. In fact, never before that had five brothers all played a game in the NHL until the Sutters accomplished that feat when Ron played his first game with the Flyers.

That lone goal in 1982-83 complemented Ron's one assist. After ten NHL games he was returned to Lethbridge where he finished the season and added 22 playoff goals in 20 games. It proved to be his ticket to the NHL to stay.

He became a full-time Flyer in 1983-84 and immediately won accolades for his strong, two-way play. "Ron became a terrific 'shadow'—taking out superstars like Wayne Gretzky—but he had other assets," said Bru-

ins general manager Harry Sinden. "His defensive capabilities were great because he worked so hard, was rugged and saw the ice well."

Sutter delivered 19 goals and 32 assists for 51 points in 79 games during his first full season. In that same season Rich played 70 games for the Flyers and had 16 goals and 12 assists.

The union of Ron and Rich was bittersweet on Broad Street. It had been hoped that the twins could make beautiful music together and perhaps even steer Philly to another Stanley Cup. And, for a time, the two were in near-perfect synch.

"Because we have the same genes everyone expected us to be the same," said Ron. "The main characteristic that fitted both of us was that we both worked hard."

Ron may not have worked harder than Rich, but he certainly scored more and proved a better all-around player. Ron's defensive abilities made him a regular Selke Trophy candidate as best NHL defensive forward while

> *"The thing about Ron Sutter that you couldn't say about most NHL players was that nobody wanted to play against him. The other thing I learned is that you win when you have a Sutter in your lineup."*

his goal-scoring improved to a point where he tallied 26 goals in 1988-89, a career high.

Rich was conspicuously less productive. The latter remained with Philadelphia through the 1985-86 season and was dealt to Vancouver on June 6, 1986.

Flyers management had given careful thought before trading Rich. But the bottom line was that he failed to display the consistency of his twin brother after his promising 16-goal performance in 1983-84.

"We had always played together," said Ron of the split. "The only time I could remember being on another team was in training camp scrimmages."

Ron had no trouble handling the split. He played some of his best hockey as a Flyer in the late 1980s and accompanied Philadelphia to the Stanley Cup finals in 1987. During the 1988-89 playoffs he totalled ten points (1-9) in nineteen playoff games.

Sutter's belligerence resulted in no less than four seasons in which his penalty minutes exceeded 100. "Ron played the game just like his older brother, Brian, did," said former St. Louis Blues coach Jacques Demers. "They both were fierce competitors.

"The thing about Ron Sutter that you couldn't say about most NHL players was that nobody wanted to play against him. The other thing I learned is that you win when you have a Sutter in your lineup."

Ron remained in the Flyers lineup until September 22, 1991. On that date he was traded to St. Louis with defenseman Murray Baron for Dan Quinn and Rod Brind'Amour.

As luck would have it, Brind'Amour evolved into a latter-day Ron Sutter and remained a Flyer ever since.

Not so for Sutter. His production decreased and he was eventually traded to Quebec City, then the Islanders—for 25 games, Phoenix of the International League in 1995-96—before moving on to Boston and most recently San Jose.

By 1997-98 Ron appeared near the end of the NHL rope. He played in 57 games for the Sharks but produced only two goals and seven assists.

Nevertheless, his trademarks—perseverance, determination, tenacity—remained intact. After all, he was a Sutter, and one of the best.

Flyer Behn Wilson punches Flame Willi Plett behind the head in a fight that emptied the benches of both teams.

Behn Wilson

When the question of defenseman Behn Wilson's potential is raised, one can only be reminded of the deathless lines of the poet John Greenleaf Whittier, "For of all sad words of tongue or pen, The saddest are these: 'It might have been.'"

At a glance, Wilson had everything a Flyers coach could desire. He was big, belligerent and brainy.

When confronting him, enemy forwards hardly could contain their feelings of intimidation. Because of all his defensive assets, Wilson added a mean streak of the kind that every general manager coveted in his backliners.

At his best, Behn reminded press box veterans of the legendary Montreal Canadiens defenseman Doug Harvey, who played tough and wise simultaneously. Unfortunately, there was precious little of that very often in Wilson's game, and thus he will forever be viewed as an enigma rather than an immortal to Philadelphia hockey fans.

This much can be said without quarrel about Wilson. "He was not your average hockey player," wrote Randi H. Pearlman. "Not by the distance of 500 hockey sticks. From the spelling of his name to his studying at the University of Toronto, which he left behind to join the Flyers—Wilson was an impressive distillation of athlete, scholar and fighter."

BEHN BEVAN WILSON

Born: Toronto, Ontario, December 19, 1958

Position: Defense

NHL Teams: Philadelphia, 1978-83; Chicago, 1983-88

Awards/Honors: Played in 1980-81 All-Star Game

Drafted by Philadelphia sixth overall in 1978, Wilson was the product of a trade which sent Orest Kindrachuk, Ross Lonsberry and Tom Bladon to Pittsburgh. The Flyers needed to rebuild, and Wilson was seen as a key part of the process. But at the time, Behn's head was elsewhere.

"I always thought that my future would lie in the university," said Wilson. "Even up until [the year before his rookie season] that looked how it was going to be, although I kept hoping for a professional career in hockey. Still, I enrolled at the University of Toronto to pursue my interest in pre-medicine."

"He was not your average hockey player. Not by the distance of 500 hockey sticks. From the spelling of his name to his studying at the University of Toronto . . . Wilson was an impressive distillation of athlete, scholar and fighter."

Right after being drafted, Wilson beat out veterans such as Jimmy Watson, Bob Dailey and Moose Dupont to secure a spot on the Philly blue line. The Broad Street Bullies angle didn't faze Wilson, and his roughneck game helped him assimilate into the existing Flyers system.

"We didn't try to knock each other out of the lineup," said Wilson. "My style had always been to play aggressive, physical type of hockey. I had to establish my ability to play that way in the NHL."

His solid rookie season encompassed 80 games, with 13 goals and 36 assists for 49 points, an existing Flyers record. His 197 penalty minutes led the team and forced management to take notice.

"Behn proved himself in many areas," said former Flyers coach Bob McCammon. "He was very mature for his age, so you really didn't think of him as just being 19 years old."

During the 1979-80 season, the Flyers went on a record-setting 35-game unbeaten streak, and Wilson became an integral figure in that starring cast when he tipped a puck past Penguins goalie Greg Millen, giving Philadelphia a 1-1 tie, equalling a then-existing record of 28 straight games without a loss.

In that year's playoffs, Wilson scored four goals and nine assists for 13 points with 66 penalty minutes, as the Flyers charged to the Stanley Cup finals against the New York Islanders. In that series, Wilson found it difficult to use his gargantuan size against an equally towering Islander squad. One faceoff in particular prompted a reporter to comment that Wilson "hid behind a linesman when [Islander forward Clark] Gillies sidled up next to him."

Though Wilson's stats for 1980-81 appeared solid enough, with a 16-goal, 63-point, 237-penalty minute effort, he was not achieving the superstar status that the Flyers had expected. He was dressing for fewer and fewer games, and his hot-and-cold play garnered enough attention from the Spectrum boo-birds to brand him in the eyes of many as a non-star.

Wilson finally was traded to Chicago for defenseman Doug Crossman in the summer of 1983. As in Philadelphia, he was unable to realize his enormous potential. He spent three seasons with the Blackhawks before missing the entire 1986-87 season due to a severe back injury suffered during the 1986 playoffs against Toronto. Wilson finished his NHL career in Chicago in 1987-88, having never achieved the point nor penalty minute totals he had with Philadelphia.

Wilson's big-league career ended just short of a decade. By ordinary standards it was a good, if not spectacular, run. He made the playoffs every year with the Flyers and Blackhawks and produced reasonably impressive numbers.

But when all was said and done, Behn Wilson's top-heavy build-up exceeded his grasp of the game, and through no fault of his own, he exited the NHL with less than rave notices.

Still, his contributions to the Flyers surpassed the mediocre level and at times were splendid. That should not be forgotten nor hidden under the press clippings that never were of Wilson's making in the first place.

Ross Lonsberry

He made pit stops in Boston, Los Angeles, and Pittsburgh, but it was in Philadelphia, more than any city, where Ross Lonsberry made his most meaningful impact.

Originally a Bruins-developed forward, Lonsberry was an all-purpose performer who, were he playing today, could best be compared to an Adam Graves-type player.

Like Dave Schultz, Bill Clement and Don Saleski, Lonsberry was a foot soldier extraordinaire who never had any problems sticking his nose in the messy corners or staking his claim in front of the enemy net in pursuit of a goal.

The most he ever collected in Flyer penalty minutes was 99—a rather small number in relation to Schultz, et al—but Lonsberry's grit had the characteristics of good sandpaper.

Check out the box scores of the 1974 and 1975 Stanley Cup championships and you will find Lonsberry's name in prominent places. For example, in Game 3 on March 12, 1974 with the series tied at one game apiece, Lonsberry delivered the key goal at 14:19 of the third period at the Spectrum to put the game out of sight of the Bruins. Philadelphia won, 4-1, and that match was the one that catapulted them toward the finish line. In Game 4 on March 14,

DAVID ROSS LONSBERRY

Born: Humbolt, Saskatchewan, February 7, 1947

Postition: Left Wing

NHL Teams: Boston, 1966-69; Los Angeles, 1969-72; Philadelphia, 1972-78; Pittsburgh 1978-81

Left wing Ross Lonsberry (18) is in the Flyers' top 20 all-time in both playoff and regular season scoring.

1974, Lonsberry delivered again. With the score tied 2-2 late in the third period, Lonsberry collaborated with defenseman Jim Watson to help arrange Bill Barber's game-winning goal at 14:35 of the third. The win gave Philly a three games-to-one lead, which the Bruins never matched.

Ross was equally as effective in the 1975 finals against the Buffalo Sabres. With the Flyers nursing a 1-0 lead just past the seven-minute mark of the third period, Lonsberry beat goalie Gerry Desjardins at 7:29. It proved to be the winning goal in a 4-1 decision that put the Flyers one game up in the finals.

The second game, also played at The Spectrum, remained scoreless past the eight-minute mark of the second period. This time Lonsberry combined with Bobby Clarke as Reg Leach outwitted Desjardins for the game's first goal. Again the Flyers were triumphant, 2-1.

He scored again in Game 4—a 4-2 Flyers loss — but his major work had been done and the Flyers went on to win the series in six games.

What is surprising about Lonsberry is that he ever became a Flyer in the first place. The native of Watson, Saskatchewan had always been a goal-scorer since he started playing organized hockey in Humbolt, Sask., at the age of 13. A star in the Western (Junior) Hockey League, Lonsberry went directly to the Bruins in 1966-67.

Coincidentally, Bobby Orr made the same jump to Boston, the difference being that Orr stayed. Lonsberry was shipped to Buffalo and then Oklahoma City and never truly impressed the Bruins brass.

On May 14, 1969 Ross was dealt to Los Angeles with Eddie Shack for Ken Turlik and the Kings' first choices in the 1971 (Ron Jones) and 1973 (Andre Savard) amateur drafts.

In Los Angeles, Lonsberry blossomed. In his first season with the Kings, he tallied 20 goals and 22 assists for 42 points. A season later he upped his total to 25 goals and 28 assists for 53 points. If the Kings had been wise they would have kept him for another decade, because that's how long the 5'11", 195-pound left wing

---

> ## *"Ross was one of our best players," said coach Fred Shero. "His stamina alone was amazing."*

---

performed nobly in the NHL. Instead, the Kings traded him to Philadelphia with Bill Flett, Ed Joyal, and Jean Potvin for Bill Lesuk, Jim Johnson, and Serge Bernier on January 28, 1972.

The Kings' mistake was obvious from the get-go. Lonsberry proved steady throughout his stint on Broad Street and even better in the clutch.

The 1973 playoffs marked his first postseason NHL experience. In 11 games he responded with four goals and three assists. In the first Stanley Cup year, he had 13 points (4-9) in 17 games.

"Ross was one of our best players," said coach Fred Shero. "His stamina alone was amazing."

Nicknamed "Roscoe," Lonsberry came through with four goals and three assists in 17 games for the Flyers' 1975 Cup run and had the same numbers a year later in 16 games as Philadelphia lost in the finals to the Montreal Canadiens.

As a defensive forward, Lonsberry's responsibility included coverage of the NHL's top right wings, a job he performed calmly and efficiently. The only other coverage he could have used was for his head. During the 1974 finals, a whiskey bottle hurled by a rowdy Boston Garden fan missed Lonsberry's head by inches and shattered next to his skates on the ice.

"I don't think anything ever scared me so much as that," Lonsberry said.

Those who watched him know that Ross was not often frightened. But by the end of the 1977-78 season, the Flyers had their eyes on a gifted young defenseman named Behn Wilson, who would be available in the first round of the draft.

To obtain that pick, the Flyers traded Lonsberry to Pittsburgh with Tom Bladon and Orest Kindrachuk.

In the end, Philadelphia got as much value out of Lonsberry as could have been expected. He was one of the key links—among many—who forged the championship squad of the mid-1970s and executed the key plays when necessary in both Stanley Cup seasons.

He concluded his career as a Penguin after the 1980-81 season, but it is worth noting that even in the very twilight of his hockey life, Lonsberry still was effective. He scored 17 goals and 33 assists for 50 points before finally bidding adieu to the NHL.

A young Kevin Dineen hustles down the ice.

Kevin Dineen

Few hockey players made a greater impact in a shorter time at The Spectrum than Kevin Dineen.

Counting the shortened lockout season, the ebullient right wing spent all of five years wearing the orange and black, yet to many Philadelphia fans, Dineen spent a lovable lifetime in The City of Brotherly Love.

Hockey immortal Gordie Howe once explained the source of such affection.

"The little bugger is one of the most competitive players I've ever seen," concluded Howe.

Dineen's competitive ways came naturally. His father, Bill Dineen, had been a teammate of Howe's on some mighty Detroit Red Wings squads. The elder Dineen got that way via some major-league hustle.

Bill was a feisty forward with both the Motor City sextet and the Chicago Blackhawks and later went on to coach in the World Hockey Association and the American Hockey League before actually going behind the Flyers' bench.

KEVIN DINEEN

Born: Quebec City, Quebec, October 28, 1963

Position: Right Wing

NHL Teams: Hartford, 1985-91, 1996-97; Philadelphia 1991-96; Carolina 1997-present

Awards/Honors: Played in 1988 All-Star Game; Bud Light/NHL Man of the Year Award, 1990-91; Captain, Philadelphia, 1993-94 season; Captain, Hartford/Carolina, 1996-present

Kevin Dineen propels a wrist shot from the left side.

"My dad made a career out of hockey," said Kevin, "so naturally, a lot of it rubbed off on me. When my dad coached the Houston Aeros, I got a chance to learn the sport from Gordie Howe."

Bill Dineen: "Gordie took a special shine to Kevin because he was the one with the most mischief in him among my sons—and a charmer as well. Gordie liked Kevin because no matter how rough he handled Kevin, picking him up by the ears and all that, Kevin would always come right back at him."

Kevin broke in with the Whalers in 1984-85 and remained in Hartford until 1991-92 when he was traded to Philly. In that first season on Broad Street, he played 64 games and scored 26 goals and 30 assists.

But the intangibles he brought to the Flyers' table impressed hockey people as much as anything. "Kevin is one of the most inspirational players I have ever known," said former Stanley Cup-winning Canadiens coach Jean Perron.

The tangibles weren't bad either. In his first full year as a Flyer (1992-93), Dineen played 83 regular sea-

son games and compiled a 35-28-63 mark. His 201 penalty minutes were the second highest PIM of his career.

"Kevin was a throwback to the old days," said Emile Francis, who managed Dineen in Hartford. "He was a puckhound who wouldn't take 'no' for an answer. He was perpetual motion all the way."

When the lockout crippled the 1994-95 campaign, Dineen played for Houston in the International League and then returned to Philadelphia once the labor dispute was settled. He was particularly effective in the playoffs, during which the Flyers reached the third round before being eliminated by the New Jersey Devils. He played in 15 playoff games with six goals and four assists as well as 18 penalty minutes.

"I loved to play more than anything else," said Dineen. "Over the course of the season, I would always look for some motivation."

Invariably, he would find it, but not always in Philly. During the 1995-96 season he was traded back to the Whalers, and when the Hartford franchise moved to Carolina and became the Hurricanes, Dineen went with

"Kevin was a throwback to the old days," said Emile Francis, who managed Dineen in Hartford. "He was a puckhound who wouldn't take 'no' for an answer. He was perpetual motion all the way."

them—as team captain.

"Kevin was one of the dozen players in the league whom every team wanted when he was in his prime," said Gerry Cheevers, the former Bruins goalie, coach and later television analyst.

Part of that prime was, fortunately, spent in Philadelphia. And in one season, 1994-95, it actually seemed as if Dineen would be one of the architects of a Stanley Cup-winning season.

The Devils destroyed that dream, but not before Dineen had completed some of the hardest digging any three playoff rounds had ever seen. For that alone, he always will be remembered with affection in Pennsylvania.

A battler in the Bobby Clarke mold, Kevin Dineen is shown checking Benoit Hogue of the Islanders.

One of the best Swedish imports ever to play defense in the NHL, Kjell Samuelsson was nicknamed "The Human Tripod."

Kjell Samuelsson

His not-so-flattering nickname was The Human Tripod. The oversized Swedish defenseman looked awkward as he snowshoed up and down the ice. But on closer scrutiny—especially from coaches and teammates—Kjell Samuelsson was every inch a hockey player—all seventy-eight inches of him.

By rights, Samuelsson had no business being a Flyer. Originally drafted by the New York Rangers in the sixth round (119th overall) of the 1984 entry draft, Kjell should have stayed on Broadway for a decade. But as it happened, the Rangers' general staff underestimated Samuelsson's talent and traded him to Philadelphia along with a second-round draft choice for goalie Bob Froese on December 18, 1986.

Until then, Kjell had played only parts of two seasons for the Broadway Blueshirts. In 1985-86 he was up for a nine-game cup of coffee during the regular season but also played in nine playoff games. He had played 30 more games for New York the following season before the trade was made.

As a Flyer, Samuelsson came into his own as an effective backliner. His reach, which favorably compared to a Roto-Rooter, enabled Kjell to poke-check pucks out of the reach of ordinary-sized defensemen. And although

KJELL SAMUELSSON

Born: Tyngsryd, Sweden, October 18, 1958

Position: Defense

NHL Teams: N.Y. Rangers, 1985-87; Philadelphia, 1987-1992, 1995-present; Pittsburgh, 1991-95

Awards/Honors: Played in 1988 All-Star Game; Won Barry Ashbee Trophy, 1988-89

Swedes once had a reputation for playing "soft" hockey, Samuelsson was among the roughest of blueliners but in a smart, relatively quiet way. His toughness was underlined by his penalty minutes.

In 1987-88, his first full year in Philadelphia, Kjell totalled a career-high 184 penalty minutes. He played in 74 games, scored six goals and 24 assists while finishing plus-28, highest plus-minus of the Flyers. Samuelsson's consistent play on the blue line earned him a spot on the Wales Conference All-Star Team, chosen over such name defenders as Chris Chelios and Larry Murphy.

"He was very hard to play against," said Peter Inhacek, a Toronto Maple Leafs forward from that era. "Kjell was like an octopus out there. He was all over you in front of the net and in the corners.

"He had good hockey sense and could body-check. Against some defensemen you could go one on one and fake like you're going to go to the left but you turn to the right. Samuelsson could never be fooled. He stayed right with you."

He stayed in Philadelphia until February 19, 1992 when Kjell was involved in a blockbuster deal with Pittsburgh—Samuelsson, along with Rick Tocchet, Ken Wregget and a third-round choice in the 1993 NHL entry draft (Dave Roche). In return the Flyers received Mark Recchi, Brian Benning and the Kings' first-round choice in the 1992 NHL entry draft (Jason Bowen).

It was a super move for Samuelsson and the Penguins. Pittsburgh won its second straight Stanley Cup while Kjell contributed mightily in the 15 playoff games in which he was involved. He played three more full seasons with the Penguins but was left unprotected after the 1994-95 campaign.

The Flyers wasted no time signing him as a free agent on July 7, 1995.

Kjell was welcomed back to The Spectrum like a long-lost relative. One of his favorite nicknames was even pulled out of cold storage for the occasion. When he had originally signed with the Flyers, some press box wag got the bright idea that Samuelsson's less than elegant skating stride reminded him of the ungainly cartoon dog Marmaduke. Kjell immediately was tagged Marmaduke, and that soon was shortened to Duke.

In any event, Duke returned to Broad Street as a surprisingly agile 37-year-old. He managed to play in 75 games and scored three goals.

Unquestionably, the most memorable of the goals was achieved on February 25, 1996 in a game at The Spectrum against the Chicago Blackhawks. The score was

"He was very hard to play against," said Peter Inhacek, a Toronto Maple Leafs forward from that era. "Kjell was like an octopus out there. He was all over you in front of the net and in the corners."

tied, 2-2, late in the third period when Kjell was posted at the visitors' blue line. Dan Quinn of the Flyers had the puck behind the net and skimmed a pass to Eric Lindros, who was camped at the bottom of the left circle.

When the puck eluded Lindros, it made its way toward the blue line in the general direction of Marmaduke. First, the defenseman knocked down the puck and then spun to get to his forehand.

"He turned in a loose circle that brought to mind a rusty-but-dependable Volvo negotiating an icy curve," wrote Les Bowen of the *Philadelphia Daily News*. The Spin-a-rama worked. Although Samuelsson's shot was moving wide to the right of goalie Ed Belfour, it ricochetted off the back of defenseman Chris Chelios' skate.

As if guided by radar, the rubber skimmed past Belfour's pad and into the net with 20.4 seconds left in regulation time. It provided the Flyers with a 3-2 victory. As for his lifetime highlight film goal, Samuelsson merely commented, "It looked better on TV than it felt like."

Injuries limited Kjell's activity during his final two seasons with the Flyers. His swan song was played in 1997-98 when he played in 49 games. Samuelsson tallied only three assists, yet was able to finish with an admirable plus-nine, one of the best plus-minuses on the team.

For more than a decade, he was one of the true unsung heroes in major-league hockey and certainly a worthy member of the Flyers on both visits to Broad Street.

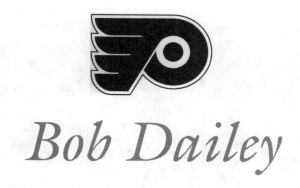

Bob Dailey

When defenseman Bob Dailey was traded from the Vancouver Canucks to the Philadelphia Flyers, he inadvertently inspired a priceless quip from then coach Fred Shero.

Columnist Stan Hochman of the *Philadelphia Daily News* asked Shero how long it would take Dailey to learn the Flyers' Xs and Os.

To which Shero offered the perfect squelch: "I've got guys who have been with me for five years and they still make mistakes!"

Actually, Shero knew he had a good one in Dailey, and the arithmetic supports that thesis—57, 39, 39, 34. Those are the kinds of points few defensemen put up in a season. Yet Dailey did just that between 1977-78 and 1980-81.

"He was a quality hockey player," reflected Shero. "Talent will out."

The Flyers acquired Dailey a couple of years after their two-year Stanley Cup run after which the Montreal Canadiens became the National Hockey League dynasty.

"Montreal had the league's best defense," said Shero, "and we were hoping that Dailey could help us close the gap."

ROBERT SCOTT "BOB" DAILEY

BORN: Kingston, Ontario, May 3, 1953

Position: Defense

NHL Teams: Vancouver, 1973-77; Philadelphia, 1977-82

Awards/Honors: Voted Best Flyers Defenseman, 1979, 1981; Played in 1977-78 All-Star Game

One of the top Flyer defenders of the late 1970s, Bob Dailey.

Dailey certainly did help, but the chasm never was completely filled, although the Flyers did reach the Stanley Cup finals in 1980 against the New York Islanders.

During that four-series run, Dailey performed in 19 games and produced a quality four goals and 13 assists for 17 points.

Seventeen points in nineteen games should have been enough to enshrine the oversized defenseman in some form of puck pantheon, even in a corner of The Spectrum, but one episode negated any thought of that. Dailey was one of six Philadelphia players on the ice when Bob Nystrom scored the sudden-death goal in Game 6 at Nassau Coliseum.

As the puck sailed past Philly goalie Pete Peeters, Dailey slammed his stick against the ice and looked down, totally spent. Al Morganti, who covered that series for the *Philadelphia Inquirer*, later commented: "Dailey played that entire series with his left shoulder so badly damaged he could hardly lift his arm."

"He was a quality hockey player," reflected Shero. "Talent will out."

In fact the pain was so severe that Dailey could not even carry his light duffel bag out to the team bus. "The shoulder was useless," added Morganti, "the arm no more than a strand of spaghetti, but Dailey had pushed to the limit."

Overlooked, as well, was the fact that Dailey had scored early in the third period of Game 6 to ignite a Flyers rally that eventually tied the count, sending the game into overtime.

"We will remember Bobby Clarke with the gap-toothed smile, skating with the Stanley Cup," said Morganti, "but for Dailey, the picture that remained was not framed by a glorious victory."

The defeat in the finals was an event that a professional such as Dailey should easily have brushed aside, and he did. He returned to the club the next autumn, playing in 53 games during the 1980-81 season. He had a season that virtually any other backliner would have coveted—at least points-wise—with 34 points (7-27) and appeared in mint condition the following campaign.

At age twenty-nine he was at the pinnacle of his career, aiming for the NHL decade mark and, if he was lucky, perhaps fifteen full big-league seasons.

But he wasn't lucky; not by a long shot, slap shot, or whatever shot.

In his twelfth game of the season, Bob was skating against the Buffalo Sabres at Memorial Auditorium when it happened and a career came crashing down on him.

"It was a routine icing," he remembered. "I went back and my skate hit a rut in the ice. I fell into the boards. I saw my foot at a right angle to my shin and said, 'Uh-oh!'

"The ankle was busted on both sides. The bone was in a hundred pieces." He was carried off the ice on a stretcher with an ankle so badly shattered that several pins and screws were required to hold it together.

"I tried to skate in March of 1982, but it was no use. The foot was swollen to three times its normal size. The doctors said, 'That's it. No more hockey.'"

Dailey tried for a comeback in 1986, enduring workouts with Flyers physical therapist Pat Croce, but although he thought his ankle felt fine, the 6'6" 230-pound backliner couldn't hack it anymore.

"You see a man that big, and you think he can live with anything," summed up Morganti. "You forget that the threshold for pain does not necessarily correlate to inches and feet. You forget that large people hurt, too."

The hurt was not easily mended, not for the Flyers and not for a gifted defenseman named Bob Dailey.

Bob Froese makes a kick save against the Rangers.

Bob Froese

For a goaltender whose most active season as a Flyer consisted of 51 games in the net, Bob Froese must have been special to gain a spot on the list.

Yes, the bouncy little stopper was special. Very special.

One might say that Froese was the best second goalie the Flyers ever had, a net minder with the misfortune of having to play behind Ron Hextall during Hexy's best years in the business.

But when the S.O.S was sounded for him, Froese cheerfully donned the pads and did what had to be done.

In 1985-86 when he was asked to play 51 times, Froese responded like an All-Star. He posted a league-leading five shutouts and also paced the NHL with a 2.55 goals-against average.

What makes this all the more remarkable was the fact that for most of his young life, Bob Froese entertained few thoughts about the National Hockey League.

And why should he?

The St. Catherines, Ontario native was a teenager before he played his first organized hockey game and militantly favored lacrosse as his sport of choice.

ROBERT GLEN "BOB" FROESE

Born: St. Catherines, Ontario, June 30, 1958

Position: Goaltender

NHL Teams: Philadephia, 1982-86; N.Y. Rangers, 1986-1991

Awards/ Honors: Second Team All-Star (1986), NHL All-Star game (1986), Shared William Jennings Trophy with Darren Jensen (1986)

But a lacrosse injury at age 14 permanently altered the direction of his career. He drifted toward goaltending and became so adept in the Ontario Hockey Association that the minor pro Saginaw Gears signed him in 1978-79.

For a time it appeared that Bob was destined to be a career minor-leaguer; if not with Saginaw then it would be the Milwaukee Admirals.

"I had good character-building years in the International League," Froese said. "If I had never made the NHL, I probably would look back on them and think they were terrible years. But now, I look back and say they were good years for me."

Gene Ubriaco, the Admirals' coach, detected a special trait in Froese that endeared him to the blocker. Bob not only had talent, he was a remarkable team player, so much so that Ubriaco felt obliged to tip off the Flyers to his find. The Philly high command trusted Gene and signed Froese as a free agent in June, 1981.

He was exported to Maine of the American Hockey League and had no business expecting anything more, because the Flyers owned a whiz-bang goaltender named Pelle Lindbergh.

But during the 1982-83 season campaign, Lindbergh made the mistake of breaking his wrist. Enter Bob Froese.

He not only won his first two major-league games but collected an assist in each!

After his second game in the NHL, a match against the Pittsburgh Penguins, the story of Froese barking at a player one time in the minor league surfaced.

"I did it [barked] once. I think it surprised the other team more than anything. The guys on our team, I could do anything and it wouldn't surprise them," Froese said. "Geez, I've always been a different guy... not crazy or anything... just Czechoslovakian."

How good was he?

How about 17 wins, two ties and only four losses? His 2.52 goals-against average stacked up favorably with Lindbergh's 2.98 in 40 games.

The Flyers knew they had a good one and decided to make him better. Hall of Famer Bernie Parent was

Stopped cold! Bob Froese stops the Rangers' Mark Pavelich at the goal mouth.

summoned as professor and Froese became his pupil.

As expected, Bob learned well and became the Flyers' regular goaltender in 1983-84. He won more than twice as many games as he lost (28-13-7) and earned the third-best goals-against average (3.14) in the NHL.

Then his luck took a downward turn.

Just as it had seemed he had won the number-one job from Lindbergh, Froese was riddled with a series of injuries, limiting his play to 17 games. But fate dealt a cruel hand to the Flyers when Lindbergh was killed in an auto accident on November 10, 1985.

The tragedy enabled Froese to reestablish his claim to the Flyers' number-one goalie role. His response was swift and sure.

"Consistency is nothing more than a measure of your mental strength," Froese said. "For a goalie to be consistent, you have to prepare. You can't just wait for the game and then try to switch it on."

Froese finished the 1985-86 season with a 2.55 goals-against average, topping the league and a 31-10-5 record. He was a full half-goal per game better than runner-up Al Jensen's 3.18.

Reemphasizing Froese's superiority were other bits of arithmetic. His save percentage (.909) and five shutouts also were league-leaders. Bob seemed poised for a long, happy run on Broad Street.

But the 1986 playoffs proved an obstacle he could not surmount. Philadelphia encountered a hot Rangers squad powered by goalie John Vanbiesbrouck. New York stung Froese, whose 3.07 average was inadequate. Vanbiesbrouck stopped 93 percent of the Flyers shots, Froese only 88 percent of the Rangers!

Philly was eliminated in five games. Froese was eliminated as a number one. The following autumn, Ron Hextall deposed Froese, and the Flyers merely waited for an opportune time trade him. Ironically, the deal sent Froese to the most unlikely of teams, the Rangers, where he would support Vanbiesbrouck.

Froese did his job well, but he never again would play a starring—nor number one—role. Nor would his average be as impressive as it had been with the orange-and-black.

Following three full seasons (1986-87 through 1988-89) on Broadway, Froese called it a career in 1990 after a 15-game season in New York.

Where does he fit on the Flyers list of good ones?

Bob Froese was one of the better regular season goalies to play for Philadelphia, and an excellent stopper when Lindbergh was lost. But one bad playoff was enough to destroy his future with the Flyers.

"Consistency is nothing more than a measure of your mental strength," Froese said. "For a goalie to be consistent, you have to prepare. You can't just wait for the game and then try to switch it on.

Bob Froese exults in winning the Jennings Trophy.

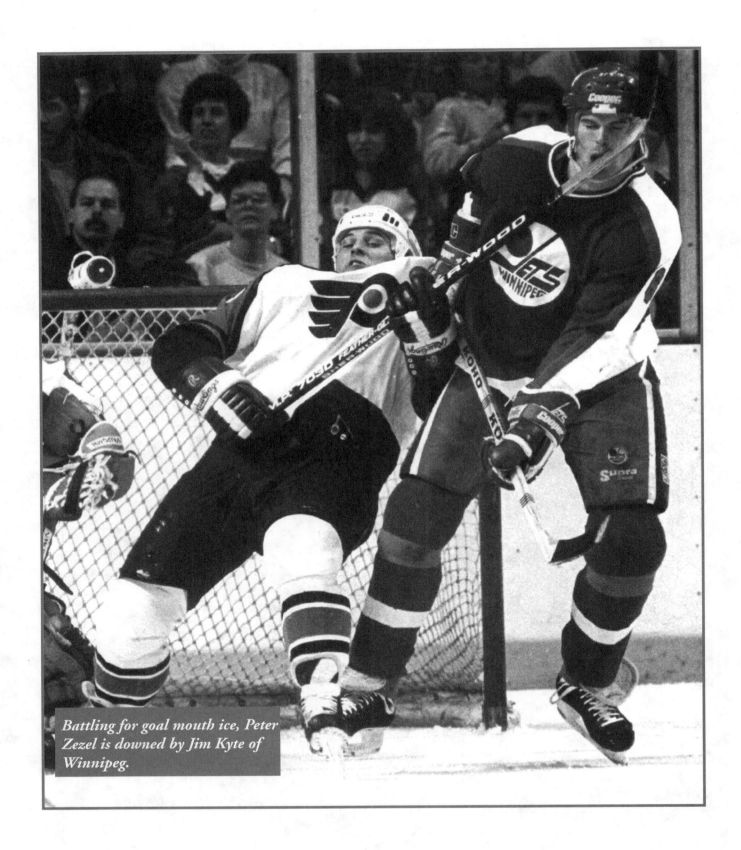

Battling for goal mouth ice, Peter Zezel is downed by Jim Kyte of Winnipeg.

Peter Zezel

Considering that he played only four and a half seasons in Philadelphia, Peter Zezel enjoyed one of the most upbeat relationships with local fans of anyone who skated at The Spectrum.

Part of the Toronto native's appeal was his enduring work ethic, and the other part was his delightful personality. Anyone who watched the center play or whom conversed with him came way convinced that this was a very good man and a darn good stick handler to boot.

He was the Flyers' first choice—41st overall—in the 1983 entry draft while playing junior hockey for the Toronto Marlboros. In two years he totalled 207 points, which was enough to catch the eyes of the general staff. A year after being drafted, he was invited to the club's training camp and made The Show on his first attempt.

"Getting drafted by the Flyers was the biggest thrill of my life," he said. "Bobby Clarke had been my idol when I was younger, and now I was in Philly alongside him."

Clarke: "When Peter first took the ice as a Flyer, some of us remarked that he reminded us of Bryan Trottier, with his build. As for the other parts of his game, we could tell right away that he was very bright and saw the whole ice."

PETER ZEZEL

Born: Toronto, Ontario, April 22, 1965

Position: Center

NHL Teams: Philadelphia, 1984-88; St. Louis, 1988-90, 95-97; Washington, 1990-91; Toronto, 1991-94; Dallas, 1994-95; New Jersey, 1997-98; Vancouver, 1998-present

One of the most popular Flyers during the 1980s was center Peter Zezel, here fending off Dave Hannan of Pittsburgh.

Zezel had come to hockey by way of soccer. He was an expert booter and played professionally for Toronto of the North American Soccer League. He also was one of only 19 players to play for the Canadian Youth National Team, which toured various parts of the world. In time, he managed to incorporate kickwork into his on-ice repertoire. It would become a permanent part of Peter's game and particularly advantageous during face-offs.

These gifts enabled him to immediately click as a freshman in the NHL. He scored 15 goals, 46 assists (a club rookie record) for 61 points to go along with an impressive plus-22 in the plus-minus category.

Coach Mike Keenan found Zezel's teamsmanship a primary asset.

During a game with Los Angeles, the Flyers were protecting a one-goal lead when the Kings pulled their goaltender for an extra attacker. Philly defenseman Mark Howe flipped the puck from his own goal line out of the Flyers' zone and toward the open net.

Zezel was close enough to the puck to add an extra tap in and get the credit for the red light himself. Instead, he resisted the temptation and Howe wound up with the goal.

"That play was typical of Peter's unselfishness," said Keenan. "It was a comment on the type of person he is and always has been."

Keenan hardly was shy about thrusting him into a pivotal role during their march to the 1985 Stanley Cup finals. "That," Peter recalled, "was a tremendous experience. It gave me a lot of confidence."

He performed in no less than 19 playoff games, tallying a goal and eight assists, cementing a regular berth along with equally young and ebullient pals, Rick Tocchet and Derrick Smith.

"The three of us had been warned about the sophomore jinx," Zezel laughed, "but we analyzed the potential problem and decided that it wouldn't happen to us."

It didn't.

Zezel played 79 games in his second year—14 more than his first—and was no less effective. His plus-minus climbed to plus-27 and his overall ice presence impressed coach Mike Keenan, who favored Peter's grit.

"He was very talented," said Keenan.

The relationship between Keenan and Zezel remained strong long after their Philadelphia years. "What I learned from Mike as a Flyer," said Zezel, "is that when I made a bad pass in practice, I would swear at myself because it mattered."

While others may have regarded Keenan as a tyrant, Zezel worked well with Mike. He remembered one game against the Islanders when his line allowed a couple of goals against the legendary Mike Bossy-Bryan Trottier-Clark Gillies line.

"Keenan came into the dressing room after the first period and was yelling at everybody and then he came up to me and kicked me in the shinpads. In the next game, we got ahead in the first period, so I grabbed a pair of goalie pads and sat in front of my stall. Mike sort of smiled. Sort of."

What he lacked at the start was consistency. "Some of the teams got wind of what I could do," said Zezel. "I had to come up with a better game plan, make some

"Being the center of attention with the fans was never bad," Zezel confessed. *"It always gave me a real nice feeling when I would give a kid an autograph and his face would light up."*

changes so they didn't read me as well."

Whatever alterations Zezel made, they worked. As a third-year NHLer, he zoomed to 33 goals, 39 assists and a career-high 72 points. In that 1986-87 season Peter helped the Flyers to the Stanley Cup finals once more. He was in 25 playoff games and produced 13 points (3-10).

Better still, he had transcended the NHL rinks as a hero. He was cast in the movie *Youngblood* with Rob Lowe

In their early Flyer years, Peter Zezel and Rick Tocchet were among the most exuberant Flyers.

and became a regular on the off-season golf circuit.

"Being the center of attention with the fans was never bad," Zezel confessed. "It always gave me a real nice feeling when I would give a kid an autograph and his face would light up."

At one point he had become such a fan favorite in Philly that he had to be accompanied by a bodyguard when he went grocery shopping. He frequently paid people to buy clothes for him while he stayed in the safety of his home.

The love affair between Zezel and the community was evident in all walks of life. Once he settled in as a year-round resident, he devoted time to "Philadelphia Pro Athletes Against Drunk Driving" and other local services.

At 5'11", 200 pounds, Zezel emerged as one of the league's top faceoff specialists. "I tried to use my feet a lot," he said, "and I cheated a bit."

Zezel never duplicated his 72-point season in Philly. He dropped 15 points the following year and it became generally accepted that his role had been altered.

"I was not a number-one center," he admitted. "I liked the role of being a good faceoff man and a little bit of everything. I wasn't going to be a 40-goal man."

At least not in Philadelphia. On November 29, 1988, Zezel was traded to St. Louis for Mike Bullard.

Peter Zezel and the Philadelphia fans exhibit their joy over a Flyer goal.

Zezel: "The trade made me realize that not everybody is going to be in one place forever. I would have loved to have played my entire career in Philadelphia, but it was out of my control."

Like a table-tennis ball, Peter bounced from team to team—St. Louis, Washington, Toronto, Dallas, St. Louis again, New Jersey and Vancouver—through 1998.

He was likeable wherever he played but never more so than when he wore the orange and black at The Spectrum.

Don Saleski

There are those who might wonder why Don Saleski deserves to be on any list of favorite Flyers.

He never was an overwhelming scorer, never a particularly heavy hitter nor a major leader on the team.

Yet there was something special about The Big Bird from Moose Jaw, Saskatchewan. Something vibrant, intelligent, winning.

It would be an exaggeration to suggest that the Flyers would not have won either of their two Stanley Cups, in 1974 and 1975, without Saleski. But he delivered a special brand of chemistry.

Saleski provided that intangible link between the Dave Schultz-Bob Kelly truculence and the high-skill performers like Rick MacLeish and Bill Barber.

Plus, he was a winner.

"The success Don had was due to his willingness to work," said Bob Clarke, who teamed with Saleski on the championship teams. "He put an effort toward what he wanted and was willing to do anything to achieve his goals."

Like Clarke, Saleski was a Western Canadian who learned his hockey in the tough towns on the prairie. Although his numbers in Regina were not spectacular, he was drafted in the sixth round of the 1969 draft by the Flyers. He later played for Winnipeg and Saskatoon before turning pro with Quebec of the American Hockey League in 1971-72. His modest nine goals and seven assists in 72 AHL games gave no hints of better things to come, but a year later he moved on to Richmond of the AHL and his numbers soared.

He scored 22 goals in 73 games and earned a one-game tryout with the Flyers. A year later, 1972-73, he made the big club precisely when Fred Shero

DONALD PATRICK "BIG BIRD" SALESKI

BORN: Moose Jaw, Saskatchewan, November 10, 1949

Position: Right Wing

NHL Teams: Philadelphia, 1971-1979; Colorado, 1978-1980

Don "Big Bird" Saleski (center) took his share of hits during his eight years with the Flyers. He recorded 118 goals and 117 assists for a total of 235 points

was turning it from a turn-the-other-cheek sextet to a skillful, marauding powerhouse.

"Don was a strong person," remembered Clarke. "He always had an idea where he was heading and he wanted badly to play in the NHL."

In his rookie season, Saleski proved he belonged. Over 78 games, he scored a dozen goals, nine assists and 21 points. Surprising were the 205 penalty minutes for a rather even-tempered personality.

"I was a role player who never achieved greatness as a goal scorer or playmaker," said Saleski, "although I did have three 20-goal seasons with Philadelphia."

In his sophomore season, 1973-74, Saleski hiked his totals to 15-25-40 the year Philadelphia won its first Stanley Cup. Over a 17-game playoff run, he was 2-7-9, not all bad for a role player.

"We had a great team," Saleski reflected. "We may have been closer as a team than any other in sports. The camaraderie on the Flyers was unparalleled. Our team spirit and the way we played and lived together was a great experience."

Once, they even went to jail together.

The episode followed a game in Toronto against the Maple Leafs. To no one's surprise, a brawl erupted and three and a half hours were required to finish the game. (Toronto won, 5-4.) The next day the Flyers learned that criminal charges had been filed against Saleski and teammates Mel Bridgman and Joe Watson.

Ontario attorney general Roy McMurtry charged them with various offenses including assault and possession of an offensive weapon—the hockey stick—as a result of what some reporters called Rollerball On Ice at Maple Leaf Gardens. Saleski, Watson and Bridgman were taken to a Toronto police station where they were photographed, fingerprinted and formally charged, but it turned out to be more of a publicity stunt on the part of McMurtry.

By the end the 1974-75 season Saleski's teammates rated him the best defensive forward. "There were a lot of guys similar to me," Don noted. "They were steady players, not superstars—Billy Clement, Simon Nolet, Dave Schultz, Bob Kelly, Orest Kindrachuk and Barry Ashbee. We knew that the only way we were going to win was by playing together and being a close-knit team."

Saleski was smart enough to know his limitations, but every so often, he would enjoy a scoring outburst as he did on April 20, 1976 against the Maple Leafs at The Spectrum.

This was during the Flyers' 1976 march to the finals. In order to get there, Philadelphia had to dispose of Toronto, and Saleski provided the big push with a three-goal hat trick in a 7-1 drubbing of the visitors.

"It was my first hat trick in eight or nine years," Don recalled. "The last previous time I had scored three goals in a game was in juniors against the Moose Jaw Canucks.

"Despite the hat trick, I never thought of myself as a goal scorer. I was a checker, a worker and someone who helped his team in as many ways as he could."

He chipped in 21 goals that year and followed with 22 in 1976-77 and then a career-high 27 in 1977-78. "He was tireless," said Clarke. "Big, heavy, great in the corners. You didn't always notice him, but he was always out there, going up and down the ice, doing his job, helping us win games."

General manager Keith Allen patiently watched Saleski mature into a meaningful member of the team after a somewhat shaky start. "Big guys usually develop slower," Allen explained. "It was true in Don's case because he missed a season because of mononucleosis right after we drafted him in 1969."

By 1978-79 Allen decided that it would be a prudent time to trade Saleski. The NHL had decided to go in a different direction, minimizing the checking, hit-

> *"We had a great team," Saleski reflected. "We may have been closer as a team than any other in sports. The camaraderie on the Flyers was unparalleled. Our team spirit and the way we played and lived together was a great experience."*

ting and fighting while accentuating a speedier style of play. Pat Quinn had replaced Shero as head coach and had decided to alter the Flyers' game plan to suit the new league policy.

Quinn utilized Saleski considerably less than Shero had, and Don made it clear that he wanted to be traded. Allen accommodated him during the 1978-79 season, sending him to the lowly Colorado Rockies.

At first, Saleski made the adjustment with no complaints. But when the 1979-80 season began, Don (Grapes) Cherry was the new Rockies coach. Don and Don got along about as smoothly as the Hatfields and McCoys. Saleski often said that it was "the low point" of his hockey career.

"When Cherry came from Boston to Colorado," Saleski recalled, "he found himself with a lot of misguided kids. They didn't have a lot of direction or confidence. Cherry didn't know how to deal with that team, didn't know how to relate to those guys or motivate them. He tried intimidation, and, in the end, it was dehumanizing."

After a bitter argument with Cherry in front of his teammates, Saleski knew that he was finished. He was demoted to Fort Worth and soon decided that he had had enough of pro hockey.

Although friends—including Flyers owner Ed Snider—urged him to remain in hockey, Don retired and in time became a highly successful business executive.

"Don moved into the business world as well as any athlete I have known," said Snider.

But Snider and most Philadelphians will remember Don Saleski as The Big Bird who helped the Flyers soar in those wonderful years of the 1970s.

The *"Little O,"*
Orest Kindrachuk.

Orest Kindrachuk

They called him "The Little O." Orest Kindrachuk was on the smallish side and tended to be overlooked among the more luminescent Flyers.

But those who knew him well understood that the native of Nanton, Alberta was special. One of them was Max McNab, general manager of the San Diego Gulls in the old Wester Pro League back in 1971-72.

Like Kindrachuk, McNab was a Western Canadian who appreciated that prairie boys like Little O tended to have bigger hockey hearts than the Easterners. At least that was the prevailing thought west of Ontario.

"I remember Orest when he played junior hockey," McNab recalled. "He was one of the few players who went up to the Flin Flon [Manitoba] rink and wasn't frightened by the Junior Bombers. Right then and there it was obvious that this kid was going to go places."

And he did.

He played three seasons for the Saskatoon (Junior) Blades in the Western Canada League and was signed by the Flyers as a free agent in 1971 after a 100-assist year (1970-71) with the Blades, which he also captained.

OREST KINDRACHUK

Born: Nanton, Alberta, September 14, 1950

Position: Center

NHL Teams: Philadelphia, 1972-78; Pittsburgh, 1978-81; Washington, 1981-82.

Awards/Honors: Captain, Pittsburgh, 1978-81

Following his junior stint, he had so promising a year at San Diego that the Flyers brought him to training camp in September 1972.

McNab: "I was hoping to get him back with San Diego, but the Flyers had a farm team in Richmond, Virginia, at the time. It was in the American League and Eddie Bush was coach.

"At camp I had my eyes on Bush whenever Kindrachuk was on the ice. Bush saw the same things I saw. Orest won faceoffs, he battled in the corners and he could even pop a few goals. I knew I'd never see him in the Western League again. And I didn't."

"I remember Orest when he played junior hockey," McNab recalled. "He was one of the few players who went up to the Flin Flon [Manitoba] rink and wasn't frightened by the Junior Bombers. Right then and there it was obvious that this kid was going to go places."

Kindrachuk played 72 games for Richmond and produced 35 goals and 51 assists. The Flyers liked him enough to offer a two-game tryout (0-0-0) and by 1973-74, he was promoted to the big club.

"They put him between Don (Big Bird) Saleski and Dave (Hammer) Schultz, and Little O helped make them better players," added McNab.

The result was a mixture of firecrackers and goals. Not that Little O played there all the time; Bill Clement and Terry Crisp alternated with the two Terminators, but Kindrachuk proved just as effective in a conspicuously low-key way.

Although he was a significant element on the Flyers' Stanley Cup-winning team in 1974, he remained a student on the sidelines. Ever since his junior days in

Saskatoon, Kindrachuk had maintained an interest in optometry, to the point of taking a season off from the Junior Saskatoon Blades to take optometry classes at the University of Saskatchewan.

There was no need for a day job testing eyesight, at least not in the mid-1970s. Kindrachuk fit snugly into the Flyers' system, playing bigger than his 5'10", 175 pounds. En route to the 1974 Stanley Cup, he scored five playoff goals and four assists for nine points in 17 games.

"He deserved some kind of handicap, working between wingers like me and Saleski," kidded Schultz.

His penalty minutes over his five-year Philadelphia career—85, 72, 101, 79, 128—reflect Kindrachuk's involvement in the action.

"Orest had all the guts in the world," said McNab.

After the Flyers won their second championship, Kindrachuk continued to raise the level of his play. His biggest scoring year (1975-76) involved 76 games during which he scored 26 goals and 49 assists for 75 points. It more than doubled his output from the Cup year.

Back problems disturbed his progress, and by 1977-78 his name frequently surfaced in trade rumors. At the time Bobby Clarke and Rick MacLeish were Philadelphia's top centers, with Little O coming in third.

The long-rumored deal finally happened on June 14, 1978, when Orest was moved to Pittsburgh with Tom Bladon and Ross Lonsberry for Pittsburgh's first choice (Behn Wilson) in the 1978 amateur draft and other considerations.

Kindrachuk became Penguins captain and responded with a 60-point (18-42) season in 1978-79 but slipped to 46 (17-29) the following year. He played only 13 games for Pittsburgh (3-9-12) in 1980-81. A herniated disk in his spine not only threatened his career but raised doubts whether Little O would be able to walk without pain. The surgery was completed, but the Penguins had decided that Kindrachuk no longer was worth the gamble.

After Pittsburgh released him, Kindrachuk was signed by Washington as a free agent on September 1, 1981 but he managed only four games and one goal for the Capitals before dropping the curtain on his big-league career.

In his book *The Broad Street Bullies*, author Jack Chevalier once described Kindrachuk as "a typical Flyer —unheralded, undrafted and unpretentious."

All things considered, one might also say of Little O that he was awfully effective.

Pete Peeters

A photo of Pete Peeters has been shown in areas from Mineola, New York to Montauk Point, New York, more than any other sports action picture.

Unfortunately, it is not the most favorable one the four-year Flyer goaltender would have preferred.

The photograph was taken on the afternoon of May 24, 1980 at Nassau Coliseum. Two players are seen. One of them is Bob Nystrom of the New York Islanders. The other is Peeters.

The time was 7:11 of the first overtime period of the sixth game of the Stanley Cup finals.

Nystrom had just taken a pass from John Tonelli (not in the photo) and deflected the puck off his stick and over the sliding pads of Peeters. The goal won the first Stanley Cup for the Islanders and sent the Flyers packing.

But not Peeters.

The Edmonton native had completed his first full season in Philadelphia, and to suggest that he was outstanding would be an understatement.

Consider his won-loss-tie record (29-5-5) during the regular season.

At the time, Pete was sharing the goal with veteran Phil Myre. The playoff loss notwithstanding, he finished the Stanley Cup round with eight wins against

PETER "PETE" PEETERS

Born: Edmonton, Alberta, August 17, 1957

Position: Goaltender

NHL Teams: Philadelphia, 1978-82, 1989-91; Boston, 1982-85; Washington, 1985-89

Awards/Honors: Vezina Trophy, 1983

five losses.

Better still, he established a record unbeaten streak of 27 games, which was the second longest in NHL history by any goalie until that point in time. (Pete would later break that mark.)

His goaltending style was clean and efficient. It had been developed with the Medicine Hat Tigers of the Western (Junior) League and refined with both the Milwaukee Admirals in the International League and Maine Mariners of the American League. He also helped the Mariners to a Calder Cup victory.

By the time he reached the NHL Peeters had refined a puck handling style to near-perfection. "Pete controlled the puck as well as the best of the goaltenders," said Hall of Fame defenseman Brad Park. "He reminded me of Eddie Giacomin. He was the best at clearing the puck because he could shoot it the length of the ice, and he could thread a needle with it when he cleared it. Plus he was fearless. Eddie never thought there was a puck he couldn't get to first and clear. Pete was just like that. Plus he could skate well. He was very sure on his feet, even when he came out of the net."

Peeters had inspired such confidence following the 1979-80 season that his return engagement (1980-81) was disappointing by comparison. In 1980-81 he again played in 40 games, won 22, lost 12 and tied five. He was two and one in the playoffs.

The front office's disappointment was reflected on the ice. By season's end, Peeters had been replaced by rookie Rick St. Croix, who was selected to start nine playoff games against Peeters' three.

It didn't require much time for the Flyers to understand that St. Croix was not the answer. The latter's goals-against average was 3.91. Peeters' was 3.71. A Swedish prospect named Pelle Lindbergh was imported to cure the red light problem.

As difficult as the 1980 Nystrom-Islanders loss was for Peeters, it was not as damaging to his Philadelphia career as the 1982 first-round playoff defeat he suffered at the hands of the underdog New York Rangers.

There are some in Philadelphia who still argue that Peeters was made the scapegoat for the upset under the orchestration of coach Bob McCammon. That was the spring during which McCammon had humorously alluded to the smaller Broadway Blueshirts as "Smurfs."

It enraged and inspired the New Yorkers, and Peeters was the most noticeable victim. In retrospect, Peeters once recalled to *GOAL Magazine*, "McCammon didn't play me much toward the end of the season. Then he said that he would be sticking me into the playoffs. It was as if he was saying, 'Well, Pete, bring us to the Stanley Cup and you have a job. Otherwise, you're gone.'"

> *". . . He reminded me of Eddie Giacomin . . . he was fearless. Eddie never thought there was a puck he couldn't get to first and clear. Pete was just like that."*

And he was.

On June 9, 1982 Peeters was dealt to the Boston Bruins for defenseman Brad McCrimmon. "The Flyers needed defense," said Pete. "It was a business move and I bore no animosity. But the thing that always worked against me in terms of my Flyers career was that rookie year. My performance and my numbers always were compared to that year. When I fell back a bit it wasn't acceptable."

For Peeters the deal proved a blessing. In his first season with the Bruins, he dropped his goals-against average from 3.71 to 2.36 and produced eight shutouts. "Getting Peeters was the greatest trade Harry Sinden ever made," said then Bruins coach Gerry Cheevers. "We couldn't ask for anything more than we got out of Pete. Even when he lets in a goal, it doesn't bother him."

Not that the Flyers were complaining. McCrimmon provided long and efficient service. But Peeters won a Vezina Trophy in 1983 and seemed on top of his game until the Islanders knocked him—and the Bruins—off. By 1983-84 he was severely slipping in Beantown, sharing Boston's goaltending with Doug Keans and Mike Moffat. His record (29-16-2) was good enough, but it was Peeters in goal when the Montreal Canadiens swept Boston in the first playoff round.

A year later, his record had dropped to 19-26-4 (3.47) and he played only one playoff game (a loss) as the Habs swept the Bruins in the postseason once more. On November 14, 1985, Peeters was traded to Washington for Pat Riggin.

His career with the Capitals ranged from mediocre to excellent. In 1988-89, for example, he posted a 20-7-3 record with a 2.85 goals-against average as Washington won its first Patrick Division title. But in the playoffs, it was the Flyers—and Ron Hextall—who knocked off Washington, and Peeters.

Ironically, that loss actually propelled Peeters back to Broad Street for one last, brief run with the Flyers.

The move began when Capitals general manager David Poile decided that his club needed a new look in goal. In June 1989, Poile offered Peeters a termination contract.

At that point the Flyers grabbed him, although they already had Hextall and Ken Wreggett on the roster. Peeters was tickled. "My ultimate goal is to be on a team that wins the Stanley Cup," said Pete. "The Flyers are capable of doing it."

It was, of course, wishful thinking. Peeters had lost his edge and it showed. He won only one of 19 games, lost 13 and tied five. His goals-against average was 3.74. His swan song came in 1990-91, when a last level of respectability was reached.

Before departing the bigs, he won nine, lost seven and tied one for a 2.88 goals-against average and even one last shutout.

His thoughts on goaltending: "When you're at the NHL level, it's a mental game. It's all confidence, and when your confidence is soaring, you don't think. You just react. That's the key for any goalie."

At times, Peeters seemed like the most confident goaltender ever to wear the orange and black. But there were too many of those other nights.

AND that infamous afternoon in 1980 at Nassau Coliseum when the Flyers' hopes for a third Stanley Cup slipped past Peeters's right pad.

A charging Scott Mellanby upends Oilers defenseman Steve Smith.

Scott Mellanby

He was a sophomore at the University of Wisconsin when the handsome native of Montreal first made a splash with the Philadelphia media.

This was March 14, 1986, when *The Inquirer* ran an Al Morganti-bylined story about the 19-year-old right wing who had just signed with the big club.

Scott Mellanby seemed too young for the National Hockey League and certainly not ready to be an impact player. But the man who brought him into the fold—general manager Bob Clarke—had no doubts about the young man's future.

"If he wasn't ready for the NHL," said Clarke, "we wouldn't have signed him. We've been watching him for a long time and we like what we see."

Mellanby's hockey roots ran deep but in a somewhat unusual direction. His father, Ralph, had been executive producer of *Hockey Night in Canada* and the man who turned Don Cherry into a television personality.

When the Flyers met the New York Islanders in the 1980 Stanley Cup finals, *Hockey Night in Canada* televised the game. Ralph Mellanby was in charge, and 14-year-old Scott came along as a "crew" member.

"At the time," Scott remembered, "Gary Dornhoefer was working with my father, and he took me out on the ice before the Flyers' practice. That was exciting

SCOTT MELLANBY

BORN: Montreal, Quebec, June 11, 1966

Position: Right Wing

NHL Teams: Philadelphia, 1986-91, Edmonton, 1991-93, Florida, 1993-present

Awards/Honors: Captain, Florida, 1997-98-present

for a kid like me. Frankly, I never imagined then that someday I would wind up in a Philadelphia jersey."

Mellanby wasn't even sure about a hockey career. He enrolled at the University of Wisconsin to get an academic education more than anything and was majoring in radio-TV when he got the call from Bob Clarke.

"Playing in the NHL was a dream I always had," said Mellanby on that Thursday in 1986. "But I had remained very cautious about it. My parents had pointed out the example of players putting everything into pro hockey. They quit school, then couldn't make it as hockey pros. I was able to get two years in and then turn pro because the Flyers gave me that opportunity."

He made the most of it.

After a two-game audition in the spring of 1986, Mellanby was invited to training camp the following September and immediately won a spot on the varsity. But the switch from collegiate hockey to the NHL hardly was a bowl of cherries.

"It was a lot more than I had expected," said Mellanby who played 71 games in 1986-87 as a Flyers rookie. "For starters, there was a lot more to do. The 80-game schedule was a grind. There were a lot more people competing for jobs, so ice time was limited."

Still, he got enough ice time to account for 11 goals and 21 assists as well as 94 penalty minutes. Considering that he was an NHL freshman, his plus-eight in the plus-minus department was a pleasant bonus.

"I had never been a great goal scorer," said Mellanby. "I figured that if I could reach 20 goals in an NHL season, well, that would be just fine. My game then was getting into the corners, working the puck out."

He got plenty of experience in a hurry. Mellanby's NHL debut coincided with the Flyers' trip to the 1987 Stanley Cup finals. The 24 postseason games were like postgraduate course in hockey tension, and Scott passed with solid grades. He scored five goals and five assists and looked every bit the well-rounded player Clarke thought he would be.

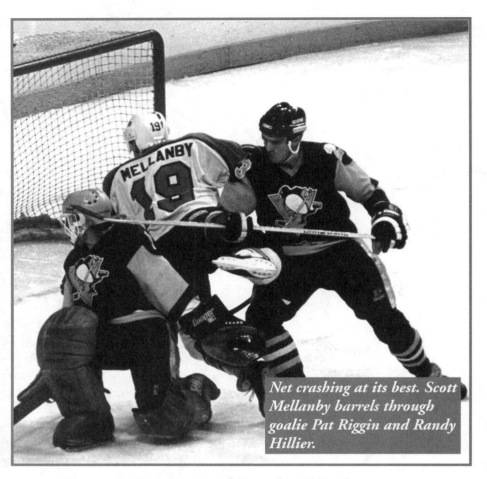

Net crashing at its best. Scott Mellanby barrels through goalie Pat Riggin and Randy Hillier.

"Scott fit in well," recalled former teammate Ron Sutter. "He was good along the boards, rarely made a mistake and played an all-round game."

Plus, he got better.

As an NHL sophomore he scored 25 goals and added 26 assists. As a junior, the numbers were 21-29-50 as well as an impressive playoff. Over 19 postseason games, he produced four goals and five assists.

At this point in time, Mellanby's career appeared ready for an orbit at a significantly higher level. He was playing all ends of the ice, doing the intangibles that appeal more to management than stats-loving fans and gaining NHL maturity.

Then, tragedy of a sort struck.

During August 1989 Mellanby was relaxing with friends at the Muskoka Sands Hotel on Lake Muskoka Sands in Gravenhurst, Ontario. A brouhaha erupted at the bar involving two men and one of Scott's friends.

When the dust had cleared, Mellanby suffered a slashed left forearm that required surgery to repair a severed nerve and tendon damage.

After hearing about the episode, Clarke declared, "Scott is a responsible individual who saw a friend in trouble and felt he had to help. The outcome was terri-

"Scott fit in well," recalled former teammate Ron Sutter. "He was good along the boards, rarely made a mistake and played an all-round game."

bly unfortunate, but we trust Scott's judgement and believe that he was justified in his actions."

Although Mellanby returned to the Flyers later in the 1989-90 season and was able to play in 57 games (6-17-23), he did not appear to have the same presence that accompanied his play before the incident.

To the Flyers' credit, they stood by their man, and Scott returned the favor in 1990-91, playing in 74 games. The 20 goals and 21 assists suggested that he was himself again and, back on track, would be everything the Flyers general staff originally hoped he would be.

But the Broad Street high command had other ideas. On May 30, 1991 Mellanby was shipped to Edmonton along with Craig Fisher and Craig Berube in exchange for Dave Brown, Corey Foster and Jari Kurri.

Mellanby's two seasons in Edmonton went reasonably well but certainly not THAT well, because general manager Glen Sather left him unprotected for the 1993 expansion draft. Scott was the fourth forward selected by the Panthers and eighth forward taken overall.

The brand of hockey that Philadelphians had hoped to see—but rarely did—finally surfaced in Miami. In 1993-94 he played 80 games and tallied 30 goals and 30 assists. Two years later he played in 79 games and achieved a career-high 32 goals and 38 assists.

That was the season in which Florida went all the way to the finals, and, on that 22-game trek, Mellanby produced three goals and six assists for nine points as well as 44 playoff penalty minutes.

When Brian Skrudland left Miami before the 1997-98 season, Mellanby was named Florida captain. He had fulfilled a career that originally was crafted in Philadelphia.

Who knows? Had Mellanby not inadvertently become involved in that off-season episode in 1989 he still might be a Flyer.

But he did, and Flyers fans are left with a five-year legacy of fine hockey from a fine individual. At this juncture, what might have been is irrelevant.

Ecstasy is a Scott Mellanby game winner. Keith Acton (25) shares the joy.

Terry Crisp played gutsy hockey for the Flyers.

Terry Crisp

Many components are necessary for construction of a championship machine. When it came to the 1974 and 1975 Stanley Cup-winning Flyers, the primary parts were obvious.

Goaltending—as in Bernie Parent—was one, and leadership—as in Bobby Clarke—was another.

But a machine, like clockwork, is more complicated than that. Some parts are less visible than others, yet without them, the machine simply will not function at its optimum capacity.

In terms of the 1974-1975 champions, Terry Crisp was one of those unobtrusive—but nonetheless pivotal—parts.

A center out of Parry Sound, Ontario, Crisp played his junior hockey in the days when NHL clubs had their own sponsored teams. Terry was in the Boston Bruins organization and made a name for himself with the Niagara Falls Flyers.

The Bruins liked him enough to pen Terry to a professional contract and assigned him to Minneapolis of the Central Professional League. He played in Minnesota for two seasons (1963-64 and 1964-65) which was enough for an invitation to Boston in 1965-66.

To say the least, Crisp's three-game exposure to the bigs that season was less than captivating. His stats read 0-0-0, which qualified Terry for a one-

TERRY ARTHUR CRISP

BORN: Parry Sound, Ontario, May 28, 1943.

Position: Center

NHL Teams: Boston, 1965; St. Louis, 1967-1972; N.Y. Islanders, 1972-73; Philadephia, 1973-77

way ticket to Oklahoma City, where he remained until the NHL expanded from six to a dozen teams in 1967.

St. Louis Blues general manager Lynn Patrick had liked what he had seen of Crisp in the CPHL and drafted him for the maiden campaign. Despite a four-game penance in the minors with Kansas City, Crisp played 73 games for the Blues (9-20-29) as well as 18 playoff games (1-5-6), which included a trip to the Stanley Cup finals where St. Louis was wiped out in four straight by Montreal.

Terry wore the Blues livery until another expansion came along in 1972, and this time he was drafted by the brand new Islanders. In Nassau, Crisp did everything general manager Bill Torrey had hoped he would for 54 games (4-16-20), but most of all Terry was to be a foil for the Isles boss.

Torrey had his eyes on the 1973 prize prospect Denis Potvin. To secure Potvin—and make the youngster even happier—Torrey believed it would be wise to obtain Denis's older brother, Jean, in advance.

Since Jean Potvin was a Flyer, a deal had to be made. On March 5, 1973 Crisp was traded to the Flyers for Jean Potvin and a player to be named later (Glen Irwin) and everyone was happy.

Torrey was tickled because he knew that Jean would make brother Denis's debut easier, and Flyers general manager Keith Allen was pleased because he now possessed a seasoned checking center who would help his burgeoning contender stay on track for a Stanley Cup run.

That run didn't happen until 1973-74, but in the meantime Crisp displayed precisely the qualities for which Allen had obtained him. This was evident in the 1973 playoffs. Philly knocked off Minnesota in a six-game opening round and then met Montreal in the second tournament. Through those eleven games, Crisp tallied three goals and two assists. But that was only half of it. His dogged play attracted the most savvy critics, including *Montreal Star* sports columnist Red Fisher. The scribe took notice of Crisp in the opening game, which Rick MacLeish won for the Flyers on a sudden-death goal.

"For the first two periods," wrote Fisher, "Crisp was the hardest-working man on the ice for the Flyers. All 5'8" inches of him. Crisp was my man because he was THAT good against the Canadiens. He was that good because he played every moment he was on the ice.

"Give me a non-scorer like Crisp who works all the time, and you can have the stars who work in fits and starts during the playoff series."

Centering for Dave (Hammer) Schultz and Don (Big Bird) Saleski, Crisp provided a line of young hus-

tlers with veteran insights and as much drive as any one of the kids had to offer.

Even Terry was amazed.

"The Flyers were having such a good season before I arrived that I felt I was just sort of dropping in for the last twelve games," Crisp recalled. "But once the playoffs arrived, I started to feel a part of it."

Crisp, who always played the game clean and never went over the 37 penalty-minute mark in any NHL season, found himself well-protected by a Broad Street Bully on either side of him. But when the term "intimidation" was mentioned to Crisp, he recoiled in mock horror.

"I don't like to hear that word 'intimidation' thrown around," Terry replied. "Anyone who plays hockey has to have guts just to lace on the skates."

Crisp continued playing his gutsy hockey in 1973-74, and with every game he proved that Keith Allen had dealt wisely in obtaining him, particularly because of his positive influence on Schultz and Saleski.

"Terry was a terrific help to me," Saleski recalled. "He was always there to show me how to get in position for passes and shots."

"Give me a non-scorer like Crisp who works all the time, and you can have the stars who work in fits and starts during the playoff series."

Jack Chevalier, who authored *The Broad Street Bullies*, the story of the Flyers' early Cup-winning years, summed up Crisp's value to the team in a few well-chosen words:

"Crispie adds flavor to a good hockey team. Like steak sauce, he blends in nicely with meat, but he doesn't do much for gristle."

He played in 17 playoff games in that delightful spring of 1974, contributing a pair of goals and another pair of assists. When the Flyers won their second Cup, Crisp's numbers were remarkable for a utility player—six points (2-4) in only nine games. Few Flyers could match that percentage.

It never was the same for Crisp after that. His game and production count dropped dramatically over the next two years, leading to retirement as a player. In 1979-80 he launched a long coaching career, first with the Junior Sault Ste. Marie Greyhounds in the Ontario Hockey League. He reached the NHL as a head coach with Calgary in 1987-88 and won a Stanley Cup behind the Flames' bench the following spring.

After leaving Calgary after the 1989-90 season, he resumed coaching with the expansion Tampa Bay Lightning in 1992-93 and remained with them until his dismissal early in the 1997-98 campaign.

He became a television commentator for the Fox network later in 1997-98 but never lost his enthusiasm for The Game.

Granted that he lacked starry talent, but The Man did come up with three Stanley Cup rings—two as a Flyer and one as Flames coach—so he must have been doing something right.

New York Rangers goalie Ed Giacomin blocks Bill Clement's shot on goal by sitting on it.

Bill Clement

Of all the swashbuckling band of Broad Streeters who brought fame and glory to Philadelphia in the mid-1970s, none was more underrated—or underplayed in terms of his skills—than this moustacheoed center from Buckingham, Quebec.

Perhaps if the Flyers' general staff had a more insightful view of Bill Clement he might have played a full decade at The Spectrum rather than four years.

Nevertheless, in that period—from 1971-72 through 1974-75—Clement did more with less time on the ice than just about any skater to wear the orange and black.

Nor should that be a surprise to anyone who had traced Clement's career from the junior level through the American League and on to the NHL. Bill always had the goods, but others' view of his delivery indubitably set him back in the eyes of some, most notably Philadelphia coach Fred Shero.

In juniors, he played for the Ottawa 67s, which happened to be an expansion team and, therefore, generally behind the eight-ball. The experience was invaluable to Clement.

"I was playing against guys who eventually would be Hall of Famers," Clement remembered. "My job was to shadow the likes of Gil Perreault and Marcel Dionne, who were the best. That's where I learned the defensive side of playing

WILLIAM H. "BILL" CLEMENT

BORN: Thurso, Quebec, December 20, 1950

POSTITION: Center

NHL Teams: Philadelphia, 1971-1975; Washington, 1975-76; Atlanta, 1976-1980; Calgary 1980-82

forward and also developed a knack for winning face-offs."

Clement played his last year with Ottawa in 1969-70 and was Philadelphia's first choice—18th overall—in the 1970 amateur draft. The Flyers assigned him to Quebec of the AHL for the 1970-71 campaign, and Bill delivered 19 goals and 39 assists for 58 points in 69 games.

He played 26 more AHL games the following year with Richmond but won a promotion to the Flyers—good for 49 games. He was in the bigs to stay.

"My first job was to prove that I could compete on a major-league level," said Clement. "The Flyers were an improving team, but they had liked what they had seen of me in Quebec. I led the Aces in scoring but didn't do much defensive work. That would come in Philadelphia."

Coach Shero had several possibilities for his third-line center, and they were named Terry Crisp, Orest Kindrachuk and Clement.

"Bobby Clarke and Rick MacLeish were the top two centers," said Clement. "Crispy, Kindrachuk and I were on the 'Taxi Squad.' We would play when Freddie would designate us. Usually, I played between Don Saleski and Dave Schultz."

Clement knew he had made it on January 28, 1972. At the time Philly had a center named Jim Johnson who had previously played for the New York Rangers and was plucked by Philadelphia in the 1967 expansion draft. He had been a Flyer ever since. Johnson was dealt to the Los Angeles Kings on that date.

"When Johnson went to the Kings," said Clement, "it told me that management felt I could stick with the big club. I felt a lot more secure once the deal was done."

In 1972-73, his first complete year in Philadelphia, Clement played in 73 games and finished with 14 goals and 14 assists. For a third-line defensive center, the 28 points represented commendable numbers.

Shero called him "a born skater" but also found himself confounded from time to time by what he regarded as erratic play. When Crisp arrived in a trade with the Islanders, Clement began seeing less ice. The less ice he was given made him tense, and the anxiety further hurt his game.

In the Flyers' first Cup-winning year, he played in 39 games (9-8-17) but reappeared for key moments in the playoffs. Although Shero might have employed him more often, Bill never held a grudge against the coach.

"Freddie was the first coach I ever had who really respected his athletes," Clement revealed. "He never had things like a 'curfew check.' He did things quietly and did them well. It was not easy to take twenty hockey players and make a unified unit out of them."

Shero had enough confidence in Clement to insert him into the lineup of Game 6 of the Stanley Cup finals between the Flyers and Boston Bruins. This was the spring of 1974, and until then, not a single expansion team had ever won the Stanley Cup.

"We had our doubts about beating the Bruins before the series began," said Clement. "After all, they had Bobby Orr, Phil Esposito and they had won Cups in 1970 and again in 1972. The feeling in our room was that if we could win one of the first two games [at Boston Garden], we would be in shape to give them a run for it.

"Boston beat us in the opener, but only after we had rallied from a two-goal deficit. Bobby Orr got their winner with less than a minute left in the third period. So even though we had lost the game, we felt good because we had played them virtually even for the night."

Game 2 also was at Boston Garden, and this time the Flyers again rallied from a two-goal deficit to send the game into sudden-death overtime.

"Clarkie got the winner at the twelve-minute mark," Clement recalled, "and that sent us back to Philly tied at one apiece. It was just what we had hoped for, and now we began to believe we could go all the way."

With Philadelphia leading the series, three games to two, Game 6 was played on May 19, 1974 at The Spectrum. According to Clement, Clarke had become virtually an unofficial assistant coach to Shero and would advise Fred whom to play on certain nights. The captain suggested that Clement be inserted in the lineup, and Shero obliged.

"Our strategy was to fire the puck into Orr's corner and have him play the puck first," Clement remembered. "We hoped to force him to give up the puck and then eliminate him if possible.

"Rick MacLeish scored for us late in the first period, and then we just played our game, grinding it out. I was hustling my butt off, although it wasn't all that easy. I had injured my knee earlier in the playoffs and at one time had a full cast on my leg, but by this time I wasn't even thinking about it."

Even after sipping champagne from The Cup, Clement was nervous. An expansion draft was coming up, and he fully expected to be left unprotected by management.

"The draft was June 12, 1974," Clement recalled, "and the man the Flyers left unprotected was Simon Nolet, not me. That was quite a boost for me at the time."

As luck would have it, the decision was propitious for Philadelphia. Clement reached his peak as a Flyer, scoring 21 goals in 68 games and 16 assists for a then career high 42 points. His penalty minute total of 42 was relatively low for a Flyer, and conceivably, it could have had an effect on Shero's thinking.

"As everyone knew," Clement continued, "Freddie was called The Fog and many people thought he was off in a daze lots of the time. That wasn't the case. The 'Fog' business was mostly a smokescreen, designed by Freddie to confuse and mislead the opposition. The fact was that he was a very private man."

Shero thought enough of Clement to play Bill in Game 6 of the Flyers-Sabres Stanley Cup final of 1975. Philadelphia led the series, three games to two, before the finale at The Auditorium in Buffalo.

"Unlike the year before," Clement asserted, "we had no doubts that we could win the Cup in 1975. First of all, the Sabres hadn't won a game at The Spectrum all year, and secondly, our tough guys were tougher than their tough guys. We had the ultimate warriors and we had Bernie Parent in goal. At that point in time Bernie was the best goalie in the world, bar none."

Game 6 was locked in a 0-0 draw through the first two periods. But at only eleven seconds of the third period, Bob Kelly beat goalie Roger Crozier on a wraparound, giving Philly a one-goal lead.

"We needed a cushion, and I'm happy to say that I was the right man in the right place at the right time," said Clement. "There was a little more than two and a half minutes left in the period—still one-nothing for us—when Orest Kindrachuk fed me a perfect pass.

"It was a breakaway from the blue line in, and as

"The draft was June 12, 1974," Clement recalled, "and the man the Flyers left unprotected was Simon Nolet, not me. That was quite a boost for me at the time."

---

soon as I got the puck everything seemed to slow down —just right. I knew that Crozier played from a crouch and that there usually was room over his right shoulder. I kept coming in and in and, at the last second, chipped the puck between his legs."

The time was 17:13 and the goal cemented the win, 2-0, and the Flyers' second straight Stanley Cup.

Logically, Clement's timely goal and superb season under trying circumstances should have guaranteed his security on Broad Street. But it was not to be, for an assortment of reasons.

"For one thing," said Clement, "I was not Freddie's kind of player in that I wasn't a physical player. I was a team player and I worked hard, but there were other factors to consider.

"The main thing was that Mel Bridgman—at the time the best junior in Canada—was going to be available in the draft and the Flyers wanted him. What they did was make a deal with Washington to get him, and that's how I wound up leaving Philadelphia."

The Flyers traded Clement with Don McLean and Philadelphia's first draft choice (Alex Forsythe) in the 1975 amateur draft for Washington's first choice in the same draft, which just happened to be Bridgman.

Bill played a season for the Capitals and then was dealt to the Atlanta Flames for Gerry Meehan, Jean Lemieux and a first-round draft choice. In 1978 Clement registered a career-high 50 points and became the backbone of the Flames' penalty-killing team.

In 1977-78 he reached a career-high point total of 50 in 70 games with 20 goals and 30 assists, clearly indicating that he could have done likewise with Philadelphia. Interestingly, that same season Bridgman tallied only 48 points (16-32), two less than Clement.

Bill's NHL career concluded in Calgary—following the Flames' move from Atlanta—in 1981-82 when he scored four goals and twelve assists in 69 games.

He has since become the prime hockey analyst for the ESPN network and also is successful as a motivational speaker.

To Philadelphia hockey fans, he is remembered as a gentleman and a scholar on a team more notorious for its brawn and bluster. Not that Bill had any problem with that.

"I always got a kick out of the story about visiting teams coming to play us in Philly," said Clement. "The opposition bus would pull up to our building and the players would say they knew they were in trouble when —after the driver had shut off the bus's motor—the bus would still be shaking."

Flyers followers have always had an appreciation for class acts. That, among other reasons, is why they have always appreciated William H. Clement.

It's hard to believe the Flyers once played the game in long pants as demonstrated by Darryl Sittler.

Darryl Sittler

His visit to Philadelphia was brief, to be sure, but noteworthy. There have been precious few Hall of Famers to have worn the orange and black, at least compared to the Original Six teams who have roamed the National Hockey League for so many more years.

Thus, when a graceful and gracious star moves to Broad Street for even a few years—as Darryl Sittler did—and gives everything that is left in his body, he is worthy of the Flyers Pantheon.

Sittler had previously established his reputation with the Toronto Maple Leafs. He made his NHL debut in 1970-71 and remained in Canada's Queen City until January 1982. It was then that the Flyers' general manager Keith Allen executed one of the club's most satisfying deals—at least for the moment.

In acquiring Sittler, who still was in his prime, the Flyers gave up Rich Costello, Hartford's second-round choice (Peter Ihnacak) in the 1982 entry draft (which Philadelphia had acquired in an earlier deal) and future considerations (Ken Strong). While none of the aforementioned trio had any significant impact, Sittler played effective hockey centering for Bill Barber and Ilkka Sinisalo.

"The line worked," Sittler remembered, "because Ilkka was so good at getting into the zone from the right side and then Billy was good at coming in after his linemates got into the zone. But the biggest thing is that we picked up the puck in the other end a lot. That was one of the reasons I got so many goals."

In 1982-83, Sittler's first full year in Philadelphia, he scored 43 goals and 40 assists for 83 points in 80 games. It marked the fifth time Darryl had scored

DARRYL GLEN SITTLER

BORN: Kitchener, Ontario, September 18, 1950

Position: Center

NHL Teams: Toronto, 1970-82; Philadelphia, 1982-84; Detroit, 1984-85

Awards/Honors: Captain, Toronto, 1975-81

40 or more goals in his NHL career. He also became the 17th man in hockey history to score 1,000 points in his career.

"Sittler's quick, efficient shot was a key to his success," said Mark Whicker of the *Philadelphia Daily News.* "The year he scored 43 goals, it happened so gradually that it was hardly noticeable.

"You looked in the summaries one day and it whispered, 'Sittler 17,' and then a few days later it said, 'Sittler 21.'"

The production came as no surprise to Flyers fans who remembered one particular night during the 1976 Philadelphia-Toronto playoffs. Sittler scored five goals against the Broad Street skaters in an 8-5 Toronto win. During one barrage, he scored twice in 32 seconds.

Because of such performances, Sittler had blossomed into one of Canada's foremost hockey heroes and remained such until he was dealt to Philadelphia. He had been a Leaf for almost a dozen years, and it was Darryl's goal that beat Czechoslovakia for the 1976 Canada Cup championship.

"He had become Steve Garvey with a stick," said Whicker.

In Philadelphia the adulation was considerably more muted but no less appreciative. "I wasn't on the ice as much with the Flyers as I was with Leafs," Sittler recalled. "And I didn't have the other team's checking line on me all the time."

He never was able to achieve the same level of excellence as he had in 1982-83 with the Flyers. In 1983-84 he played in 76 games but slipped to 27 goals and 36 assists for 63 points.

On the debit side was the inescapable fact that during the three years when Sittler centered for the Flyers, they never made it past the first playoff round.

Then, in October 1984, opportunity knocked and general manager Bob Clarke answered. The Detroit Red

"He had become Steve Garvey with a stick," said Whicker.

Wings wanted Sittler, and Clarke obliged. In return the Flyers received a pair of young, energetic players, Murray Craven and Joe Paterson.

Once again Sittler was involved in a deal that was beneficial to Philadelphia, only this time he was not the Flyer. Craven and Paterson formed part of a new nucleus that would enable the Flyers to reach the Stanley Cup finals twice before the decade of the 1980s had ended.

As for Sittler, his final NHL season, 1984-85, was just short of a disaster in Detroit. He tallied only eleven goals and sixteen assists for 27 points in 61 games. His last hurrah was a two-assist-in-two-playoff-games run for the Red Wings, after which he retired.

There was, however, an ironic postscript. In 1992 the Flyers drafted Darryl's son, Ryan, who had played in a New Jersey "Squirt" hockey league when the Sittlers were Philadelphia residents.

Ryan was the Flyers' first choice (seventh overall) and then went on to play for the University of Michigan in the Central Collegiate Hockey League. By 1998 he still had yet to make it to the NHL although he had been skating in the minors.

Darryl returned to the Maple Leafs organization in August 1991, assisting in the areas of marketing, community relations and alumni relations. It was a fitting denouement to his career, but one should not forget the brief but productive run he had in Philadelphia.

Larry Zeidel

One might wonder why a defenseman who played one season for the Flyers should appear alongside such legends as Bobby Clarke and Bernie Parent. But Larry Zeidel's episode was so special, so unique and so filled with the spirit that infused the club, he HAD to be part of this lineup.

When the NHL expanded from six to twelve teams in the summer of 1967, Zeidel was one of the few Jewish players in professional hockey.

In Yiddish there's a word for what he did—it's called *chutzpah*. Translated, it means an inordinate amount of nerve, and nerve is what Zeidel had.

A rugged type, Zeidel played briefly in the NHL for Detroit and Chicago before being demoted to the minors in 1954. He bounced around such cities as Edmonton, Hershey, Seattle and Cleveland and seemed destined to finish his long career in the bush leagues, until the NHL's first expansion. Even then, nobody thought Larry had a chance to crack the NHL because he was then 39 years old and completely forgotten by the big-league moguls.

So when the NHL managers convened in Montreal in June, 1967 to find 120 additional men to stock the six new expansion clubs, nobody was surprised that Larry Zeidel hadn't become a Minnesota North Star, a Los Angeles King or a Pittsburgh Penguin. In fact, the least surprised man in the world was Larry Zeidel because he had *chutzpah*.

"I looked at those draft picks," said Zeidel, whose scarred face suggests an overhead view of a railroad freight yard. "I had to laugh. I knew I was better

LAZARUS "LARRY" ZEIDEL

Born: Montreal, Quebec, June 1, 1928

Position: Defense

NHL Teams: Detroit, 1951-53; Chicago, 1953-54; Philadephia 1967-69

The rugged Larry Zeidel played with "chutzpah" for the Flyers.

than half the guys they were pickin'. Then I thought about some of the fellows in the NHL. I thought of Jean Ratelle. He was a first-rate center with the Rangers. I played against him years ago when he was with Baltimore. I could handle him then, so why can't I handle him now?"

Although Larry Zeidel wouldn't admit it, twelve NHL managers had the answer: "You're too old." But people with *chutzpah* don't listen—they act.

One thing bugged him—he wasn't absolutely certain that his body could take seven months of NHL hockey. So he made an appointment with a doctor at the Western Reserve University medical center in Cleveland for a checkup. "I told him I got great blood lines," Zeidel said. "My father was skating after he was fifty. My mother still washes bed sheets in the bathtub. You gotta have blood for that."

The doctor listened carefully and then tested him with an electrocardiograph machine (which records the sound of a person's heartbeat and prints a pattern of it). When he got through he told Larry Zeidel, who was 39 years old, that he had the heart of a 20-year-old. But that wasn't enough. Zeidel demanded the doctor put it in writing because big things were about to happen. Hockey was just about to be confronted with its first case of Madison Avenue hard sell.

"In order to sell myself, I needed a third-party testimonial," said Larry. "I needed something to shut up the people who'd say, 'He's too old, he's too old.' When I got the letter from the doctor, I knew I was in business."

Zeidel had always had class. When he was earning $7,000 a year with the Hershey Bears, he drove around in a new Lincoln Continental convertible. If he was going to sell himself, he'd do it right. He read an article in *Fortune* magazine about job hunting. "The key," he explained, "is getting a resume. I went to a couple of pros. They said you gotta go first class. We had the pictures taken, just like Hollywood, and then made up the brochure."

Apart from the eight-by-ten-inch glossy photos and the report from the doctor, the brochure had ten pages. The cover, in black and white, read "Resume" in italicized capital letters and then, in smaller type, "With References and Testimonials," and again in big type, "Larry Zeidel," and finally, in very small type, "Professional Hockey Player * Sales Promotion * Public Relations Executive." Underneath on the left was a picture of Larry in a hockey uniform and on the right was a picture of him wearing a Brooks Brothers suit, sitting behind a desk holding a phone.

The contents were appropriately unbashful. Page two opened with a quotation from Bud Poile, who wrote while he was manager of the San Francisco Seals: "...Larry

is a smart hockey man and would make a fine coach." Page ten concluded with a letter from Guild, Bascom and Bonfigli, a Seattle advertising agency, thanking him for the appearance of the agency's beer ads in *Western Hockey World*. Larry had once been a salesman for the magazine.

"Two things bugged me when it [the resume] was finished," he remembered. "I was afraid they'd only think of me for the front office. I wanted to play. And I wasn't sure who to send it to. I didn't want the managers to think I was goin' over their heads."

In August 1967 he mailed the presentation to everyone important on each of the twelve teams. Pretty soon the replies began to drift in. "I certainly am quite impressed with the material you sent me," wrote Bruce A. Norris, president of the Detroit Red Wings. "I know you always played well for and against us. I think with your approach that you should have a fine business career. If anything develops of mutual interest, I certainly will contact you." He didn't.

Writing on behalf of general manager Emile Francis, the Rangers' secretary said thanks but no thanks, adding that New York was building a young defense. To add insult to injury, the secretary misspelled Larry's last name. Sam Pollock of the Canadiens also said no. The Los Angeles Kings replied that they had no openings in sales, promotions, or public relations. The Blackhawks, Maple Leafs, Penguins, North Stars and Blues never answered. There were two nibbles, however.

Frank J. Selke, then manager of the Oakland Seals, said he would discuss the matter with his coach, Bert Olmstead. William J. Putnam, president of the Flyers, told Larry to keep in touch. "I agree with your feeling," wrote Putnam, "that age itself does not limit a player—it is mental attitude." Three weeks later, Selke wrote that there was no opening in his organization. There was no further response from Putnam.

But Larry Zeidel's resume—with references and testimonials—was making the rounds in the Philadelphia offices. In time, it landed on the desk of Keith Allen, the Flyers' coach. "The brochure," said Allen, "put the spark in our particular minds. He had played for me in Seattle so I knew a little about him. He's the same type of individual as Gordie Howe; he's got the enthusiasm of a kid."

Allen talked to Bud Poile, his boss, about Larry. But even though Larry had done some quiet scouting among American League prospects for Poile prior to the draft, Poile, being one of the shrewdest men in hockey, wasn't about to do Zeidel any favors. For one thing, the Flyers had bought the entire Quebec Aces for the American Hockey League and were overloaded with

"In order to sell myself, I needed a third-party testimonial," said Larry. "I needed something to shut up the people who'd say, 'He's too old, he's too old.' When I got the letter from the doctor, I knew I was in business."

defensemen. Also, they had just made some excellent draft choices—Ed Van Impe and John Miszuk from Chicago, Joe Watson and Dick Cherry from Boston and Jean Gauthier from Montreal. And, more important, it happened to be September.

"Larry's timing was bad," said Poile. "He should have sent the brochure out in October when everybody's sorry about their choices. In September, the managers all think they're going to win the Stanley Cup."

By the first of October, Poile began to see signs that indicated that he might not have a Cup winner. Dick Cherry had quit hockey to become a teacher. Joe Watson and Ed Van Impe were holdouts and refused to report to camp, and season ticket sales were dragging at the Spectrum.

By this time, Larry Zeidel considered his $200 investment an artistic success but a practical flop. He was ready to sign for another season with the Cleveland Barons when Poile showed a flicker of interest in obtaining him. "But," said Poile, "I can't do business with Bright [Paul Bright, owner of the Barons]."

Zeidel, who was then selling season tickets for the Barons, phoned Bright and told him that he ought to make some money on him (Zeidel) while there was still time. Bright agreed, but unfortunately Poile and Bright wouldn't agree on anything.

"Marie, my wife, told me there was only one thing to do, get the two of them on the phone together," said Larry. This could be done by making a conference call, but after Larry dialed, nobody wanted to talk.

"Here I am payin' for the call and all I get is complete silence. So I say, 'Fellas, what's it gonna be?' Then they all started arguing. Finally Poile said he'll give me a five-game trial and Bright asks me if I'll take it, and I say, 'Sure, I'll take my chances,' and we made the deal."

The dice were loaded, though. Poile insisted that Zeidel sign a letter giving him the right to drop Larry at will, for by this time things were looking up for the Flyers. Van Impe and Watson had finally signed their contracts, Miszuk and Gauthier were going good and the younger John Hanna and Noel Price, both with extensive NHL experience, were now with the team. So the Flyers planned to keep Zeidel for a month, attract some Jewish fans and then let him sell tickets. To Poile it made sense—nobody would get hurt.

But coach Keith Allen wasn't concerned with the motives of the deal. Right away he started Zeidel with Joe Watson and right away the Flyers started winning and climbed to first place in the Western Division.

On November 4, the Flyers were scheduled to meet tougher competition then they had met in their division—the Montreal Canadiens. That afternoon, Bernie Parent, the young goalie, and Larry Zeidel were in their room at the Queen Elizabeth Hotel in Montreal. Parent had the shakes. His questions to Zeidel showed how scared he was: "How many shots do you think they'll take at me?" "Do you really like hockey?" "We don't have a chance, do we?"

Larry Zeidel made a big impression on the young Parent. "You gotta think positive—think positive," he kept repeating. He pulled out a poem, "I Can," and read it to Parent. He fed the kid everything he had. "You gotta have a goal—a singleness of purpose."

"Yeah," Parent replied, "but they've got Jean Beliveau, Henri Richard and Ralph Backstrom."

"Forget it. They'll shoot from way out. Think positive, let the old subconscious come through for you."

Five hours later, the game was over, Philadelphia 4, Montreal 1. Bernie Parent had thought "positive." A week later, the Flyers went to Boston and defeated the Bruins. A week after that Philadelphia defeated the Rangers. Larry Zeidel started every game with Joe Watson at his side. Bud Poile was disappointed, though, for Zeidel's success was keeping younger players off the ice. "It hurts me because I have to keep John Hanna in civvies," he said.

In spite of Poile's disappointment, Zeidel helped lead the Flyers to the Western Division championship and the Clarence Campbell Bowl. Unfortunately, unlike the Flyers' successful wind-up to their 1967-68 season, Larry's saga did not have a particularly happy ending. He showed up at training camp the following fall and discovered that manager Poile had imported a couple of new defensemen. Unperturbed, Zeidel continued to drive as hard as he ever had, but this time, it appeared that the Flyers were determined to keep him on the sidelines.

About a month after the Flyers' season began, Poile asked Zeidel to report to the Flyers' farm team in Quebec City. A proud man, Larry Zeidel refused. "I believed I was good enough to stay in the NHL and my record proved it," he said.

Neither side would budge, so Zeidel spent the remainder of the 1968-69 season on the sidelines. By no coincidence, the Flyers faltered badly and failed to defend their championship successfully.

The player with *chutzpah* retired from hockey in 1969 and went into the investment counseling business. Ironically, Bud Poile, the man who halted Zeidel's incredible comeback in midstream, was fired that same year.

Roman Cechmanek took over the Flyers goal during the 2000-2001 season.

Roman Cechmanek

He wasn't supposed to be the Flyers' premier goaltender–not by a long shot.

Brian Boucher enjoyed a sensational run for a young goalie through the playoffs of 1999-2000. With a 1.91 goals-against average that season, Boucher appeared to have a mortgage on the acreage around Philadelphia's goal.

Then a strange thing happened in the 2000-2001 season. For starters, Boucher's goals-against average ballooned to 3.27 and–poof! Just like that–the Flyers lost faith in the kid from Rhode Island.

Meanwhile, the Flyers' European scout discovered a goaltending jewel in the rough who had starred for the Czech Republic team. That team won the 2000 World's Men Ice Hockey Championship in St. Petersburg, Russia, and Cechmanek was named to the Tournament Media All-Star First Team as the best goaltender.

Cechmanek was drafted by the Flyers as the longest of the long shots. He was plucked in the sixth round (171st overall) of the 2000 NHL entry draft. It was not the kind of selection that would raise eyebrows anywhere but in Roman's hometown of Zlin in the Czech Republic.

Imported to North America, Cechmanek played three games for the American League Philadelphia Phantoms in 2000-2001. But more importantly, in 59 games as a Flyers rookie, he arrested attention with a 2.01 goals-against average. Better still, his won-lost record was 35-15-6.

In plain English, Roman the Czech had booted Boucher out of the starting job.

ROMAN CECHMANEK

BORN: Gottwaldov, Czechoslovakia, March 2, 1971

Position: Goaltender

NHL Teams: Philadelphia Flyers, 2000-present

Awards/Honors: 2001 Second All-Star Team, 2001 Bobby Clarke Trophy, 2001 All-Star Game

Defining Cechmanek's style was as difficult as beating him with a shot. He often seemed scrambly rather than scientific and was wont to take gambles.

Once in a game at First Union Center against the New Jersey Devils, Patrik Elias sped free on a breakaway for the visitors. Instead of staying in position, Roman dove head first at the skater and at the last split second threw his stick at the puck.

It was an illegal maneuver—yet applied so subtly that no penalty was called on the play. Elias was thwarted and the Flyers went on to win the game.

If his regular season was hugely successful—he was named to the NHL's Second All-Star Team and a finalist for the Vezina Trophy—Cechmanek's playoff ended in disaster.

Facing the Buffalo Sabres in the first round, Philadelphia could do very little right. With Buffalo leading three games to two, Cechmanek virtually disintegrated in the sixth game. And when the dust had cleared, Buffalo, which scored on five of its first nine shots, clinched the series with an 8-0 victory.

The thirty-year-old Cechmanek, who had backed up Dominik Hasek when the Czechs won the gold in the 1998 Olympics, had flopped in the biggest game of

Cechmanek often seems scrambly rather than scientific.

his NHL career. He had given up five goals by the 3:25 mark of the second period before being replaced by Boucher.

Not that the disaster was all the goalies' fault; all Flyers shared in the defeat.

"We couldn't say anything bad about Roman," Philadelphia defenseman Eric Desjardins said. "He was strong throughout the series. It's a team sport—you win as a team and lose as a team."

Because of Cechmanek's mediocre playoffs, Boucher was given another shot as first goalie for the 2001-2002 season. For much of the campaign, it was touch and go between the two net minders. Boucher and Cechmanek split the time almost evenly, with Roman appearing in 46 games (24-13-6, 2.05 goals-against average) and Brian in 41 (18-15-4, 2.42 goals-against average). Cechmanek had all but sewn up the job and GM Bobby Clarke's confidence in him just past the midway point of the season when he suffered a severe high ankle sprain in a game against the New York Rangers in Madison Square Garden—a game in which former Flyer Eric Lindros notched a hat trick.

Boucher played well in Cechmanek's absence, but when Roman returned late in the season he allowed just two goals his last two starts before the postseason. When it came time to face the seventh-seeded Ottawa Senators in the opening playoff round, Cechmanek was designated as the starting goalie. It marked the first time since Ron

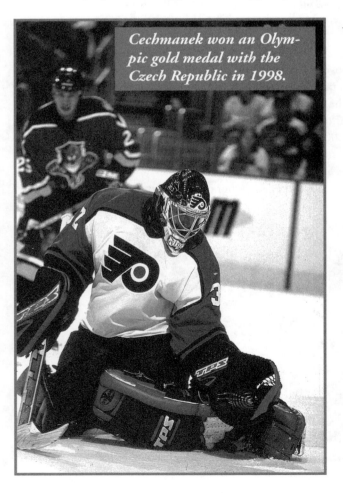

Cechmanek won an Olympic gold medal with the Czech Republic in 1998.

Hextall played in Philadelphia that the Flyers began the playoffs with the same goaltender in consecutive seasons.

Why did coach Bill Barber make such a move? "He's an experienced guy who has put up some great numbers for us this year," Barber said. "He's made big saves. This was not an easy decision. It wasn't just Cechmanek and then it was over with. This was a very difficult decision in the sense that it was not just me personally. I used staff, we sat down and talked about this for a month now."

Certainly Roman's credentials were getting better with more experience. He became the first goalie to beat Hasek four times in the regular season and he had gotten hot in the home stretch after recovering from his injury. But once the chips were down against Ottawa, Cechmanek could not top his foe at the other end of the rink, Patrick Lalime.

True, Cechmanek opened with a shutout on Ruslan Fedotenko's first overtime goal and he did finish with an impressive goals-against average of 1.85, not to mention a .936 save percentage. But Lalime came away at 1.39 and .946 as Ottawa won the next four games to annex the series.

During the summer of 2002 Ken Hitchcock replaced Bill Barber as head coach of the Flyers, while Brian Boucher was traded to Phoenix. The Flyers could have landed a top goalie such as Curtis Joseph or Mike Richter among the available free agents but chose to stick with Cechmanek.

Hitchcock pointed out that some of Roman's critics might have misinterpreted some of the goalie's questionable moves, such as the time he skated to the bench seemingly to berate his teammates.

According to Hitchcock, European goalies have a slightly different mindset than their North American counterparts. While it may have seemed to some Philadelphians that Cechmanek was committing an egregious sin, Hitchcock counted that it was nothing of the kind.

But by the fall of 2002, that was all academic. What Flyer fans sought in their goalie's third season as a big-leaguer was a mature net minder ready to lift the Flyers to higher playoff level. Whether Roman was ready for such a challenge remained to be seen.

Eric Desjardins earned a reputation as one of the NHL's toughest defensemen during the 1990s.

Eric Desjardins

Although he's not likely to gain entrance to the hockey Hall of Fame, Eric Desjardins will be remembered as:
    • One of the best National Hockey League defenseman in the decade from 1990-1991 through 2000-2001.
    • As a key element on Montreal's Stanley Cup-winning Canadiens of 1992-1993.
    • A component in one of the most one-sided deals in hockey history.

Combining solid skating, a good shot and well-distributed physicality, Desjardins was drafted from Granby, Quebec by Montreal in the second round (38th overall) of the 1987 NHL entry draft. He became a Canadiens regular by 1990-91, displaying ability not only as a defenseman but as a playmaker and scorer as well. This blend reached its highest point in Montreal during the Cup-winning campaign. Eric tallied 13 goals and 32 assists over 82 games and then in the playoff run added four goals and ten assists in twenty postseason matches.

From all appearances the French-Canadian was destined to remain in Francophone, Montreal for his entire career. However, a strange thing happened midway through the 1994-95 season. The Montreal high command had its eyes on Flyers scoring ace Mark Recchi.

The Habs seemed so intent on landing the little sniper, they not only parted with Desjardins and Gibert Dionne but also threw in John LeClair. The rest was simply glorious history for Philadelphia hockey.

ERIC DESJARDINS

Born: Rouyn, Quebec, June 14, 1969

Position: Defenseman

NHL Teams: Montreal Canadiens 1988-1995; Philadelphia Flyers, 1995-present

Awards/Honors: 1992, 1996 All-Star Game, 1994-2000 Barry Ashbee Trophy, 1998 Canadian Olympian, 1999 Yanick Dupre Memorial Class Award, 1999, 2000 Second All-Star Team

LeClair immediately became one of the league's top power forwards, while Desjardins enjoyed career years with the Flyers. His best was 1999-2000, when he totaled 14 goals and 41 assists for a lifetime regular season high of 55 points.

His attacking ability crystallized in Game 2 of the Flyers-Devils Eastern Conference Finals at the First Union Center.

With New Jersey in command and apparently ready to close out the period with a 2-1 lead, Desjardins swooped in from the blue line, accepted a cross-ice pass and fired a laser past goalie Martin Brodeur. The momentum of the game and the series shifted in the Flyers' favor as they won the game 4-3 and eventually took an overwhelming 3-1 lead in a series that they would eventually lose in a heartbreaking seventh and deciding game. During the playoffs Desjardins led all NHL defenseman in points with 12 (two goals, ten assists) and for the second straight season was named to the NHL's Second All-Star Team.

"Eric became one of our better players," said Flyers general manager Bob Clarke.

Eric's value transcended the ice. He became a team leader and in March 2000 was named club captain when former Flyer Eric Lindros was stripped of the title.

But after a little more than a year, Desjardins, who slumped through the first eight games in October of 2001, said he felt more responsibility as captain and didn't want the added pressure.

"When I first took this, I looked at it as a big challenge," Eric said. "It was tough last year; I didn't feel comfortable. I never felt like I was doing everything right. That was a big concern and it was affecting my play."

His coach at the time, Bill Barber, was supportive of Eric. "He's been a great captain for us. He's weathered a lot of the load the last few years. It takes a lot of courage to step aside." Desjardins was succeeded by veteran center Keith Primeau.

As he entered the 2002-2003 season, Desjardins already had 14 major-league seasons under his belt.

Some critics suggested that he was losing his wheels while others prophesied that the arrival of a new coach in Ken Hitchcock would be just the tonic to rejuvenate the veteran.

Whatever the case, Desjardins already has distinguished himself as the defenseman's defenseman.

Desjardins was named a team captain in March 2000.

Simon Gagne

Simon Gagne and Hall of Famer Henri Richard have one thing in common. They both are leap-year babies.

Richard, the legendary Montreal Canadiens center, was born on February 29, 1936, while Gagne's birth date is February 29, 1980.

It is Gagne's wish that he follow his fellow French-Canadian in another way, and that is to eventually be inducted into hockey's Pantheon.

Certainly the native of suburban Quebec City is off to a good start. He scored 20 goals in his rookie year, 1999-2000, 27—in only 69 games—in his sophomore season and 33 goals in 2001-2002.

A graduate of the fast Quebec Major Junior League, Gagne scored 50 goals in his final year with Quebec. The Flyers, who did not select until the 22nd pick in the first round, were fortunate to land the 6' 0", 190-pounder.

Simon comes from good hockey stock. His grandfather Roger played four seasons in the American Hockey League in the late 1940s, including the 1947-48 Calder Cup Champion Cleveland Barons. His father, Pierre, tried out for the Flyers' AHL team, the Quebec Aces, in 1967.

In his first two seasons Gagne also displayed surprising poise in playoff action. As a freshman in 1999-2000 he dressed for 17 postseason games, producing five goals and five assists. A year later, despite poor production by his older teammates, Gagne delivered three goals in six games.

Gagne showed similar aplomb in international competition. Playing for Canada's silver medal team at the 1999 World Junior Championships, he led the tournament with seven goals, four of which came in one game to tie a Team Canada record set by Mario Lemieux in 1983.

SIMON GAGNE

Born: Ste. Foy, Quebec, February 29, 1980

Position: Left Wing

NHL Teams: Philadelphia, 1999-present

Awards/Honors: 2002 Canadian Olympian, 2001 All-Star Game, 2000 All-Rookie Team

*Gagne's talents have gar-
nered praise from the great
Mario Lemieux.*

Simon's consistency has been his virtue ever since he made the difficult jump directly from the amateur ranks to the majors without a single game of minor-league experience.

The then 19-year-old Gagne netted his first goal on the power play on October 12, 1999 against the Washington Capitals. Mark Recchi took the original shot, which was deflected by John LeClair and stopped by goalie Olaf Kolzig until the "wide-eyed" Gagne pumped it home.

"The rebound," Simon said, "came to me, and I just hammered at it. I've replayed that goal in my mind again and again. All those great players out there [Recchi, LeClair, Lindros, Desjardins, Kolzig], and then there was me."

He was named to the NHL All-Rookie Team and was tied for first in power play goals (8), second in goals (20), second in power play assists (13), second in power play points (21), third in assists (28) and fourth in points (48–14th all-time among Flyers' rookies.)

So popular was Gagne when he completed his career with the Quebec Remparts that the junior team actually retired his number 12 jersey.

At the time, one of Simon's idols was the legendary Mario Lemieux. To Gagne's astonishment he actually dressed next to Le Magnifique during the 2001 All-Star Game in Denver. Simon was the youngest player of all the stars and even captured the attention of Lemieux himself.

*Simon Gagne was named to
the NHL All-Rookie Team
in 2000*

"He's going to be a star in this league," Mario Lemieux said after Gagne scored twice in the game.

"It was amazing to hear him say that," said Gagne. "Then you hear people comparing me to the other guys—it's such an honor."

Gagne received another honor when he was prominently mentioned in a *Sports Illustrated* feature by Kostya Kennedy.

"While Gagne doesn't possess the physical presence of a Joe Thornton or a Vincent LeCavalier," wrote Kennedy, "he's a more daring puck handler and has an exceptional ability to accelerate."

There's no question that the Flyers will build their offense around Gagne in the years to come.

"He's part of our youth movement," said Flyers chairman Ed Snider.

A big part, at that. Even when things go wrong—as they did in 2001-2002 when the Flyers went out of the playoffs in the first round—Gagne seems to do what's right.

In this case the arithmetic proves the point. His Plus/Minus rating at the end of the campaign was right near the top of the league—his 31 ranked third in the NHL, behind teammate Jeremy Roenick's 32 and Detroit's Chris Chelios's 40.

Ken Hitchcock was named the 15th head coach in Flyers history before the 2002-2003 season.

Ken Hitchcock

If ever the Flyers found the right coach for the right place at the right time, it is Ken Hitchcock for the 2002-2003 season.

"We did our background research on Ken as well as some other potential coaches, and each of us, including Mr. Snider, Ron Ryan, Paul Holmgren and myself, felt that Ken was the best coach available and we consider him one of the best coaches in the National Hockey League," said general manager Bob Clarke in making the announcement. "He has been successful at every level right from kids' hockey on through to, and including, the NHL. We are very lucky to get a coach like Ken for our hockey club."

"I've always had the philosophy that the people you work with are the most important thing," said Hitchcock. "Being able to work with the Flyers family– Mr. Snider, Bob Clarke, Paul Holmgren and Ron Ryan–has really given me the opportunity to feel a real strong bond to build a competitive team. This is a really proud moment for me. There is a feeling for me of coming home."

Hitchcock, 50, is the 15th head coach in Flyers history and not a day has passed without Hitchcock calling one of his veterans to advise him of the kind of commitment he expects for the 2002-03 season on a team that has underachieved for far too long in the Eastern Conference.

The biggest commitment is to discipline in Philadelphia–a commitment to effort and defense up front and a commitment to transition, transition, transition on defense. Most of all, a commitment to discipline as a team.

KEN HITCHCOCK

Born: Edmonton, Alberta, December 17, 1951

Position: Head Coach

NHL Teams: Philadelphia (assistant), 1990-1993; Dallas Stars, 1996-2002; Philadelphia, 2002-present

Awards/Honors: 1996-1997, 1997-1998, 1998-1999, 1999-2000, 2000-2001 Division Title, 1997, 1998, 1999 Stanley Cup, 2002 Canadian Olympian Assistant Coach

A native of Edmonton, Alberta, Hitchcock came into coaching by the back door, so to speak. He had worked as a salesman in Edmonton and coached hockey on an amateur level. When he found that he adjusted naturally to working with young players, Hitchcock decided to make hockey his primary profession. His first job of note was in Camloops, British Columbia.

As head coach of the Western Hockey League Blazers, Hitchcock not only developed such future NHL stars as Scott Niedermayer, but also compiled an enviable record beginning with his rookie season, 1984-85, when he went an astounding 52-17-2 before losing in the finals. He continued to have success, posting 49-, 55- and 45-win seasons. In winning two Western Hockey League Championships, his last year may have been the best, with a record of 56-16-0. He was honored as the league's top coach following the 1986-87 and 1989-90 seasons.

After four seasons as an assistant on the Flyers to Bill Dineen, he moved to the International Hockey League and the success continued; in his two seasons with Kalamazoo he notched 48- and 43-win seasons, which was enough to promote him to the parent club Dallas Stars in the middle of the 1995-96 season.

In no time at all, he turned Dallas into an NHL powerhouse. Starting in 1996-97, he led the Stars to five straight division titles and in the 1998-99 season he compiled a record of 51-19-12, won the President's Trophy with the league's best record and was nominated for the Jack Adams Award as Coach of the Year.

Translating the regular season triumphs to the playoffs seemed simple enough, and the Stars went on to win 16 games while losing seven en route to the first Stanley Cup in franchise history in a six-game victory over the Buffalo Sabres. A year later he took Dallas to the finals again before being ousted by New Jersey in a six-game final.

Following a disappointing start to Dallas's 2001-02 season, Hitchcock was fired by Dallas. He left as the Stars' career leader in regular season victories

(277), most career playoff wins (47), highest regular season winning season percentage by a coach (.610) and highest playoff winning percentage by a coach (.588).

During his stay in Dallas, he was credited with elevating Mike Modano's game to a higher level, converting Brett Hull into an effective two-way player and maximizing the effort of experienced stars.

Flyers forward Mark Recchi felt confident about his new boss, saying, "I think he learned a lot in Dallas, and he has grown as a coach. I think it's a very welcome situation and he's going to try to right the ship."

Urbane and thoroughly well read, Hitchcock is as much at home discussing civil war tactics–his passion–as he is penalty-killing techniques. Maybe that's why Fly-

Hitchcock coached the Dallas Stars to the Stanley Cup in 1999.

ers team chairman Ed Snider vowed Hitchcock would be around for the full term of his contract, ending the five-coaches-in-five-years merry-go-round.

How "natural" a fit Hitchcock will be on Broad Street will be determined in the years ahead. Critics said—as did Snider—that the next Flyer failure will be blamed on the players, not the coach. "At that point, you know it's not the coach," Snider said.

Thoroughly schooled in hockey strategy, Hitchcock has been regarded as an Xs and Os man extraordinaire. When he came to Philadelphia to accept the head coach-ing job, he simplified his mission, saying that the situation he was inheriting was similar to the one he encountered when he moved to Dallas midway through 1995-96.

"I think philosophy-wise, it could be a good match," he said. "It doesn't feel a lot different than the team did in Dallas."

If Hitchcock's track record with the Stars is any barometer, Ken's match with the Flyers will be the best coach-team blend since Fred Shero led Philly to a pair of Stanley Cups in 1974 and 1975.

Keith Primeau

The term "power forward" was not created specifically for Keith Primeau, but the hulking center certainly has displayed the traits of a Cam Neely and Clarke Gillies among legendary National Hockey League robust scorers.

Primeau established his credentials long before coming to Broad Street.

He was so highly regarded as junior player in Niagara Falls, Ontario, that the Detroit Red Wings selected him third overall in the first round of the 1990 NHL entry draft.

After a couple of trips to the minors, Primeau became a big-leaguer to stay in 1992-93. A season later he hit for 31 goals and established his credentials as a belligerent scorer. That same season he collected 173 penalty minutes, a career high.

Primeau's value was evident during the Stanley Cup finals between the Red Wings and the New Jersey Devils in June 1995. Because of injuries, Primeau struggled to the point where medics set up a hyperbaric chamber in the corridor near the dressing room in an effort to rehabilitate Keith for the games. His injury was considered a major reason why Detroit was swept in four games by the eventual Stanley Cup champions.

A contract dispute eventually led to Primeau being traded to Hartford in October 1996. When the Whalers moved to North Carolina, he remained a mainstay of the Hurricanes until he was dealt to Philadelphia for Rod Brind'Amour, Jean-Marc Pelletier and a second-round pick in the 2000 NHL entry draft on January 23, 2000.

KEITH PRIMEAU

Born: Toronto, Ontario, November 24, 1971

Position: Center

NHL Teams: Detroit, 1990-1996; Hartford 1996-1997; Carolina, 1997-1999; Philadelphia 1999-present

Awards/Honors: 1999 All-Star Game, 1998 Canadian Olympian, Flyers Captain, 2001-present

Primeau's impact was evident in the 1999-2000 playoffs when he totalled 13 points (2 goals, 11 assists), in 18 games before the Flyers fell to the eventual champion New Jersey Devils in the Eastern Conference Finals, four games to three. Keith's dramatic goal ending Game 4 of the semifinals at Pittsburgh (2-1 Flyers win in five overtimes) ended the longest game in modern history, 152:01–only a pair of six-overtime playoff contests in the 1930s were longer–and propelled the Flyers to an eventual elimination of the Penguins. The game's elapsed time of six hours, 56 minutes set an NHL record.

The following season Keith netted a new career high in goals (34) which also led the team, as did his 11 power play markers, but couldn't help to avoid the Flyers' ouster in round one against the Buffalo Sabres.

The primary reason he was obtained by Philadelphia was for guidance he could provide for young Flyers such as Simon Gagne. It explained why Primeau was named captain of the Flyers–replacing Eric Desjardins–during the 2001-2002 season.

"Keith has helped my confidence a great deal," said Gagne.

By using his physical presence to advantage, Primeau has been able to intimidate enemy defensemen without playing dirty.

"When he plays big, like a bull, people follow him," said defenseman Dan McGillis. "And he makes lanes for others, giving space for smaller players. He takes a lot of key faceoffs, and he's got a little mean streak in him."

Although Primeau had an off year in 2001-2002, opponents still believe he remains a major threat. "He controls a lot of the play," Buffalo Sabres forward Chris Gratton said. "If you pay [too much] attention to him, it leaves someone else open, and he's doing a great job of finding the open man."

Primeau has also been known to distract goaltenders. In a 2001 playoff game against Buffalo, Keith drove hard to the net late in the third period with the Flyers up by two. With Sabres defenseman James Patrick clawing all over him, Primeau crashed through the crease and into the right post, taking

out Buffalo goalie Dominik Hasek. The Dominator was so incensed by the play because he thought Primeau was going after his knees, he slammed his blocker on the ice and the tantrum earned Hasek a 10-minute misconduct.

"I don't know what happened. He just came unglued," said Primeau of Hasek. "We went to the net, but no more or less than in the past. Part of my game is to create chances through my physical play."

Thanks to teammate Mark Recchi, Primeau scored his first career hat trick in a 5-2 Flyers win against the Calgary Flames (March 8, 2001).

"When Recchi has the puck, I can be on the other side of the ice and know I still have a chance to get the puck because he has it," said Primeau. "I used to always have to be the first guy in on a forecheck. And now I don't have to be."

Veteran Keith Primeau was named team captain during the 2001-2002 season.

Primeau maneuvers past former Flyers captain Eric Lindros during the 2001-2002 season.

One reason why Flyers Chairman Ed Snider decided to avoid the expensive free agent market in the summer of 2002 was his faith in veterans such as Recchi and Primeau delivering the goods again.

The question that only Keith could answer is whether he had the wheels–and the will–to produce.

Jeremy Roenick

If ever Hollywood required a National Hockey League performer to be understudy to Chevy Chase, Jim Carrey, or Mike Myers, Jeremy Roenick would be the man.

To call the New Englander a character would be the understatement of the half-century. And anyone who had the good fortune of catching Roenick and his wife Tracy in TV commercials would quickly second the motion.

Friends have suggested that "JR", as he likes to be known, was vaccinated as a youth with a phonograph needle. Others have noted that a conversation with Jeremy is a sure preventative from laryngitis.

Just about everybody agreed a long time ago that Roenick is simply a helluva guy, who likes to talk, who likes people, and can play hockey better than most people.

Not that Roenick is the eternal clown; far from it.

"Everyone thinks he's this flashy Hollywood goofball," Tocchet says. "He has got a serious side to him. Now he's starting to realize the fine line, when to shut it down. You don't have to drive downtown and do some celebrity bowling thing when you have a couple of big games coming up."

Big games have been a part of Roenick's career ever since he made the jump from junior hockey in Hull, Quebec to the NHL in 1988-89. He had been drafted by Chicago in the first round, eighth overall, of the 1988 NHL entry draft.

Many believed that Jeremy would wind up being as much a fixture in the Windy City as the Merchandise Mart. Over a period of seven seasons, Roenick had become the darling of State Street and a very good reason to be a Blackhawks fan.

JEREMY ROENICK

BORN: Boston Massachusets, January 17, 1970

Position: Center

NHL Teams: Chicago, 1989-1996; Phoenix, 1996-2001; Philadelphia, 2001-present

Awards/Honors: 1991-1994, 1999-2001 All-Star Game, 1998, 2002 U.S. Olympian

Between 1991-92 and 1993-94 he put together successive seasons of 103, 107, and 107 points, respectively.

A dispute with management–many Chicago fans never forgave the club for letting this happen–led to Jeremy being traded to Phoenix in exchange for Alexei Zhamnov, Craig Mills, and a first-round pick in the 1997 NHL entry draft (Ty Jones) on August 16, 1996.

As a Coyote, Roenick found happiness in the sun but never achieved the high points standing he had with the Blackhawks. "I thought I could go along like I did when I was scoring 100 points a season," he said. "Then, I learned the facts of life. I learned that you get only so much out of your body. It took me a while to admit I wasn't producing at the same level as I did early in my career and that my body wasn't recovering as quickly from the pounding I was giving it."

He has played a pounding game as far back as anyone can remember.

"He's a real soldier," his former coach Mike Keenan said. "He'll volunteer for any mission. He leads the way–and he'll lay his body on the line for a teammate."

Roenick did just that for the Coyotes until he became a free agent in the summer of 2001. The Flyers quickly signed him on July 2, 2001 and Jeremy wasted no time in revealing his delight about coming to Broad Street.

"All I'm looking forward to is a championship," said Roenick. "It was really hard to think about the Stanley Cup in Phoenix with the atmosphere there. The Flyers are a much more talented team than the Chicago team I played on in the 1992 Stanley Cup finals that lost to Pittsburgh."

Playing both in the East and West has given Jeremy a good perspective on various geographic contrasts. "It is a lot tighter in the East," Roenick explained. "That is for sure. There is not as much room to maneuver. The trap is very prevalent in the East. It takes a lot to get used to the style of play. The West is more my style, but I have thoroughly enjoyed playing in the East."

A member of two American Olympic teams, Roenick has acknowledged that the experience was a high point in his hockey career–but not high enough.

"There is no question the Stanley Cup is Number One. If I ranked them one to ten, I would rank the Stanley Cup as a ten. The Olympics are a seven. I have been in my share of All-Star Games. I don't need them that much."

Some say that what Jeremy needs most of all is attention, lots and lots of it. But he has never apologized for his love of the limelight.

Free agent Jeremy Roenick signed with the Flyers in 2001 with Stanley Cup aspirations.

"Why wouldn't I love the spotlight? I do not shy away from any of that. Not many people get to do it. I like to keep things loose and keep people smiling. If they are going to watch, you might as well give them something to watch. I do like it and enjoy it. I like the camera. I like the microphone. I am not afraid to make a fool of myself."

Nevertheless, when it came to the hockey rink Roenick was a team player. In his first season as a Flyer he led all Philadelphia players in scoring. He finished the campaign having performed in 75 games and scored 21 goals and 46 assists for 67 points and a plus/minus of 32, which ranked second in the NHL.

But the elusive accomplishment–playing for a Stanley Cup winner–remains a major challenge.

"If I could do my part to win a Cup and have my name up there with those guys, I don't know if there's much more of a compliment you could get," he concluded.

Whether he wins the prize or not, this much is certain: Jeremy Roenick has earned his money as an NHL celebrity.

Roenick has been known to lay his body on the line for a teammate.

Roenick has been a member of two American Olympic teams.

The Best, Worst, and Most Unusual In Philadelphia Hockey

Worst Dirty Player. Joe Desson, Philadelphia Falcons. A quiet, bespectacled gentleman off-ice, Desson was apt to go haywire any time during a game, and frequently without warning. And heaven help the referee who happened to cross Desson's path at the wrong time. Desson's major problem was the temper he never fully controlled. When Desson wasn't fighting, he was as good as any defenseman in any league.

Early in the 1944-45 season, Desson flattened an official and was suspended for two weeks by EAHL president Tom Lockhart, though, as always, Joe was the acme of penitence after his explosion. "All I want is another chance," he said. "I will try to mend my ways."

But his niche on the notorious list was permanently carved when, as a member of the New Haven Blades, he flattened—and nearly killed—referee Mickey Slowik during an Eastern League game at New Haven Arena. This time Lockhart suspended Desson for life, one of the few times so stiff a sentence was meted out in hockey.

Worst Playing Conditions During A Game. During Game 3 of the 1975 Stanley Cup finals, the fans in Buffalo's War Memorial Auditorium got a glimpse of what hockey must look like in Foggy Old London. The Philadelphia Flyers and Buffalo Sabres were forced to decide the Stanley Cup champion in a pea soup-like atmosphere. The 70-degree heat combined with the ice and the players' movements to produce a screen of fog that made seeing the puck almost impossible—particularly for the goalies, Bernie Parent of the Flyers and Roger Crozier of the Sabres.

"I couldn't see any shots from center ice," said Parent. "I'm sure it was the same for Crozier."

The game had to be delayed eleven times because of the thickness of the fog. During each unscheduled intermission, several arena attendants were called out onto the ice to fan the fog with a sheet to make it disappear, at least temporarily.

When that failed, the players came out and skated around the fog-congested area to keep it from building up. The only players who weren't annoyed at the delays were the fourth-stringers on both teams who received more ice time than they had in weeks.

Worst Team. The Quivering Quakers.

Although organized amateur hockey was played in Philadelphia as far back as the turn of the century, the professionals didn't make their debut until the autumn of 1927 when the Philadelphia Arrows were admitted to the powerful Canadian-American League.

One of the foremost minor hockey leagues on the continent, the Can-Am, as it was known, had been organized in 1926 with representatives from New Haven, Springfield, Quebec City, Boston, and Providence.

When the league decided to expand to six teams, Philadelphia was granted a franchise for the 1927-28 season and a contest was held by the new entry to select a name. Some 4,286 letters later, a panel of sportswriters selected *The Arrows*.

"It was selected," commented *The Philadelphia Evening Ledger*, "because it denotes speed, and ice hockey is known to be a speedy game."

But speed appeared to be foreign to the Arrows in their maiden year. They finished dead last and showed no improvement the following season. However, in 1929-30, the Arrows climbed to second place only to be eliminated from the playoffs by Boston.

The team, which had been controlled by an out-of-towner, Irwin P. Wener of New Haven, was taken over by a group of Philadelphians in June 1929. Heading the group of notables was Irwin P. Griscom III. Associated with Griscom in the purchase of Wener's stock was F. Eugene Dixon, captain of the United States Davis Cup tennis team, George D. Widener, the noted turfman, as well as J. Haseltine Carstairs, John Story Smith, and Alexander Thayer.

Despite the new blood and new money, the Arrows continued to spend their seasons in the lower reaches of the Can-Am. Meanwhile, the seeds of big-league hockey for Philadelphia were being planted—of all places—in Pittsburgh, at the other end of the state.

Prior to the start of the 1928-29 National Hockey League season, Benny Leonard, who had been the lightweight champion of the world, bought the NHL's Pittsburgh franchise and operated it in the Steel City as the Pirates, with no financial success.

On October 18, 1930, the NHL Board of Governors approved Leonard's request to move the Pittsburgh franchise to Philadelphia. Ebullient Benny reacted as if he had been granted a license to coin money. He promptly spelled out elaborate plans for the "new" club, renamed the Quakers, and promised Philadelphians a brand new ice palace that would replace the already antiquated Arena.

"The present building won't be large enough to hold the crowds," Benny boasted. "We are expecting a larger one to be erected three years from now. If it isn't, I intend to bring New York capital in here and erect a modified Madison Square Garden that will house hockey, six-day bicycle races and wrestling."

Leonard's transplanted Pittsburgh club was nothing to crow about either artistically or financially. As the Pirates, they finished dead last in the American Division of the NHL during the 1929-30 campaign. Their record of five wins, 36 losses, and three ties was generally regarded as the joke of the NHL; it was hardly surprising that one of the leading jokesters on the Pirates, Joe Miller, was their goaltender.

Miller accompanied Leonard to Philadelphia, but Benny's optimism was not diminished one iota. "I think ice hockey has the greatest future of any sport in America," Leonard predicted. "So I'm willing to risk my money. I've lost plenty so far, but I'm not crying. It's the coming sport in Philadelphia, and two years from now you'll say I was right."

Leonard's choice as general manager/coach of the Quakers was Cooper Smeaton, a widely respected hockey man who had been referee-in-chief of the NHL at the time of his appointment. Smeaton had been through the hockey wars and was thankful to be alive when Leonard phoned him about the job. Being a referee was not a very safe job in those "frontier" days of pro hockey.

Smeaton had survived a number of close calls. Once, while officiating a match between Ottawa and Quebec in Quebec City, Cooper called several plays against the home club that enraged the already hostile French-Canadian audience.

Ottawa won the game by one goal and Smeaton was generally considered the culprit by the audience, a fact of which the referee was acutely aware. "Lucky for me," said Smeaton, "the referee and linesman used to share the visiting team's dressing room since we didn't have a changing room of our own. I realized how fortunate I was moments after the final buzzer that night in Quebec."

The hard-nosed, outspoken Smeaton was Leonard's kind of man and served to stoke up more of Benny's enthusiastic fire. "This is a major-league operation," Leonard boasted prior to the Quakers' opening game. "The Quakers are to ice hockey what the Athletics [then world champions] are to baseball."

Leonard was half right. He did have a major-league operation, everywhere but on the ice. His trainer, Archie Campbell, was as big-league as general manager/coach Smeaton. Campbell, after returning from service in World War I, worked for a good number of hockey and football teams.

Campbell had been around sports operations a lot longer than Leonard. One look at the Quakers' roster and Archie saw the handwriting on the wall. "Benny knew his hockey," said Campbell, "but I could tell as far as that team was concerned, he didn't have a chance."

Plain and simple, the Quakers didn't have the talent. Forwards Hibbert "Hib" Milks and Gerald Lowrey were the best of a mediocre lot. Dubious about Joe Miller's goaltending capabilities, Smeaton also signed 21-year-old Welsh-born Wilf Cude. A high-strung personality, Cude spent a horrendous season guarding the Quakers' goal. The experience, no doubt, brought on Cude's premature retirement from the sport in what is regarded as one of the most unusual retirement episodes in the game.

"I was having my afternoon steak before a game," said Cude, "and I poured a helluva lot of catsup on it. I'd just started to eat the steak when my wife, Beulah, made some casual remark about a trivial subject. For no good reason, I picked up my steak and threw it at her.

"She ducked and the steak wound up smacking against the wall. The catsup splattered and the steak hung there on the wall. Slowly it began to slip down and I stared at it. Between the time that steak hit the wall and then hit the floor, I decided I'd had enough of goaltending. When it landed I had made my decision to retire."

Judging by the Quakers' record in their first weeks of operation one could understand Cude's edginess, not to mention Smeaton's. Philadelphia opened the 1930-31 season at the Arena on November 11, 1930 and lost 3-0 to the New York Rangers. They scored only one goal in their first three games—all losing affairs—before tying Ottawa, 2-2. A momentous occasion—the Quakers' first victory—took place on November 25, 1930, at the Arena. The Toronto Maple Leafs were beaten, 2-1.

Leonard began to get the message, but his enthusiasm still ran high. "We're off to a slow start here this year," he admitted, "but I'm positive that Philadelphians will take to major hockey in another year or two. They have to become educated to it."

Leonard underestimated the Philadelphia fans. They were quite educated and were quick to realize that Benny had assembled what was to become the worst team in big-league hockey history. They did not win a single game from November 29, 1930, to January 10, 1931 and set a league record, losing 15 consecutive matches. The record stood until the Washington Capitals eclipsed the Quakers' ineptitude, dropping 17 consecutive games during the 1974-75 season.

Somewhat depressed by now but still hopeful, Leonard made a few trades and imported Stan Crosset, a towering defenseman from Port Hope, Ontario. Crosset's experience in the NHL—and one episode in particular—symbolized more than anything the ill-starred life of the Quakers.

The Quakers were in Detroit for a game against the Falcons (later the Red Wings), and Smeaton gathered his men together for a pregame skull session. He addressed himself mainly to Crosset, warning him against trying to split the vaunted Detroit defense of Reg Noble and Harvey "Rocky" Rockburn.

"These two guys have perfected the art of sandwiching attackers," said Smeaton. "Noble steers people into Rockburn and then Rockburn creams you. If you try to split them you can get hurt. And I mean hurt!"

Crosset appeared to be listening, but then in the second period Crosset stole the puck from a Detroit skater and did precisely what Smeaton had told him not to do.

Archie Campbell, the Quakers' trainer, watched the play in awe from the Philadelphia bench.

"Noble got him first," Campbell remembers, "then Rockburn sent him flying off his feet. It was no ordinary hoist, either. The big fellow seemed to take off like an airplane. Then he made a perfect three-point landing on elbows and stomach and started to skid along the ice. The wind had probably been knocked out of him before he ever touched the ice."

Many professional hockey players have mastered the art of the "swan dive," a maneuver designed to capture the referee's attention and obtain a penalty against the opposition. But everyone in the arena knew this time that Crosset was in trouble before he even landed.

"He was helpless," says Campbell. "He slid on his stomach from midice right over the boards with his stick extended in front of him. When the stick hit the boards, it jabbed Crosset's chin and knocked him out cold."

Unknown to Crosset, he had actually committed a foul on the play while he was in midair. It seems that his stick had snagged Rockburn, opening a bloody wound over Rocky's eye. While Crosset was stretched out unconscious on the ice he was given a five-minute major penalty by the referee for drawing blood!

Meanwhile, trainer Campbell dashed out on the ice to care for the injured Crosset. He waved smelling salts in front of the still Quaker until Stan came to his senses. Campbell then escorted him to the penalty box, helped him on the bench, and then dangled more smelling salts until Crosset realized that he was neither in the dressing room nor on the Quakers' bench.

"What in heaven's name an I doing *here*?" he asked of Campbell.

And calmly as possible, Archie tried to explain.

It was Crosset who helped the Quakers as much as goalie Cude, who played spectacularly in the Philadelphia nets after his rather shaky start. Wilf's problem was that he was new to the NHL and consequently unfamiliar with the big guns on the opposition. Soon after he took over the goaltending job from Joe Miller, Cude went up against the mighty Montreal Maroons.

Coach Smeaton realized that his young goalie needed some special advice about the Montreal sharpshooters, particularly after Wilf's busy first period against the Maroons. So between the first and second periods, Smeaton warned the Quakers to keep an eye on the "Big S" line of Nels Stewart, Hooley Smith, and Babe Siebert.

"Don't let that big lug Stewart stand too near our goal crease," warned Smeaton. "They don't call him 'Ole Poison' for nothing."

Edgy over the lecture, Cude broke in: "The hell

with Stewart! I want my defense to keep an eye on that fellow wearing a cap. He's the one causing all my trouble."

The heretofore subdued Quakers dressing room suddenly erupted with laughter, all except the befuddled Cude. Finally, coach Smeaton, wearing a big grin, leaned toward his net minder and whispered: "Wilfie, my boy, the chap with the cap *is* Nels Stewart."

Benny Leonard was quite willing to tolerate such shenanigans as long as his team put up a good fight, and that they did even though frequently undermanned.

On Christmas Day 1930, they pleased Benny to no end while at the same time lost 8-0 to the Bruins at Boston Garden. The Quakers and Bruins indulged in a Pier Six free-for-all that began when Hib Milks was heavily checked by George Owen of Boston.

Nearly every player from both teams participated in the brawl with one notable exception—goalie Crude. This was as good a time as any for Wilfie to take a brief sabbatical from his trying job. And what Wilf saw from his vantage point in the crease was astonishing by any hockey-fight standards.

"Even the officials took a couple on the chin before it was over," wrote Charles L. Coleman in *The Trail of the Stanley Cup.* "As the referees seemed to be making very little headway in suppressing the fight, the police were called in. Only two constables went over the boards at first, and they looked plaintively back for aid as they approached the melee. They were eventually joined by reinforcements."

After what seemed like hours of flailing sticks, crunching punches, and continuous bloodletting, the fighting eventually subsided. Referee Mickey Ion assessed major penalties with $15 fines to Owen, Eddie Shore, and Dit Clapper of the Bruins and to Milks, D'Arcy Coulson, and Allan Shields of Philadelphia.

From the Quakers' viewpoint, Clapper was the major culprit. He not only scored a hat trick against Cude but also knocked out Wally Kilrea of Philadelphia with a right cross to the chin.

A month later the Quakers showed their class, returning to Boston Garden for the first time since the 8-0 debacle. This time, goalie Cude looked like an Indian rubber man, contorting himself successfully to help the Quakers to a 3-3 tie. It was such a remarkable performance that it even earned a line in the official NHL history. Cude followed that with a pair of wins over Detroit, but it was too little, too late to save the Quakers.

The NHL governors realized the depth of the Quakers' financial problems late in the season when the Montreal Canadiens decided to release defenseman Bert McCaffrey, who surely would have helped the Philadel-phia blue line corps. The waiver price was $5,000 and it was anticipated that Leonard would grab at the opportunity to bolster his team with an eye toward next season. Instead, Leonard declined. Philadelphia had reached the bottom of the barrel.

Gallantly if not gloriously, the Quakers completed their one and only season of NHL play on March 21, 1931, at the Forum in Montreal. Their opponents were the Canadiens, paced by Howie Morenz. Instead of lacka-daisically playing out the string, the Quakers battled the Montrealers as if it were the final game for the Stanley Cup.

Matching the Canadiens goal for goal—the final score was 4-4—Philadelphia had the Forum crowd on *their side,* which stimulated the Montrealers to even more determined efforts. On one of his spectacular rushes down ice, Morenz dispatched a mighty shot at the Quakers' net. Cude lost sight of the rubber.

Before he could lift his glove to deflect the puck, it smashed against his jaw and sent him reeling backwards into the net while blood splattered across the goal crease. Cude was carried from the ice, suffering a torn jaw that required heavy stitching. Hugh McCormack, a former London, Ontario, goaltender-turned-sportswriter, then put on the pads and preserved the 4-4 tie.

Rather than departing the NHL in a blaze of glory, the Quakers made their exit in a pool of red ink. On September 26, 1931, NHL president Frank Calder made it official that Philadelphia had agreed to suspend its franchise for one year.

Players belonging to the Quakers were distributed among the clubs that finished lowest in the league. One of them, left wing Syd Howe—no relation to Gordie Howe—was signed by Toronto and later dealt to Ottawa and St. Louis before landing in Detroit with the Red Wings. He was the only member of the Philadelphia sextet to gain permanent eminence. In June 1965 Howe was elected to the Hockey Hall of Fame. The others are just a vague memory to those who watched one of sport's most pathetic teams in action.

Most Unusual Link Between Philadelphia Hockey and the New York Rangers.

The short, miserable life of Benny Leonard's Quakers did not spell the end of professional hockey in Philadelphia. If anything, the Quakers' demise proved to be a stimulus to the Arrows, who not only continued operating but did something the Quakers never did: they began winning hockey games.

Herb Gardiner, who was originally signed to manage the Arrows in October 1929, emerged as a minor-league Mister Hockey in Philadelphia. He delivered a championship to the City of Brotherly Love in the 1932-33 season when the Arrows compiled a record of 29 victories, only 12 losses, and seven ties to finish in first place, seven points ahead of runner-up Providence.

Unfortunately, the Depression had hit the United States in the underbelly and many professional sports teams reeled from lack of attendance. There was talk of folding Philadelphia's sextet prior to the 1934-35 season because of losses at the gate. But on October 15, 1934, the club was saved when the Arrows receivers decided to run the team. Gardiner was retained as manager and members of the team who had been owned by Fitz-Eugene Dixon were to be lent to the Arrows.

This tenuous arrangement had its pitfalls, mostly on the ice where the Arrows fumbled and stumbled around, looking more like the defunct Quakers than anything else. Attendance at the Arena remained low, and it was obvious that some transfusion of talent was necessary to save pro hockey in Philadelphia.

As Benny Leonard once predicted, the SOS sign was detected in New York City where Rangers manager Lester Patrick decided he would kill—or save—two hockey teams with one shot. Patrick's theory was that a good big-league club was only as solid as its farm system, and thus he became one of the first leaders to develop a strong minor-league system, with each club's name bearing the initial letter R.

Thus, the Eastern Amateur Hockey League farm club was the Rovers. And when Patrick decided to swing a deal with the Arrows and pump life into them with new bodies, Philadelphia's team became known as the Ramblers. Patrick's plan received the blessing of Colonel John S. Hammond, chairman of the board of Madison Square Garden, who envisioned the Rangers operating the Philadelphia sextet for at least five years. The way the Colonel saw it, everybody would benefit.

"After the first year," said Hammond, sounding more and more like ebullient Benny Leonard, "I can assure Philadelphia a championship team."

The difference between Leonard and Hammond is that the Colonel delivered. What's more, he dispatched to Philadelphia some of the most gifted and colorful players ever to lace on skates. Many, such as Babe Pratt, Phil Watson, Bryan Hextall, and Joe Cooper, became legendary figures in the game.

When the 1935-36 edition of the Ramblers took the ice, they appeared powerful enough to take on some of the best clubs in the NHL. This pleased Patrick to no end. Lester was particularly delighted with the Colville boys, Mac and Neil, who teamed up with Alex Shibicky

to form a front line that he believed would someday be as good as the famed Cook Brothers—Bill and Bun—who together with Frank Boucher won two Stanley Cups for the Rangers.

Thanks to Watson, the Ramblers were as amusing as they were artistic. A native of Montreal, Watson grew up in a rather unique household. His father, a native of Glasgow, was a printer on a Montreal newspaper and spoke no French. His mother, a French-Canadian private nurse, had mastered neither English nor any of the Scottish dialects.

The semantic set-toss in the Watson household was to have a lasting effect on Phillipe Henri's command of the English language, although his father had insisted that young Phil speak only English during his first six years.

However, shortly after his sixth birthday Phil got a job as an interpreter for a garbage-collector who covered an English-speaking district of Montreal and whose knowledge of the language was inadequate. It was an attractive position for a child of his years, since it paid a nickel a day, plus lunch.

Unfortunately for Phil, his mother returned home from work early one afternoon, learned of his employment, and, despite the strenuous objections of her husband, put him in a French private school 14 miles from Montreal. Young Phil remained in the school for ten years, at the end of which he had forgotten English entirely and could speak only French.

"After graduation," wrote Robert Lewis Taylor, who was the biographer of another noted Philadelphian, W. C. Fields, "Watson returned to his family; renewing his acquaintance with his father by means of signs, he looked around for something to do. Mr. Watson, impressed by the athletic medals he had won at school, encouraged his son to take up a sport."

Since Phil preferred skating to bicycle-riding, billiards, or baseball, he decided to become a professional hockey player and eventually made his way to Philadelphia.

By the time Watson arrived on Broad Street his spoken English was audible but hardly understandable, and immediately he was singled out for all types of jokes.

A favorite pastime of the Colvilles was to read Watson's fan mail to him at those semiformal gatherings attended by the entire squad. Watson would be seated in a chair, and one of the brothers, with a handful of spurious documents, over which he and the other Colville had labored at length, would take the floor facing him.

"Here's a number," Neil Colville once opened, "from a girl who signs herself Eloise Bockwurst."

Immediately, Watson's eyes lit up with joy and he chirped, "Good! Is nice. *Continuez.*"

"Dear Mr. Watson," Colville read, "in the many years I've been going to hockey games I've seen some cheesy performances, but nothing to compare with your exhibition of last Tuesday. You skate like you were carrying a walrus on your back. You're so ugly too. I'm..."

By this time Watson was in high dudgeon. "I keel all these damn *Americans*," he cried. "I queet. I go home!"

When Watson wasn't carrying on in the Philadelphia dressing room, Walter "Babe" Pratt could be counted on for some form of raillery. Once Pratt was playing in a game being refereed by an official well-fortified with brandy. Whenever there was a faceoff in Babe's defensive zone, he would take the draw, and whenever Pratt prepared to take the draw the referee leaned over Babe's shoulder to drop the puck.

"Sir," said Pratt politely to the referee. "Would you mind leaning over my opponent's shoulder when you drop the puck? You're making *me* drunk."

Another time, Pratt was asked to describe his team. "This is a great team," boasted Babe. "We have an unbeatable combination: hungry rookies and thirsty veterans."

Under Herb Gardiner's able management, the Ramblers blossomed. "Gardiner developed in that season," said Tom Lockhart, former New York Rangers business manager, "what was probably the greatest team Philadelphia has ever had on ice."

The team finished in first place with 27 victories, 18 losses, and three ties, nine points ahead of runner-up Providence. The Ramblers then whipped Providence in the best-of-five playoff finals, three games to one. It was enough to catapult Watson and Pratt into the NHL in the 1936-37 season, but Philadelphia remained stronger than ever.

Clint Smith and Bryan Hextall took over where Watson had left off in what now became the International-American League, a seven-team, two-division offshoot of the Can-Am and International Leagues. Philadelphia was spotted in the Eastern Division along with Springfield, Providence, and New Haven. Syracuse, Pittsburgh, and Cleveland comprised the Western Division.

As expected, the Ramblers captured the Eastern title with a record of 26 wins, 14 losses, and eight ties for 60 points, while in the West, Syracuse was the victor with 27 victories, 16 losses, and five ties for 59 points. Philadelphia had the top point mark in the league.

In the playoffs, however, after dropping the opening game to the Ramblers, 2-0, Syracuse won three in a row to capture the series. Nobody knew it at the time, but the golden era of minor-league hockey in Philadelphia was coming to an end.

Best Fighter—Not Counting Dave Schultz.

In 1941-42 Philadelphia's entry in the American Hockey League was called the Rockets. It was an independent club that boasted a two-fisted slugger named Ossie Asmundsen. The bloodiest fight of Asmundsen's career was against Vic Myles of the New Haven Eagles on the night of December 6, 1941, Pearl Harbor Eve, at the Philadelphia Arena.

"Men who had been watching hockey for years," commented writer Earl Eby, "say it was the worst they had ever witnessed."

The fight erupted late in the third period when Myles cracked the Philadelphia skater over the head with his stick. Asmundsen counterattacked, but officials quickly intervened and gave each player a two-minute roughing penalty.

"As they were about to enter the penalty box," wrote Eby, "Myles hit Asmundsen in the mouth with his bare fist. And as quick as a rattlesnake strikes, Asmundsen brought his stick down on Myles's head. Then the two men came together. They landed on the ice, and both of them, well-versed in the art, began bringing up the sharp blades of their skates. Asmundsen once succeeded in sinking the ends of his blades in Myles's back."

By now the bloodbath had become so bitter that Rocket goalie Alfie Moore motioned for the police to intervene before one of the gladiators was killed.

"Three policemen stood in the penalty box after being summoned by Moore," said Eby, "but they looked on, hardly believing their eyes. After a few minutes the two battlers were so exhausted they fell apart, and it was then they were separated. The ice in front of the penalty box was crimson."

After being examined by doctors on the scene, Myles emerged from the infirmary with five stitches in his scalp, while Asmundsen suffered loosened teeth, a bruised nose, and a scratched face. The Rockets won the hockey game, 3-1.

The Best Non-NHL Fight in Philadelphia.

It happened in 1943 when the Philadelphia Falcons were playing at the old Arena against a tough Eastern Hockey League team called the Coast Guard Cutters.

Operating out of Curtis Bay in Baltimore, the Cutters were populated by hockey players who had enlisted at the start of World War II. The Falcons were a patchwork sextet comprised of homebrews, such as goalie

Barney Geisel and the slick youngsters Marty Madore and Tommy Brennan. Like the Philadelphia Rockets whom they succeeded, the Falcons made up in fight what they lacked in finesse. Though unfortunately for them, the Eastern League was bulging with battlers in that wartime year.

Most of the fighters were sprinkled down the long Coast Guard Cutters roster, whose team was filled with such big-leaguers as New York Rangers captain Art Coulter, Johnny Mariucci, the "badman" of the Chicago Blackhawks, and Frankie Brimsek, Mister Zero of the Boston Bruins.

In addition to the NHL aces who had enlisted in the Coast Guard, the Cutters also boasted several first-rate minor professionals including Manny Cotlow, an awesome Jewish defenseman who played in the American Hockey Association.

One night in February, 1943, Cotlow led the Cutters—also known as "Hooligan's Navy"—into Philadelphia's Arena and single-handedly started his own private war.

Cotlow, who wore his black hair slicked down on both sides of a center part, started the ruckus by taking on Marty Madore late in the second period. Although calmed by the officials, Cotlow and Madore went at it again when they reached the penalty box, which, unlike today's separate benches, was a communal seat.

Enraged by Cotlow, several Philadelphia rooters attacked the huge Coast Guard defenseman. "They leaned over the rails," said Philadelphia hockey writer Stan Baumgartner, "and began to swing fists—some of which landed on Cotlow's chin and cheek. Coast Guard players rushed to Cotlow's aid. Bob Dill and Art Coulter climbed to the concrete walk circling the ice and began using their sticks as a gunman would use a blackjack.

"The pointed end of their sticks flattened the soft hats of two would-be Dempseys. Police rushed to the scene. Everyone started swinging. The penalty box looked like a sardine can. Another battle started on the ice with the referee and linesman soon on their knees in a hand-to-hand struggle with the players of both teams. The police finally got control and the spectators shooed back to their seats."

The Cutters, who rarely lost to anybody, won the game, 9-4.

The Most Unusual Memory of Emile Francis. The little goalie who would eventually become coach and general manager of the New York Rangers actually got his start in Philadelphia. It was in the 1943-44 campaign when Red Mackenzie, coach of the Falcons, signed Francis.

The Cat's most vivid memory, however, was about a trip to New York City for a game with the New York Rovers.

"The thing I remember most," he said, "was my first trip to New York with the Falcons. We took the train into Penn Station and then Red Mackenzie hustled us off the platform. I thought we were going first class and would take cabs to Madison Square Garden.

"Instead, Mackenzie said, 'All right, you guys, everybody into the subway.' We wound up taking the subway two stops to 50th Street, where the old Garden used to be. That was probably the only time in my life I regretted being a goalkeeper. It was murder riding the New York subway with the huge goal bag on my shoulder."

The Best Threatening Sign on a Philadelphia Dressing Room.

Philadelphia Falcons coach Red Mackenzie brooked no tomfoolery from his players, and anyone who considered challenging his authority had to first consider the sign on the dressing room door in Philadelphia: "TRAINS LEAVING FOR CANADA EVERY HOUR ON THE HOUR."

Worst Philadelphia Hockey Rink.
"The [old Philadelphia] Arena," said former Philadelphia Falcons goalie Emile Francis, "was a very dangerous place for a player.

"For staters, you had to step down into that hole and the boards were only three feet high, at the most, and up above that were the railings. It's a miracle nobody got killed with that kind of arrangement.

"If you rolled a guy up against the boards, the boards were so low the guy would end up cracking against the steel fence, and that could really hurt a man."

"The Hammer's" Best Battles.
JOHN VAN BOXMEER, MONTREAL CANADIENS: After being relentlessly poked at by Van Boxmeer, Schultz devastated the Habs rookie with a vicious roundhouse right that knocked him out cold. Thanks to NBC, who televised the game, the world became aware of the Hammer's power as a legitimate heavyweight.

DALE ROLFE, NEW YORK RANGERS: During the 1974 semifinals, Schultz skated over to a melee breaking out in front of the Rangers' goal. After receiving some punches from Blueshirts defenseman Rolfe, the Hammer used Rolfe's face as a punching bag, connecting a dozen times until Rolfe's knees buckled and he collapsed to the ice.

BRYAN HEXTALL, ATLANTA FLAMES: Hextall and Schultz arrived at the front of the Atlanta net simultaneously; both got their sticks up, but the Hammer drew first blood as he head-butted the Flames' tough guy. With a gash over his eye and his nose covered in blood, Hextall was shell-shocked. Schultz went on to score the overtime game winner, which was followed by a newspaper article that said "Schultz's pounding of Hextall was the turning point of the game."

TERRY O' REILLY, BOSTON BRUINS: The setting was Game 2 of the Stanley Cup finals, when with his team down 1-0 in the series, the Hammer zeroed in on O'Reilly, one of the Bruins' premier ice cops. After being bombarded early in the game, O'Reilly locked up with Schultz. It was the fierce right fist of the Hammer, though, that settled the fracas. Schultz later assisted on Bobby Clarke's game-winning goal in overtime.

"That fight and the goal not only gave us the win, but also a psychological lift in the series," said the Hammer in his autobiography, *Hammer—Confessions of a Hockey Enforcer*. No longer were we afraid of the Bruins."

The Flyers went on to win the game and ultimately the Cup.

Best Night for an Opponent Against the Flyers. A Montreal Canadiens castoff and a failure with the New York Rangers, Gordon (Red) Berenson fulfilled his scoring potential after he was traded to the St. Louis Blues. A smooth skater and one of the NHL's first helmeted players, Berenson reached the apex of his career on November 7, 1968, at The Spectrum.

It all started routinely enough. At 16:42 of the first period, Berenson faked his way past Flyers defenseman Ed Van Impe and with quick, long strides wheeled in on goaltender Doug Favell. Berenson dipped to his right. Favell dropped to the ice. Berenson put the puck on his backhand and flicked it into the net for his first goal of the season.

The first period ended with the score 1-0, and that's the way it stayed until 10:26 of the second period when again Berenson lured Favell to the ice and tucked the puck behind him. Then at 14:42 of the same period, Berenson bore down the center of the ice and, from just inside the blue line, fired a blur that hit the goal post and ricocheted into the net. Berenson skidded right after the puck and grabbed it in his fist. "It was my first three-goal hat trick," he would say later, "and I wanted a memento."

Before the second period ended Berenson was well on his way to a second hat trick. At 15:14 he took a pass from Camille Henry and flicked a wrist shot past Favell for his fourth goal. And number five came with less than a minute remaining in the period. Now the Philadelphia fans were chanting "We want Red!"

The record for goals scored in a single game belonged to Syd Howe of the Detroit Red Wings. Howe had scored six times against the Rangers in 1944. Berenson tied the mark at 14:04 of the third period on a breakaway slap shot. Final score: St. Louis 8, Philadelphia 0.

"What I liked about it," Berenson said later in the dressing room, "is that they were all clean-cut goals, right out of the textbook. Not one rebound." He also paid tribute to the Philadelphia fans, who had urged him on with shouts of, "Go, Red, go!"

"Sure I heard the crowd," he said, "it really gave me a big thrill. I'd like to think the fans in St. Louis would do the same thing if some visiting player came to town and had a good night."

Berenson's description of his six-goal game as a "good night" is like saying the Blizzard of '88 left a little snow on the ground. But in Berenson's case he really meant it. He had, in fact, refused coach Scotty Bowman's offer for some extra shifts after his sixth goal so he could try for seven.

"I was getting tired," Berenson explained. "I didn't want to miss a check and have [goalie] Jacques [Plante] lose his shutout. Scoring goals is nice, but I just want to be a hockey player—one who scores a few more goals than he has scored on him. Personally, I'd feel awful if I had gone out and tried for number seven without doing my checking."

Most Unusual Good Luck Charm.
Her nickname was "The Songbird of the South."

Along Tin Pan Alley, Kate Smith was regarded as one of the finest vocalists of all time. And when she wasn't singing, she was writing hits as well.

Kate's signature tune, "When the Moon Comes Over the Mountain," was written by Ms. Smith along with Harry Woods and Howard Johnson in 1931.

She was one of the top stars of radio and hardly one you would associate with the National Hockey League, let alone the Flyers.

Nevertheless, Kate Smith became a Flyer legend because club executive Lou Sheinfeld decided that her classic rendition of "God Bless America" made a worthy alternate, as a game opener, to "The Star Spangled Banner."

Kate's pregame rendition of "God Bless America" became a symbol of victory for the Flyers. Her recorded version of the song was first played at The Spectrum on December 11, 1969. Philly won the game and Smith became the team's good luck charm.

She performed the song live at The Spectrum three times, and the Flyers won all three games. The most famous occurrence came before Game 6 of the 1974 finals. The Flyers won the game 1-0 to claim the Cup.

Most Unusual Coach.

Nicknamed "The Fog," Fred Shero was at once one of the most progressive and enigmatic coaches in NHL annals. He also was the only coach to deliver two Stanley Cups to Philadelphia.

Called everything from the Casey Stengel of hockey to a latter-day W. C. Fields, Shero was a mystery man to Philadelphia sportswriters, his players and even his family. Shero was an emotional man, although his sentiments were almost always locked deep inside. Even after great wins, Shero liked to sit by himself, perhaps concentrating and conquering his emotions so they wouldn't be visible to the outside world.

Shero often expressed himself with personal notes placed in a player's locker or a handwritten quote on the locker room blackboard. After the Flyers came back from a 4-1 deficit to defeat the New York Rangers, Shero scribbled the score in the locker room with a sign reading: "This game will never be forgotten by me. Money doesn't live forever. But great moments do."

At the beginning of each month and during special moments in the season, Shero used the blackboard to write "meaningful" notes to his players. One day during the season, he wrote: "Those who live on past glories will only have the glories of the past to live on." His players watched, listened and loved the man.

Bernie Parent was named the 1974 Stanley Cup's Most Valuable Player after Bobby Clarke, the other prime contender, announced that no one but Parent deserved the award. At the official presentation, Parent took the key that went along with the prize, said he needed 23 more for his teammates, and handed it to his mentor, Fred Shero. That morning, Shero did show emotion, allowing more tears to flow than perhaps ever before during his reign in Philadelphia.

Many experts credit Shero with being the first to see the value of European hockey. He was astute enough to realize, however, that he had to adapt the Soviets' skills and methods to the NHL. Freddie borrowed ideas from the Soviets and put together his own collection of rules, which were simple and to the point, such as:

- Never pass diagonally in our zone unless 100 percent certain.
- Never go backward in our end except on a power play. (Passing backward in our end to a teammate to elude opposition is okay.)
- Never throw a puck out blindly from behind their net.
- Wings on wings between blue lines except when able to intercept a stray pass.
- Never allow men in our defensive zone to be outnumbered.
- No forward must ever turn his back to the puck at any time. Know where the puck is at all times. Only defensemen are allowed to turn their backs for a fraction of a second on a swing to the corner in our end.

In his book Dave Schultz added the following about Shero: "Although Freddie had an ideal sense of how these rules should be executed and how these techniques should be learned, some of my teammates were not so believing.

"One day he had us out on the ice for practice and told the guys he wanted three-man passing drills with three pucks rather than one. Bob Kelly told Fred that was impossible.

"'Bull,' said Freddie. 'I saw fifteen-year-olds do it when I was in Moscow.'

"We did it."

A Chronology of Sixty-Nine Momentous Events in Flyers History

1. **October 11, 1967:** The Flyers meet the California Seals in Oakland for their first-ever NHL game. The final score: Seals 5, Flyers 1.

2. **October 18, 1967:** The visiting Flyers defeat St. Louis, 2-1, for Philadelphia's first franchise win.

3. **October 19, 1967:** In their first game at The Spectrum, the Flyers top Pittsburgh, 1-0.

4. **November 7, 1968:** St. Louis's Red Berenson scores six goals in one game against the Flyers, setting an NHL record for most goals in a road game.

5. **February 17, 1968:** The Spectrum's roof blows off and the Flyers are forced to play their remaining games on the road.

6. **June 12, 1969:** Philadelphia selects Bobby Clarke of the Flin Flon Bombers in the second round (17th overall) of the 1969 NHL entry draft.

7. **April 4, 1970:** The Flyers drop their sixth consecutive game, a 1-0 loss to Minnesota, and are eliminated from the playoffs after needing a win or a tie in their final six games to reach the postseason. On the lone goal, Bernie Parent lost sight of the puck in the afternoon sun shining through one of the Spectrum exits.

8. **January 31, 1971:** The Flyers trade Parent to Toronto for Bruce Gamble, Mike Walton and a number-one draft pick. Walton is then sent to Boston for Rick MacLeish and Danny Schock.

9. **February 8, 1972:** Goalie Bruce Gamble suffers a heart attack in the first period of a game in Vancouver but continues to play. The final score is Flyers 3, Canucks 1.

10. **March 29, 1973:** Bobby Clarke becomes the first Flyer to record 100 points in a season during a 4-2 win over Atlanta. He finishes the season with 35 goals and 52 assists for 113 points.

11. **April 10, 1973:** Gary Dornhoefer scores the overtime game winner, giving the Flyers a 3-2 win over Minnesota and a 3-2 edge in the series. The series culminates in the Flyers' first playoff win.

12. **May 15, 1973:** The Flyers reacquire Bernie Parent's rights and a second-round draft choice for Doug Favell and the Flyers' first-round draft choice.

13. **October 11, 1973:** Kate Smith performs "God Bless America" for the first time at The Spectrum. The Flyers win the game, their season opener, 2-0, over the Maple Leafs.

14. June, 1973: Bobby Clarke is awarded the Hart Trophy as the NHL's Most Valuable Player.

15. May 19, 1974: Rick Macleish scores the lone goal and Bernie Parent records a shutout as Philadelphia defeats Boston in six games for the Stanley Cup. The Flyers become the first NHL expansion team to capture the championship.

16. May 24, 1974: The Flyers obtain Reggie Leach from the California Golden Seals for Larry Wright, Al MacAdam, George Pesut and a first-round draft pick.

17. June, 1974: Bernie Parent (along with Chicago's Tony Esposito) receives the Vezina Trophy as the league's top goaltender and Flyers coach Fred Shero wins the Jack Adams Trophy as Coach of the Year.

18. May 27, 1975: Philadelphia wins their second straight Stanley Cup, defeating the Buffalo Sabres 2-0 in Game 6 of the finals. Bernie Parent becomes the first ever NHL player to win back-to-back Conn Smythe Trophies as playoff MVP.

19. June 18, 1975: Bobby Clarke wins his second Hart Trophy and Bernie Parent wins the Vezina Trophy.

20. January 11, 1976: The Flyers defeat the Soviet Red Army Team 4-1 at The Spectrum, the first NHL team to do so.

21. April 1, 1976: Reggie Leach becomes the second NHL player to score 60 goals in a season.

22. April 3, 1976: Bobby Clarke sets the Flyers' record for most points in a season with 119, by assisting on Bill Barber's 50th goal.

23. May 6, 1976: Reggie Leach scores five goals in a 6-3 semifinal playoff win over Boston.

24. May 16, 1976: Montreal completes a sweep over the Flyers in the Stanley Cup finals. Despite Philadelphia's loss, Reggie Leach wins the Conn Smythe Trophy.

25. December 11, 1977: Flyer Tom Bladon sets an NHL record for points by a defenseman in a single game with eight (four goals, four assists) in an 11-1 victory over Cleveland.

26. May 12, 1977: Flyers defenseman Barry Ashbee passes away from leukemia.

27. October 11, 1979: Bernie Parent's uniform #1 is retired. Parent himself was forced to retire due to an injury sustained when a stick inadvertently hit him in the eye in a game against the Rangers.

28. January 6, 1980: A win over Buffalo gives the Flyers 35 consecutive games without a loss. It is the longest such streak in professional sport history.

29. May 24, 1980: The Flyers lose in overtime to the New York Islanders in the Stanley Cup finals.

30. June, 1980: Flyers coach Pat Quinn wins the Jack Adams Trophy.

31. May 15, 1984: Bobby Clarke retires from hockey and is named Flyers vice president and general manager.

32. September 25, 1984: Bernie Parent becomes the first Flyer to be inducted into the Hall of Fame.

33. November 15, 1984: Bobby Clarke's uniform #16 is retired.

34. April 13, 1985: Tim Kerr sets two NHL playoff records: one for most goals in one period (four) and fastest four goals (8:16) in a second period. The final score is Flyers 6, Rangers 5.

35. May 30, 1985: The Flyers are defeated by the Edmonton Oilers in five games for the Stanley Cup.

36. June 12, 1985: Flyers goalie Pelle Lindbergh is awarded the Vezina Trophy and Flyers coach Mike Keenan wins the Jack Adams Trophy.

37. August 22, 1985: Bill Barber retires after playing his entire 12-year career in Philadelphia.

38. November 10, 1985: Pelle Lindbergh is killed in a car accident. He is honored before a game by the Flyers four nights later.

39. April 6, 1986: Tim Kerr sets a new NHL record by scoring 34 power play goals in a season.

40. May 28, 1987: The Flyers force the Oilers to a Game 7 in the Stanley Cup finals on J. J. Daignault's overtime game-winning goal.

41. May 31, 1987: Edmonton wins the Stanley Cup by defeating Philadelphia, 3-1, in Game 7. Despite being on the losing side, Flyers goalie Ron Hextall wins the Conn Smythe Trophy.

42. June 15, 1987: Ron Hextall receives the Vezina Trophy.

43. June 10, 1987: Bobby Clarke is inducted into the Hall of Fame.

44. December 8, 1987: In a win over Boston, Ron Hextall becomes the first goaltender to cleanly score a goal in an NHL game.

45. April 11, 1989: Ron Hextall becomes the first goaltender to score a playoff goal by netting his second career tally in an 8-5 win over Washington.

46. June 30, 1992: The rights to Eric Lindros are awarded to the Flyers after Philadelphia sends Ron Hextall, Steve Duchesne, Kerry Huffman, Mike Ricci, Peter Forsberg, Chris Simon, first-round draft picks in 1993 and 1994 and $15 million in cash to the Quebec Nordiques.

47. February 9, 1995: Montreal trades John LeClair, Eric Desjardins and Gilbert Dionne to Philadelphia for Mark Recchi and the Flyers' third-round draft choice.

48. July 6, 1995: Eric Lindros wins the Hart Trophy as league MVP.

49. October 5, 1996: The Flyers lose to the Florida Panthers in the first-ever game at the CoreStates Center.

50. June 7, 1997: The Detroit Red Wings sweep the Flyers in the Stanley Cup finals.

51. February 28, 1998: Eric Lindros scores the game-winning goal at the New York Rangers, recording his 500th point in the NHL. In 352 games he became the fifth fastest to reach 500 points in NHL history.

52. April 13, 1998: John LeClair records 50th goal of the season at Buffalo. He became the first American-born player to reach the 50-goal mark three times and the second Flyer to record three consecutive 50-goal seasons.

53. November 20, 1998: Goaltender Ron Hextall allows one goal on 19 shots to record a 3-1 win at Carolina to register his 233rd win as a Flyer. With the win, Hextall moves past Bernie Parent into first place on the Flyers' all-time list in wins.

54. February 20, 1999: Eric Lindros is scoreless at Ottawa, ending his 18-game point-scoring streak from January 7 through February 18 (14 goals, 21 assists). Lindros ties Bobby Clarke for the longest such streak in team history.

55. March 10, 1999: Mark Recchi is acquired from Montreal for Danius Zubrus, a second-round pick in 1999 (Matt Carkner), and the New York Islanders' sixth-round pick in 2000 (Scott Selig).

56. March 21, 1999: Flyers defeat the Detroit Red Wings 5-4 at the First Union Center, ending a team-record 12-game winless streak from February 24 through March 16 (0-8-4). The Flyers also posted a 15-game undefeated streak from December 12, 1998 through January 13, 1999 (10-0-5). The Flyers became the only team in NHL history to record both a streak of 10 or more games undefeated and a streak of 10 or more games winless in the same season.

57. October 24, 1999: John Vanbiesbrouck records his third consecutive shutout, a career first, and becomes only the fourth goaltender during the 1990s to post three consecutive shutouts.

58. April 8, 2000: John LeClair scores his 40th goal, becoming the first player in Flyers history to score 40 or more goals in five consecutive seasons.

59. May 4, 2000: Keith Primeau scores at 12:01 of the fifth overtime period to give the Flyers a 2-1 win at Pittsburgh in Game 4 of the Easter Conference Semifinals. It is the longest game in modern NHL history (152:01). In addition, the game's elapsed time of six hours, 56 minutes sets an NHL record. The Flyers' 72 shots and game's combined 130 shots both were team records for an overtime game.

60.   May 23, 2000: Eric Lindros plays his last game in a Flyer uniform after Scott Stevens hits Lindros in Game 7 of the Eastern Conference Finals to give him a concussion.

61.   December 10, 2000: The Flyers name Bill Barber the 14th head coach in team history, replacing Craig Ramsay. The Flyers defeat the New York Islanders 5-2 at the First Union Center for Barber's first win as head coach.

62.   March 13, 2001: Mark Recchi posts a goal and two assists in a 5-2 win vs. St. Louis. His goal vs. St. Louis is his 1,000th career NHL point.

63.   March 31, 2001: Goaltender Roman Cechmanek stops all 21 shots faced to record a 1-0 win vs. the Detroit Red Wings, his 10th shutout of the season: His 10 shutouts are the most by a Flyers goaltender since Bernie Parent registered 12 during the 1974-75 season.

64.   June 14, 2001: Head coach Bill Barber wins the Jack Adams Award as "the NHL coach adjudged to have contributed the most to his team's success." Barber is the first winner to receive this award after taking his position during the season and the eighth head coach to win in his first NHL season.

65.   July 2, 2001: The Flyers sign unrestricted free agent center Jeremy Roenick to a five-year contract.

66.   August 20, 2001: The Flyers trade the rights to restricted free agent center Eric Lindros to the New York Rangers in exchange for right wing Pavel Brendl, left wing Jan Hlavac, defenseman Kim Johnsson and a conditional third-round pick in the 2003 NHL entry draft.

67.   April 14, 2002: Flyers finish the regular 2001-2002 season in first place (Atlantic Division) with a 42-27-10-3 record. They finish second overall in the Eastern Conference.

68.   April 30, 2002: Head coach Bill Barber is fired.

69.   May 14, 2002: Ken Hitchcock is hired as new head coach.

Appendix A

Flyers Career Stats by Player

BARRY ASHBEE

REGULAR SEASON

Year	Team	League	GP	G	A	PTS	PIM
1956-57	Barrie	OHA	34	0	4	4	-
1957-58	Lakeshore	OHA	-	-	-	-	-
1958-59	Barrie	OHA	53	8	22	30	-
1959-60	Kingston	EPHL	62	2	11	13	72
1960-61	Kingston	EPHL	64	4	11	15	75
1961-62	N. Bay-Kingston	EPHL	35	2	7	9	87
1962-63	Hershey	AHL	72	0	17	17	94
1963-64	Hershey	AHL	72	3	6	9	142
1964-65	Hershey	AHL	36	1	10	11	100
1965-66	Boston	NHL	14	0	3	3	14
1966-67		DID	NOT	PLAY			
1967-68	Hershey	AHL	65	5	15	20	86
1968-69	Hershey	AHL	71	5	29	34	130
1969-70	Hershey	AHL	72	5	25	30	80
1970-71	Philadelphia	NHL	64	4	23	27	44
1971-72	Philadelphia	NHL	73	6	14	20	75
1972-73	Philadelphia	NHL	64	1	17	18	106
1973-74	Philadelphia	NHL	69	4	13	17	334

PLAYOFFS

Year	Team	League	GP	G	A	PTS	PIM
1956-57	Barrie	OHA	-	-	-	-	-
1957-58	Lakeshore	OHA	-	-	-	-	-
1958-59	Barrie	OHA	-	-	-	-	-
1959-60	Kingston	EPHL	-	-	-	-	-
1960-61	Kingston	EPHL	5	0	0	0	14
1961-62	N. Bay-Kingston	EPHL	8	-	-	-	-
1962-63	Hershey	AHL	15	0	2	2	34
1963-64	Hershey	AHL	6	0	0	0	12
1964-65	Hershey	AHL	14	0	0	0	22
1965-66	Boston	NHL	-	-	-	-	-
1966-67		DID	NOT	PLAY			
1967-68	Hershey	AHL	5	0	1	1	4
1968-69	Hershey	AHL	11	2	5	7	14
1969-70	Hershey	AHL	7	0	1	1	24
1970-71	Philadelphia	NHL	-	-	-	-	-
1971-72	Philadelphia	NHL	-	-	-	-	-
1972-73	Philadelphia	NHL	11	0	4	4	20
1973-74	Philadelphia	NHL	17	0	4	4	22

NHL Totals

Regular season					*Playoffs*				
GP	G	A	PTS	PIM	GP	G	A	PTS	PIM
284	15	70	85	291	17	0	4	4	22

BILL BARBER

REGULAR SEASON

Year	Team	League	GP	G	A	PTS	PIM
1970-71	Kitchener OHA		61	46	59	105	129
1971-72	Kitchener OHA		62	44	63	107	89
1972-73	Richmond	AHL	11	9	5	14	4
	Philadelphia	NHL	69	30	34	64	46
1973-74	Philadelphia	NHL	75	34	35	69	54
1974-75	Philadelphia	NHL	79	34	37	71	66
1975-76	Philadelphia	NHL	80	50	62	112	104
1976-77	Philadelphia	NHL	73	20	35	55	62
1977-78	Philadelphia	NHL	80	41	31	72	34
1978-79	Philadelphia	NHL	79	34	46	80	22
1979-80	Philadelphia	NHL	79	40	32	72	17
1980-81	Philadelphia	NHL	80	43	42	85	69
1981-82	Philadelphia	NHL	80	45	44	89	85
1982-83	Philadelphia	NHL	66	27	33	60	28
1983-84	Philadelphia	NHL	63	22	32	54	36
1984-85	Philadelphia	NHL	DID NOT PLAY				

PLAYOFFS

Year	Team	League	GP	G	A	PTS	PIM
1970-71	Kitchener	OHA	-	-	-	-	-
1971-72	Kitchener	OHA	-	-	-	-	-
1972-73	Richmond	AHL	-	-	-	-	-
	Philadelphia	NHL	11	3	2	5	22
1973-74	Philadelphia	NHL	17	3	6	9	18
1974-75	Philadelphia	NHL	17	6	9	15	8
1975-76	Philadelphia	NHL	16	6	7	13	18
1976-77	Philadelphia	NHL	10	1	4	5	2
1977-78	Philadelphia	NHL	12	6	3	9	2
1978-79	Philadelphia	NHL	8	3	4	7	10
1979-80	Philadelphia	NHL	19	12	9	21	23
1980-81	Philadelphia	NHL	12	11	5	16	0
1981-82	Philadelphia	NHL	4	1	5	6	4
1982-83	Philadelphia	NHL	3	1	1	2	2
1983-84	Philadelphia	NHL	-	-	-	-	-
1984-85	Philadelphia	NHL	DID NOT PLAY				

NHL Totals

Regular Season					Playoffs				
GP	G	A	PTS	PIM	GP	G	A	PTS	PIM
903	420	463	883	623	129	53	55	108	109

TOM BLADON

REGULAR SEASON

Year	Team	League	GP	G	A	PTS	PIM
1972-73	Philadelphia	NHL	78	11	31	42	26
1973-74	Philadelphia	NHL	70	12	22	34	37
1974-75	Philadelphia	NHL	76	9	20	29	54
1975-76	Philadelphia	NHL	80	14	23	37	68
1976-77	Philadelphia	NHL	80	10	43	53	39
1977-78	Philadelphia	NHL	79	11	24	35	57
1978-79	Pittsburgh	NHL	78	4	23	27	64
1979-78	Pittsburgh	NHL	57	2	6	8	35
1980-81	Edmonton	NHL	1	0	0	0	0
	Winnipeg NHL		9	0	5	5	10
	Detroit	NHL	2	0	0	0	2
1981-82	Adirondack	AHL	41	3	15	18	28

PLAYOFFS

Year	Team	League	GP	G	A	PTS	PIM
1972-73	Philadelphia	NHL	11	0	4	4	2
1973-74	Philadelphia	NHL	16	4	6	10	25
1974-75	Philadelphia	NHL	13	1	3	4	12
1975-76	Philadelphia	NHL	16	2	6	8	14
1976-77	Philadelphia	NHL	10	1	3	4	4
1977-78	Philadelphia	NHL	12	0	2	2	11
1978-79	Pittsburgh	NHL	7	0	4	4	12
1979-78	Pittsburgh	NHL	1	0	1	1	0
1980-81	Edmonton	NHL	-	-	-	-	-
	Winnipeg NHL		-	-	-	-	-
	Detroit	NHL	-	-	-	-	-
1981-82	Adirondack	AHL	18	3	3	6	16

NHL Totals

Regular Season					*Playoffs*				
GP	G	A	PTS	PIM	GP	G	A	PTS	PIM
610	73	197	270	392	86	8	29	37	70

MEL BRIDGMAN

REGULAR SEASON

Year	Team	League	GP	G	A	PTS	PIM
1972-73	Victoria	WHL	4	1	1	2	0
1973-74	Victoria	WHL	62	26	39	65	149
1974-75	Victoria	WHL	66	66	91	157	175
1975-76	Philadelphia	NHL	80	23	27	50	86
1976-77	Philadelphia	NHL	70	19	38	57	120
1977-78	Philadelphia	NHL	76	16	32	48	203
1978-79	Philadelphia	NHL	76	24	35	59	184
1979-80	Philadelphia	NHL	74	16	31	47	136
1980-81	Philadelphia	NHL	77	14	37	51	195
1981-82	Philadelphia	NHL	9	7	5	12	47
	Calgary	NHL	63	26	49	75	94
1982-83	Calgary	NHL	79	19	31	50	103
1983-84	New Jersey	NHL	79	23	38	61	121
1984-85	New Jersey	NHL	80	22	39	61	105
1985-86	New Jersey	NHL	78	23	40	63	80
1986-87	New Jersey	NHL	51	8	31	39	80
	Detroit	NHL	13	2	2	4	19
1987-88	Detroit	NHL	57	6	11	17	42
	Adirondack	AHL	2	1	2	3	0
1988-89	Vancouver	NHL	15	4	3	7	10

PLAYOFFS

Year	Team	League	GP	G	A	PTS	PIM
1972-73	Victoria	WHL	-	-	-	-	-
1973-74	Victoria	WHL	-	-	-	-	-
1974-75	Victoria	WHL	12	12	6	18	34
1975-76	Philadelphia	NHL	16	6	8	14	31
1976-77	Philadelphia	NHL	7	1	0	1	8
1977-78	Philadelphia	NHL	12	1	7	8	36
1978-79	Philadelphia	NHL	8	1	2	3	17
1979-80	Philadelphia	NHL	19	2	9	11	70
1980-81	Philadelphia	NHL	12	2	4	6	39
1981-82	Philadelphia	NHL	-	-	-	-	-
	Calgary	NHL	3	2	0	2	14
1982-83	Calgary	NHL	9	3	4	7	33
1983-84	New Jersey	NHL	-	-	-	-	-
1984-85	New Jersey	NHL	-	-	-	-	-
1985-86	New Jersey	NHL	-	-	-	-	-
1986-87	New Jersey	NHL	-	-	-	-	-
	Detroit	NHL	16	5	2	7	28
1987-88	Detroit	NHL	16	4	1	5	12
	Adirondack	AHL	-	-	-	-	-
1988-89	Vancouver	NHL	7	1	2	3	10

NHL Totals

Regular Season					Playoffs				
GP	G	A	PTS	PIM	GP	G	A	PTS	PIM
977	252	449	701	1625	125	28	39	67	298

ROD BRIND'AMOUR

REGULAR SEASON

Year	Team	League	GP	G	A	PTS	PIM
1988-89	Michigan State	CCHA	42	27	32	59	63
	St. Louis	NHL	-	-	-	-	-
1989-90	St. Louis	NHL	79	26	35	61	46
1990-91	St. Louis	NHL	78	17	32	49	93
1991-92	Philadelphia	NHL	80	33	44	77	100
1992-93	Philadelphia	NHL	81	37	49	86	89
1993-94	Philadelphia	NHL	84	35	62	97	85
1994-95	Philadelphia	NHL	48	12	27	39	33
1995-96	Philadelphia	NHL	82	26	61	87	110
1996-97	Philadelphia	NHL	82	27	32	59	41
1997-98	Philadelphia	NHL	81	36	38	73	54
1998-99	Philadelphia	NHL	82	24	50	74	47
1999-00	Philadelphia	NHL	12	5	3	8	4
	Carolina	NHL	33	4	10	14	22
2000-01	Carolina	NHL	79	20	36	56	47
2001-02	Carolina	NHL	81	23	32	55	40

PLAYOFFS

Year	Team	League	GP	G	A	PTS	PIM
1988-89	Michigan State	CCHA	-	-	-	-	-
	St. Louis	NHL	5	2	0	2	4
1989-90	St. Louis	NHL	12	5	8	13	6
1990-91	St. Louis	NHL	13	2	5	7	10
1991-92	Philadelphia	NHL	-	-	-	-	-
1992-93	Philadelphia	NHL	-	-	-	-	-
1993-94	Philadelphia	NHL	-	-	-	-	-
1994-95	Philadelphia	NHL	15	6	9	15	8
1995-96	Philadelphia	NHL	12	2	5	7	6
1996-97	Philadelphia	NHL	19	13	8	21	101
1997-98	Philadelphia	NHL	5	2	2	4	7
1998-99	Philadelphia	NHL	6	1	3	4	0
2000-01	Carolina	NHL	6	1	3	4	6
2001-02	Carolina	NHL	23	4	8	12	16

NHL Totals

Regular Season					Playoffs				
GP	G	A	PTS	PIM	GP	G	A	PTS	PIM
983	325	511	836	811	116	38	51	89	73

DAVE BROWN

REGULAR SEASON

Year	Team	League	GP	G	A	PTS	PIM
1980-81	Spokane	WHL	9	2	2	4	21
1981-82	Saskatoon	WHL	62	11	33	44	344
1982-83	Philadelphia	NHL	2	0	0	0	5
	Maine	AHL	71	8	6	14	418
1983-84	Philadelphia	NHL	19	1	5	6	98
	Springfield	AHL	59	17	14	31	150
1984-85	Philadelphia	NHL	57	3	6	9	165
1985-86	Philadelphia	NHL	76	10	7	17	277
1986-87	Philadelphia	NHL	62	7	3	10	274
1987-88	Philadelphia	NHL	47	12	5	17	114
1988-89	Philadelphia	NHL	50	0	3	3	100
	Edmonton	NHL	22	0	2	2	56
1989-90	Edmonton	NHL	60	0	6	6	145
1990-91	Edmonton	NHL	58	3	4	7	160
1991-92	Philadelphia	NHL	70	4	2	6	81
1992-93	Philadelphia	NHL	70	0	2	2	78
1993-94	Philadelphia	NHL	71	1	4	5	137
1994-95	Philadelphia	NHL	28	1	2	3	53
1995-96	San Jose	NHL	37	3	1	4	46

PLAYOFFS

Year	Team	League	GP	G	A	PTS	PIM
1980-81	Spokane	WHL	-	-	-	-	-
1981-82	Saskatoon	WHL	5	1	0	1	4
1982-83	Philadelphia	NHL	-	-	-	-	-
	Maine	AHL	16	0	0	0	107
1983-84	Philadelphia	NHL	2	0	0	0	12
	Springfield	AHL	-	-	-	-	-
1984-85	Philadelphia	NHL	11	0	0	0	59
1985-86	Philadelphia	NHL	5	0	0	0	16
1986-87	Philadelphia	NHL	26	1	2	5	59
1987-88	Philadelphia	NHL	7	1	0	1	27
1988-89	Philadelphia	NHL	-	-	-	-	-
	Edmonton	NHL	7	0	0	0	6
1989-90	Edmonton	NHL	3	0	0	0	0
1990-91	Edmonton	NHL	16	0	1	1	30
1991-92	Philadelphia	NHL	-	-	-	-	-
1992-93	Philadelphia	NHL	-	-	-	-	-
1993-94	Philadelphia	NHL	-	-	-	-	-
1994-95	Philadelphia	NHL	3	0	0	0	0
1995-96	San Jose	NHL	-	-	-	-	-

NHL Totals

Regular Season					Playoffs				
GP	G	A	PTS	PIM	GP	G	A	PTS	PIM
729	45	52	97	1789	80	2	3	5	209

ROMAN CECHMANEK

REGULAR SEASON

Year	Team	League	GP	W	L	T	SO	AVG
2000-01	Philadelphia	AHL	3	1	1	-	-	1.12
2000-01	Philadelphia	NHL	59	35	15	6	10	2.01
2001-02	Philadelphia	NHL	46	24	13	6	4	2.05

PLAYOFFS

Year	Team	League	GP	W	L	SO	AVG
2000-01	Philadelphia	NHL	6	2	4	-	3.11
2001-02	Philadelphia	NHL	4	1	3	1	1.85

Regular Season						*Playoffs*				
GP	W	L	T	SO	AVG	GP	W	L	SO	AVG
105	59	28	12	14	2.02	10	3	7	1	2.61

BOBBY CLARKE

REGULAR SEASON

Year	Team	League	GP	G	A	PTS	PIM
1967-68	Flin Flon	WCHL	59	51	117	168	148
1968-69	Flin Flon	WCHL	58	51	86	137	123
1969-70	Philadelphia	NHL	76	15	31	46	68
1970-71	Philadelphia	NHL	77	27	36	63	78
1971-72	Philadelphia	NHL	78	35	46	81	87
1972-73	Philadelphia	NHL	78	37	67	104	80
1973-74	Philadelphia	NHL	77	35	52	87	113
1974-75	Philadelphia	NHL	80	27	89	116	125
1975-76	Philadelphia	NHL	76	30	89	119	136
1976-77	Philadelphia	NHL	80	27	63	90	71
1977-78	Philadelphia	NHL	71	21	68	89	83
1978-79	Philadelphia	NHL	80	16	57	73	68
1979-80	Philadelphia	NHL	76	12	57	69	65
1980-81	Philadelphia	NHL	80	19	46	65	140
1981-82	Philadelphia	NHL	62	17	46	63	154
1982-83	Philadelphia	NHL	80	23	62	85	116
1983-84	Philadelphia	NHL	73	17	43	60	70

PLAYOFFS

Year	TM	LG	GP	G	A	PTS	PIM
1967-68	Flin Flon	WCHL	15	4	10	14	2
1968-69	Flin Flon	WCHL	18	9	16	25	0
1969-70	Philadelphia	NHL	-	-	-	-	-
1970-71	Philadelphia	NHL	4	0	0	0	0
1971-72	Philadelphia	NHL	-	-	-	-	-
1972-73	Philadelphia	NHL	11	2	6	8	6
1973-74	Philadelphia	NHL	17	5	11	16	42
1974-75	Philadelphia	NHL	17	4	12	16	16
1975-76	Philadelphia	NHL	16	2	14	16	28
1976-77	Philadelphia	NHL	10	5	5	10	8
1977-78	Philadelphia	NHL	12	4	7	11	8
1978-79	Philadelphia	NHL	8	2	4	6	8
1979-80	Philadelphia	NHL	19	8	12	20	16
1980-81	Philadelphia	NHL	12	3	3	6	6
1981-82	Philadelphia	NHL	4	4	2	6	4
1982-83	Philadelphia	NHL	3	1	0	1	2
1983-84	Philadelphia	NHL	3	2	1	3	6

NHL Totals

Regular Season					*Playoffs*				
GP	G	A	PTS	PIM	GP	G	A	PTS	PIM
1144	358	852	1210	1453	136	42	77	119	152

BILL CLEMENT

REGULAR SEASON

Year	Team	League	GP	G	A	PTS	PIM
1970-71	Quebec	AHL	69	19	39	58	88
1971-72	Richmond	AHL	26	8	9	17	20
	Philadelphia	NHL	49	9	14	23	39
1972-73	Philadelphia	NHL	73	14	14	28	51
1973-74	Philadelphia	NHL	39	9	8	17	34
1974-75	Philadelphia	NHL	68	21	16	37	42
1975-76	Washington	NHL	46	10	17	27	20
	Atlanta	NHL	31	13	14	27	29
1976-77	Atlanta	NHL	67	17	26	43	27
1977-78	Atlanta	NHL	70	20	30	50	34
1978-79	Atlanta	NHL	65	12	23	35	14
1979-80	Atlanta	NHL	64	7	14	21	32
1980-81	Calgary	NHL	78	12	20	32	33
1981-82	Calgary	NHL	69	4	12	16	28

REGULAR SEASON

Year	Team	League	GP	G	A	PTS	PIM
1970-71	Quebec	AHL	1	0	0	0	0
1971-72	Richmond	AHL	-	-	-	-	-
	Philadelphia	NHL	-	-	-	-	-
1972-73	Philadelphia	NHL	2	0	0	0	0
1973-74	Philadelphia	NHL	4	1	0	1	4
1974-75	Philadelphia	NHL	12	1	0	1	8
1975-76	Washington	NHL	-	-	-	-	-
	Atlanta	NHL	2	0	1	1	0
1976-77	Atlanta	NHL	3	1	1	2	0
1977-78	Atlanta	NHL	2	0	0	0	2
1978-79	Atlanta	NHL	2	0	0	0	0
1979-80	Atlanta	NHL	4	0	0	0	4
1980-81	Calgary	NHL	16	2	1	3	6
1981-82	Calgary	NHL	3	0	0	0	2

NHL Totals

Regular Season					*Playoffs*				
GP	G	A	PTS	PIM	GP	G	A	PTS	PIM
719	148	208	356	383	50	5	3	8	26

MURRAY CRAVEN

REGULAR SEASON

Year	Team	League	GP	G	A	PTS	PIM
1980-81	Medicine Hat	WHL	69	5	10	15	18
1981-82	Medicine Hat	WHL	72	35	46	81	49
1982-83	Detroit	NHL	31	4	7	11	6
	Medicine Hat	WHL	28	17	29	46	35
1983-84	Detroit	NHL	15	0	4	4	6
	Medicine Hat	WHL	48	38	56	94	53
1984-85	Philadelphia	NHL	80	26	35	61	30
1985-86	Philadelphia	NHL	78	21	33	54	34
1986-87	Philadelphia	NHL	77	19	30	49	38
1987-88	Philadelphia	NHL	72	30	46	76	58
1988-89	Philadelphia	NHL	51	9	28	37	52
1989-90	Philadelphia	NHL	76	25	50	75	42
1990-91	Philadelphia	NHL	77	19	47	66	53
1991-92	Philadelphia	NHL	12	3	3	6	8
	Hartford	NHL	61	24	30	54	38
1992-93	Hartford	NHL	67	25	42	67	20
	Vancouver	NHL	10	0	10	10	12
1993-94	Vancouver	NHL	78	15	40	55	30
1994-95	Chicago	NHL	16	4	3	7	2
1995-96	Chicago	NHL	66	18	29	47	36
1996-97	Chicago	NHL	75	8	27	35	12
1997-98	San Jose	NHL	57	12	17	29	25
1998-99	San Jose	NHL	43	4	10	14	18
1999-00	San Jose	NHL	19	0	2	2	4

PLAYOFFS

Year	Team	League	GP	G	A	PTS	PIM
1980-81	Medicine Hat	WHL	5	0	0	0	2
1981-82	Medicine Hat	WHL	-	-	-	-	-
1982-83	Detroit	NHL	-	-	-	-	-
	Medicine Hat	WHL	-	-	-	-	-
1983-84	Detroit	NHL	-	-	-	-	-
	Medicine Hat	WHL	4	5	3	8	4
1984-85	Philadelphia	NHL	19	4	6	10	11
1985-86	Philadelphia	NHL	5	0	3	3	4
1986-87	Philadelphia	NHL	12	3	1	4	9
1987-88	Philadelphia	NHL	7	2	5	7	4
1988-89	Philadelphia	NHL	1	0	0	0	0
1989-90	Philadelphia	NHL	-	-	-	-	-
1990-91	Philadelphia	NHL	-	-	-	-	-
1991-92	Philadelphia	NHL	-	-	-	-	-
	Hartford	NHL	7	3	3	6	6
1992-93	Hartford	NHL	-	-	-	-	-
	Vancouver	NHL	12	4	6	10	4
1993-94	Vancouver	NHL	22	4	9	13	18
1994-95	Chicago	NHL	16	5	5	10	4
1995-96	Chicago	NHL	9	1	4	5	2
1996-97	Chicago	NHL	2	0	0	0	2
1997-98	San Jose	NHL	6	1	1	2	0

NHL Totals

Regular Season					Playoffs				
GP	G	A	PTS	PIM	GP	G	A	PTS	PIM
1071	266	493	759	524	118	27	43	70	64

TERRY CRISP

REGULAR SEASON

Year	Team	League	GP	G	A	PTS	PIM
1963-64	Minneapolis	CPHL	42	15	20	35	22
1964-65	Minneapolis	CPHL	70	28	34	62	22
1965-66	Boston	NHL	3	0	0	0	0
	Oklahoma City	CPHL	61	11	22	33	35
1966-67	Oklahoma City	CPHL	69	31	42	73	37
1967-68	St. Louis	NHL	73	9	20	29	10
1968-69	Kansas City	CHL	4	1	1	2	4
	St. Louis	NHL	57	6	9	15	14
1969-70	Buffalo	AHL	51	15	34	49	14
	St. Louis	NHL	26	5	6	11	2
1970-71	St. Louis	NHL	54	5	11	16	13
1971-72	St. Louis	NHL	57	13	18	31	12
1972-73	N.Y. Islanders	NHL	54	4	16	20	6
	Philadelphia	NHL	12	1	5	6	2
1973-74	Philadelphia	NHL	71	10	21	31	28
1974-75	Philadelphia	NHL	71	8	19	27	20
1975-76	Philadelphia	NHL	38	6	9	15	28
1976-77	Philadelphia	NHL	2	0	0	0	0

PLAYOFFS

Year	Team	League	GP	G	A	PTS	PIM
1963-64	Minneapolis	CPHL	-	-	-	-	-
1964-65	Minneapolis	CPHL	5	0	2	2	0
1965-66	Boston	NHL	-	-	-	-	-
	Oklahoma City	CPHL	9	1	5	6	0
1966-67	Oklahoma City	CPHL	11	3	7	10	0
1967-68	St. Louis	NHL	18	1	5	6	6
1968-69	Kansas City	CHL	-	-	-	-	-
	St. Louis	NHL	12	3	4	7	20
1969-70	Buffalo	AHL	-	-	-	-	-
	St. Louis	NHL	16	2	3	5	2
1970-71	St. Louis	NHL	6	1	0	1	2
1971-72	St. Louis	NHL	11	1	3	4	2
1972-73	N.Y. Islanders	NHL	-	-	-	-	-
	Philadelphia	NHL	11	3	2	5	2
1973-74	Philadelphia	NHL	17	2	2	4	4
1974-75	Philadelphia	NHL	9	2	4	6	0
1975-76	Philadelphia	NHL	10	0	5	5	2
1976-77	Philadelphia	NHL	-	-	-	-	-

NHL Totals

Regular Season					*Playoffs*				
GP	G	A	PTS	PIM	GP	G	A	PTS	PIM
534	67	134	201	135	110	15	28	43	40

BOB DAILEY

REGULAR SEASON

Year	Team	League	GP	G	A	PTS	PIM
1973-74	Vancouver	NHL	76	7	17	24	143
1974-75	Vancouver	NHL	70	12	36	48	103
1975-76	Vancouver	NHL	67	15	24	39	119
1976-77	Vancouver	NHL	44	4	16	20	52
	Philadelphia	NHL	32	5	14	19	38
1977-78	Philadelphia	NHL	76	21	36	57	62
1978-79	Philadelphia	NHL	70	9	30	39	63
1979-80	Philadelphia	NHL	61	13	26	39	71
1980-81	Philadelphia	NHL	53	7	27	34	141
1981-82	Philadelphia	NHL	12	1	5	6	22

PLAYOFFS

Year	Team	League	GP	G	A	PTS	PIM
1973-74	Vancouver	NHL	-	-	-	-	-
1974-75	Vancouver	NHL	5	1	3	4	14
1975-76	Vancouver	NHL	2	1	1	2	0
1976-77	Vancouver	NHL	-	-	-	-	-
	Philadelphia	NHL	10	4	9	13	15
1977-78	Philadelphia	NHL	12	1	5	6	22
1978-79	Philadelphia	NHL	8	1	2	3	14
1979-80	Philadelphia	NHL	19	4	13	17	22
1980-81	Philadelphia	NHL	7	0	1	1	18
1981-82	Philadelphia	NHL	-	-	-	-	-

NHL Totals

Regular Season					*Playoffs*				
GP	G	A	PTS	PIM	GP	G	A	PTS	PIM
561	94	231	325	814	63	12	34	46	105

ERIC DESJARDINS

REGULAR SEASON

Year	Team	League	GP	G	A	PTS	PIM
1986-87	Granby	QMJHL	66	14	24	38	75
1987-88	Granby	QMJHL	62	18	49	67	138
1987-88	Sherbrooke	AHL	3	0	0	0	6
1988-89	Montreal	NHL	36	2	12	14	26
1989-90	Montreal	NHL	55	3	13	16	51
1990-91	Montreal	NHL	62	7	18	25	27
1991-92	Montreal	NHL	77	6	32	38	50
1992-93	Montreal	NHL	82	13	32	45	98
1993-94	Montreal	NHL	84	12	23	35	97
1994-95	Montreal	NHL	9	0	6	6	2
1994-95	Philadelphia	NHL	34	5	18	23	12
1995-96	Philadelphia	NHL	80	7	40	47	45
1996-97	Philadelphia	NHL	82	12	34	46	50
1997-98	Philadelphia	NHL	77	6	27	33	36
1998-99	Philadelphia	NHL	68	15	36	51	38
1999-00	Philadelphia	NHL	81	14	41	55	32
2000-01	Philadelphia	NHL	79	15	33	48	50
2001-02	Philadelphia	NHL	65	6	19	25	24

PLAYOFFS

Year	Team	League	GP	G	A	PTS	PIM
1987-88	Granby	QMJHL	5	0	3	3	10
1987-88	Sherbrooke	AHL	4	0	2	2	2
1988-89	Montreal	NHL	14	1	1	2	6
1989-90	Montreal	NHL	6	0	0	0	10
1990-91	Montreal	NHL	13	1	4	5	8
1991-92	Montreal	NHL	11	3	3	6	4
1992-93	Montreal	NHL	20	4	10	14	23
1993-94	Montreal	NHL	7	0	2	2	4
1994-95	Philadelphia	NHL	15	4	4	8	10
1995-96	Philadelphia	NHL	12	0	6	6	2
1996-97	Philadelphia	NHL	19	2	8	10	12
1997-98	Philadelphia	NHL	5	0	1	1	0
1998-99	Philadelphia	NHL	6	2	2	4	4
1999-00	Philadelphia	NHL	18	2	10	12	2
2000-01	Philadelphia	NHL	6	1	1	2	0
2001-02	Philadelphia	NHL	5	0	1	1	2

NHL Totals

Regular Season					Playoffs				
GP	G	A	PTS	PIM	GP	G	A	PTS	PIM
971	123	384	507	638	157	20	53	73	87

KEVIN DINEEN

REGULAR SEASON

Year	Team	League	GP	G	A	PTS	PIM
1981-82	U. of Denver	WCHA	26	10	10	20	70
1982-83	U. of Denver	WCHA	36	16	13	29	108
1983-84	Cdn. National	-	52	5	11	16	2
	Cdn. Olympic	-	7	0	0	0	0
1984-85	Hartford	NHL	57	25	16	41	120
	Binghampton	AHL	25	15	8	23	41
1985-86	Hartford	NHL	57	33	35	68	124
1986-87	Hartford	NHL	78	40	39	79	110
1987-88	Hartford	NHL	74	25	25	50	217
1988-89	Hartford	NHL	79	45	44	89	167
1989-90	Hartford	NHL	67	25	41	66	164
1990-91	Hartford	NHL	61	17	30	47	104
1991-92	Hartford	NHL	16	4	2	6	23
	Philadelphia	NHL	64	26	30	56	130
1992-93	Philadelphia	NHL	83	35	28	63	201
1993-94	Philadelphia	NHL	71	19	23	42	113
1994-95	Houston	IHL	17	6	4	10	42
	Philadelphia	NHL	40	8	5	13	39
1995-96	Philadelphia	NHL	26	0	2	2	50
	Hartford	NHL	20	2	7	9	67
1996-97	Hartford	NHL	78	19	29	48	141
1997-98	Carolina	NHL	53	7	16	23	100
1998-99	Carolina	NHL	67	8	10	18	97
1999-00	Ottawa	NHL	67	4	8	12	57
2000-01	Columbus	NHL	66	8	7	15	126
2001-02	Columbus	NHL	59	5	8	13	62

PLAYOFFS

Year	Team	League	GP	G	A	PTS	PIM
1981-82	U. of Denver	WCHA	-	-	-	-	-
1982-83	U. of Denver	WCHA	-	-	-	-	-
1983-84	Cdn. National	-	-	-	-	-	-
	Cdn. Olympic	-	-	-	-	-	-
1984-85	Hartford	NHL	-	-	-	-	-
	Binghampton	AHL	-	-	-	-	-
1985-86	Hartford	NHL	10	6	7	13	18
1986-87	Hartford	NHL	6	2	1	3	31
1987-88	Hartford	NHL	6	4	4	8	8
1988-89	Hartford	NHL	4	1	0	1	10
1989-90	Hartford	NHL	6	3	2	5	18
1990-91	Hartford	NHL	6	1	0	1	16
1991-92	Hartford	NHL	-	-	-	-	-
	Philadelphia	NHL	-	-	-	-	-
1992-93	Philadelphia	NHL	-	-	-	-	-
1993-94	Philadelphia	NHL	-	-	-	-	-
1994-95	Houston	IHL	-	-	-	-	-
	Philadelphia	NHL	15	6	4	10	18
1995-96	Philadelphia	NHL	-	-	-	-	-
	Hartford	NHL	-	-	-	-	-
1996-97	Hartford	NHL	-	-	-	-	-
1997-98	Carolina	NHL	-	-	-	-	-
1998-99	Carolina	NHL	6	0	0	0	8

NHL Totals

Regular Season					Playoffs				
GP	G	A	PTS	PIM	GP	G	A	PTS	PIM
1184	355	405	760	2217	59	23	18	41	127

GARY DORNHOEFER

REGULAR SEASON

Year	Team	League	GP	G	A	PTS	PIM
1961-62	Niagara Falls Jr. "A"	OHA	50	8	31	39	-
1962-63	Niagara Falls Jr. "A"	OHA	38	16	34	50	-
1963-64	Minneapolis	CPHL	39	21	30	51	67
	Boston	NHL	32	12	10	22	20
1964-65	Boston	NHL	20	0	1	1	13
	San Fransisco	WHL	37	10	25	35	59
1965-66	Hershey	AHL	54	16	20	36	56
	Boston	NHL	10	0	1	1	2
1966-67	Hershey	AHL	71	19	22	41	110
1967-68	Philadelphia	NHL	65	13	30	43	134
1968-69	Philadelphia	NHL	60	8	16	24	80
1969-70	Philadelphia	NHL	65	26	29	55	96
1970-71	Philadelphia	NHL	57	20	20	40	93
1971-72	Philadelphia	NHL	75	17	32	49	183
1972-73	Philadelphia	NHL	77	30	49	79	168
1973-74	Philadelphia	NHL	57	11	39	50	125
1974-75	Philadelphia	NHL	69	17	27	44	102
1975-76	Philadelphia	NHL	74	28	35	63	128
1976-77	Philadelphia	NHL	79	25	34	59	85
1977-78	Philadelphia	NHL	47	7	5	12	62

PLAYOFFS

Year	Team	League	GP	G	A	PTS	PIM
1961-62	Niagara Falls Jr. "A"	OHA	-	-	-	-	-
1962-63	Niagara Falls Jr. "A"	OHA	38	16	34	50	-
1963-64	Minneapolis	CPHL	39	21	30	51	67
	Boston	NHL	32	12	10	22	20
1964-65	Boston	NHL	20	0	1	1	13
	San Fransisco	WHL	-	-	-	-	-
1965-66	Hershey	AHL	3	1	1	2	14
	Boston	NHL	-	-	-	-	-
1966-67	Hershey	AHL	5	0	1	1	7
1967-68	Philadelphia	NHL	3	0	0	0	15
1968-69	Philadelphia	NHL	4	0	1	1	20
1969-70	Philadelphia	NHL	-	-	-	-	-
1970-71	Philadelphia	NHL	2	0	0	0	0
1971-72	Philadelphia	NHL	-	-	-	-	-
1972-73	Philadelphia	NHL	11	3	4	7	18
1973-74	Philadelphia	NHL	14	5	6	11	43
1974-75	Philadelphia	NHL	17	5	5	10	33
1975-76	Philadelphia	NHL	16	3	4	7	43
1976-77	Philadelphia	NHL	9	1	0	1	22
1977-78	Philadelphia	NHL	4	0	0	0	5

NHL Totals

Regular Season					Playoffs				
GP	G	A	PTS	PIM	GP	G	A	PTS	PIM
787	214	328	542	1291	80	17	19	36	203

ANDRE "MOOSE" DUPONT

REGULAR SEASON

Year	Team	League	GP	G	A	PTS	PIM
1968-69	Montreal	OHA	38	2	14	16	32
1969-70	Omaha	CHL	64	11	26	37	258
1970-71	N.Y. Rangers	NHL	7	1	2	3	21
	Omaha	CHL	54	15	31	46	308
1971-72	Providence	AHL	18	1	8	9	95
	St. Louis	NHL	60	3	10	13	147
1972-73	St. Louis	NHL	25	1	6	7	51
	Philadelphia	NHL	46	3	20	23	164
1973-74	Philadelphia	NHL	75	3	20	23	216
1974-75	Philadelphia	NHL	80	11	21	32	276
1975-76	Philadelphia	NHL	75	9	27	36	214
1976-77	Philadelphia	NHL	69	10	19	29	168
1977-78	Philadelphia	NHL	69	2	12	14	225
1978-79	Philadelphia	NHL	77	3	9	12	135
1979-80	Philadelphia	NHL	58	1	7	8	107
1980-81	Quebec	NHL	63	5	8	13	93
1981-82	Quebec	NHL	60	4	12	16	100
1982-83	Quebec	NHL	46	3	12	15	69

PLAYOFFS

Year	Team	League	GP	G	A	PTS	PIM
1968-69	Montreal	OHA	-	-	-	-	-
1969-70	Omaha	CHL	12	1	8	9	75
1970-71	N.Y. Rangers	NHL	-	-	-	-	-
	Omaha	CHL	11	0	7	7	45
1971-72	Providence	AHL	-	-	-	-	-
	St. Louis	NHL	11	1	0	1	20
1972-73	St. Louis	NHL	-	-	-	-	-
	Philadelphia	NHL	11	1	2	3	29
1973-74	Philadelphia	NHL	16	4	3	7	67
1974-75	Philadelphia	NHL	17	3	2	5	49
1975-76	Philadelphia	NHL	15	2	2	4	46
1976-77	Philadelphia	NHL	10	1	1	2	35
1977-78	Philadelphia	NHL	12	2	1	3	13
1978-79	Philadelphia	NHL	8	0	0	0	17
1979-80	Philadelphia	NHL	19	0	4	4	50
1980-81	Quebec	NHL	1	0	0	0	0
1981-82	Quebec	NHL	16	0	3	3	18
1982-83	Quebec	NHL	4	0	0	0	8

NHL Totals

Regular Season					Playoffs				
GP	G	A	PTS	PIM	GP	G	A	PTS	PIM
810	59	185	244	1986	140	14	18	32	352

PELLE EKLUND

REGULAR SEASON

Year	Team	League	GP	G	A	PTS	PIM
1981-82	AIK	Sweden	23	2	3	5	2
1982-83	AIK	Sweden	34	13	17	30	14
1983-84	AIK	Sweden	35	9	18	27	24
1984-85	AIK	Sweden	35	16	33	49	10
1985-86	Philadelphia	NHL	70	15	51	66	12
1986-87	Philadelphia	NHL	72	14	41	55	2
1987-88	Philadelphia	NHL	71	10	32	42	12
1988-89	Philadelphia	NHL	79	18	51	69	23
1989-90	Philadelphia	NHL	70	23	39	62	16
1990-91	Philadelphia	NHL	73	19	50	69	14
1991-92	Philadelphia	NHL	51	7	16	23	4
1992-93	Philadelphia	NHL	55	11	38	49	16
1993-94	Philadelphia	NHL	48	1	16	17	8
	Dallas	NHL	5	2	1	3	2

PLAYOFFS

Year	Team	League	GP	G	A	PTS	PIM
1981-82	AIK	Sweden	-	-	-	-	-
1982-83	AIK	Sweden	3	1	4	5	2
1983-84	AIK	Sweden	6	6	7	13	2
1984-85	AIK	Sweden	-	-	-	-	-
1985-86	Philadelphia	NHL	5	0	2	2	0
1986-87	Philadelphia	NHL	26	7	20	27	2
1987-88	Philadelphia	NHL	7	0	3	3	0
1988-89	Philadelphia	NHL	19	3	8	11	2
1989-90	Philadelphia	NHL	-	-	-	-	-
1990-91	Philadelphia	NHL	-	-	-	-	-
1991-92	Philadelphia	NHL	-	-	-	-	-
1992-93	Philadelphia	NHL	-	-	-	-	-
1993-94	Philadelphia	NHL	-	-	-	-	-
	Dallas	NHL	9	0	3	3	4

NHL Totals

Regular Season					Playoffs				
GP	G	A	PTS	PIM	GP	G	A	PTS	PIM
594	120	335	455	109	66	10	36	46	8

DOUG FAVELL

REGULAR SEASON

Year	Team	League	GP	W	L	T	SO	AVG
1967-68	Philadelphia	NHL	37	15	15	6	4	2.27
1968-69	Philadelphia	NHL	21	3	12	5	1	3.56
1969-70	Philadelphia	NHL	15	4	5	4	1	3.15
1970-71	Philadelphia	NHL	44	16	15	9	2	2.66
1971-72	Philadelphia	NHL	54	18	25	9	5	2.81
1972-73	Philadelphia	NHL	44	20	15	4	3	2.83
1973-74	Toronto	NHL	32	14	7	9	0	2.71
1974-75	Toronto	NHL	39	12	17	6	1	4.05
1975-76	Toronto	NHL	3	0	2	1	0	5.63
1976-77	Colorado	NHL	30	8	15	3	0	3.90
1977-78	Colorado	NHL	47	13	20	11	1	3.58
1978-79	Colorado	NHL	7	0	5	2	0	5.37

PLAYOFFS

Year	Team	League	GP	W	L	SO	AVG
1967-68	Philadelphia	NHL	2	0	2	0	4.00
1968-69	Philadelphia	NHL	1	0	1	0	5.00
1969-70	Philadelphia	NHL	-	-	-	-	-
1970-71	Philadelphia	NHL	2	0	2	0	4.00
1971-72	Philadelphia	NHL	-	-	-	-	-
1972-73	Philadelphia	NHL	11	5	6	1	2.60
1973-74	Toronto	NHL	3	0	3	0	3.31
1974-75	Toronto	NHL	-	-	-	-	-
1975-76	Toronto	NHL	-	-	-	-	-
1976-77	Colorado	NHL	-	-	-	-	-
1977-78	Colorado	NHL	2	0	2	0	3.00
1978-79	Colorado	NHL	-	-	-	-	-

NHL Totals

Regular Season						Playoffs				
GP	W	L	T	SO	AVG	GP	W	L	SO	AVG
373	123	153	69	18	3.17	21	5	16	1	3.12

BOB FROESE

REGULAR SEASON

Year	Team	League	GP	W	L	T	SO	AVG
1975-76	St. Catherine's	OHA	39	-	-	-	0	5.00
1976-77	Niagara Falls	OHA	39	-	-	-	2	4.68
1977-78	Niagara Falls	OHA	52	-	-	-	0	4.71
1978-79	Saginaw	IHL	21	-	-	-	0	3.31
	Milwaukee	IHL	14	-	-	-	1	3.52
1979-80	Maine	AHL	1	0	1	0	0	5.00
	Saginaw	IHL	52	-	-	-	0	3.78
1980-81	Saginaw	IHL	43	-	-	-	3	2.98
1981-82	Maine	AHL	33	16	11	4	2	3.28
1982-83	Philadelphia	NHL	25	17	4	2	4	2.52
	Maine	AHL	33	18	11	3	2	3.36
1983-84	Philadelphia	NHL	48	28	13	7	32	3.14
1984-85	Philadelphia	NHL	17	13	2	0	1	2.41
	Hershey	AHL	4	1	2	1	0	3.67
1985-86	Philadelphia	NHL	51	31	10	3	5	2.55
1986-87	Philadelphia	NHL	3	3	0	0	0	2.67
	N.Y. Rangers	NHL	28	14	11	0	0	3.74
1987-88	N.Y. Rangers	NHL	25	8	11	3	0	3.53
1988-89	N.Y. Rangers	NHL	30	9	14	4	1	3.78
1989-90	N.Y. Rangers	NHL	15	5	7	1	0	3.33
1990-91	N.Y. Rangers	NHL	DID NOT PLAY					

PLAYOFFS

Year	Team	League	GP	W	L	SO	AVG
1975-76	St. Catherine's	OHA	4	-	-	0	5.00
1976-77	Niagara Falls	OHA	-	-	-	-	-
1977-78	Niagara Falls	OHA	3	-	-	0	4.36
1978-79	Saginaw	IHL	-	-	-	-	-
	Milwaukee	IHL	7	-	-	0	4.14
1979-80	Maine	AHL	-	-	-	-	-
	Saginaw	IHL	4	-	-	0	3.66
1980-81	Saginaw	IHL	13	-	-	2	2.16
1981-82	Maine	AHL	-	-	-	-	-
1982-83	Philadelphia	NHL	-	-	-	-	-
	Maine	AHL	-	-	-	-	-
1983-84	Philadelphia	NHL	3	0	2	0	4.28
1984-85	Philadelphia	NHL	4	0	1	0	4.52
	Hershey	AHL	-	-	-	-	-
1985-86	Philadelphia	NHL	5	2	3	0	3.07
1986-87	Philadelphia	NHL	-	-	-	-	-
	N.Y. Rangers	NHL	4	1	1	0	3.64
1987-88	N.Y. Rangers	NHL	-	-	-	-	-
1988-89	N.Y. Rangers	NHL	2	0	2	0	6.67
1989-90	N.Y. Rangers	NHL	-	-	-	-	-
1990-91	N.Y. Rangers	NHL	DID NOT PLAY				

NHL Totals

Regular Season						Playoffs				
GP	W	L	T	SO	AVG	GP	W	L	SO	AVG
242	128	72	20	13	3.10	18	3	9	0	3.98

SIMON GAGNE

REGULAR SEASON

Year	Team	League	GP	G	A	PTS	PIM
1996-97	Beauport	QMJHL	51	9	22	31	39
1997-98	Quebec	QMJHL	53	30	39	69	26
1998-99	Quebec	QMJHL	61	50	70	120	42
1999-00	Philadelphia	NHL	80	20	28	48	22
2000-01	Philadelphia	NHL	69	27	32	59	18
2001-02	Philadelphia	NHL	79	33	33	66	32

PLAYOFFS

Year	Team	League	GP	G	A	PTS	PIM
1997-98	Quebec	QMJHL	12	11	5	16	23
1998-99	Quebec	QMJHL	13	9	8	17	4
1999-00	Philadelphia	NHL	17	5	5	10	2
2000-01	Philadelphia	NHL	6	3	0	3	0
2001-02	Philadelphia	NHL	5	0	0	0	2

NHL Totals

Regular Season					Playoffs				
GP	G	A	PTS	PIM	GP	G	A	PTS	PIM
228	80	93	173	72	28	8	5	13	4

RON HEXTALL

REGULAR SEASON

Year	Team	League	GP	W	L	T	SO	AVG
1981-82	Brandon	WHL	30	12	11	0	0	5.71
1982-83	Brandon	WHL	44	13	30	0	0	5.77
1983-84	Brandon	WHL	46	29	13	2	0	4.27
1984-85	Hershey	AHL	11	4	6	0	0	3.68
	Kalamazoo	IHL	19	6	11	1	0	4.35
1985-86	Hershey	AHL	53	30	19	2	5	3.41
1986-87	Philadelphia	NHL	66	37	21	6	1	3.00
1987-88	Philadelphia	NHL	62	30	22	7	0	3.50
1988-89	Philadelphia	NHL	64	30	28	6	0	3.23
1989-90	Philadelphia	NHL	8	4	2	1	0	4.15
	Hershey	AHL	1	1	0	0	0	3.67
1990-91	Philadelphia	NHL	36	13	16	5	0	3.13
1991-92	Philadelphia	NHL	45	16	21	6	3	3.40
1992-93	Quebec	NHL	54	29	16	5	0	3.45
1993-94	N.Y. Islanders	NHL	65	27	26	6	5	3.08
1994-95	Philadelphia	NHL	31	17	9	4	1	2.89
1995-96	Philadelphia	NHL	53	31	13	7	4	2.17
1996-97	Philadelphia	NHL	55	31	16	5	5	2.56
1997-98	Philadelphia	NHL	46	21	17	7	4	2.17
1998-99	Philadelphia	NHL	23	10	7	4	0	2.53

PLAYOFFS

Year	Team	League	GP	W	L	SO	AVG
1981-82	Brandon	WHL	3	0	2	0	9.32
1982-83	Brandon	WHL	-	-	-	-	-
1983-84	Brandon	WHL	10	5	5	0	3.75
1984-85	Hershey	AHL	-	-	-	-	-
	Kalamazoo	IHL	-	-	-	-	-
1985-86	Hershey	AHL	13	5	7	1	3.23
1986-87	Philadelphia	NHL	26	15	11	2	2.77
1987-88	Philadelphia	NHL	7	2	4	0	4.75
1988-89	Philadelphia	NHL	15	8	7	0	3.32
1989-90	Philadelphia	NHL	-	-	-	-	-
	Hershey	AHL	-	-	-	-	-
1990-91	Philadelphia	NHL	-	-	-	-	-
1991-92	Philadelphia	NHL	-	-	-	-	-
1992-93	Quebec	NHL	6	2	4	0	2.90
1993-94	N.Y. Islanders	NHL	3	0	3	0	6.08
1994-95	Philadelphia	NHL	15	10	5	0	2.81
1995-96	Philadelphia	NHL	12	6	6	0	2.13
1996-97	Philadelphia	NHL	8	4	3	0	2.97
1997-98	Philadelphia	NHL	1	0	0	0	3.00

NHL Totals

Regular Season						*Playoffs*				
GP	W	L	T	SO	AVG	GP	W	L	SO	AVG
608	296	214	69	23	2.97	93	47	43	2	3.03

PAUL HOLMGREN

REGULAR SEASON

Year	Team	League	GP	G	A	PTS	PIM
1975-76	Minnesota	WHA	51	14	16	30	121
	Johnstown	NAHL	6	3	12	15	12
	Philadelphia	NHL	1	0	0	0	2
	Richmond	AHL	6	4	4	8	23
1976-77	Philadelphia	NHL	59	14	12	26	201
1977-78	Philadelphia	NHL	62	16	18	34	190
1978-79	Philadelphia	NHL	57	19	10	29	168
1979-80	Philadelphia	NHL	74	30	35	65	267
1980-81	Philadelphia	NHL	77	22	37	59	306
1981-82	Philadelphia	NHL	41	9	22	31	183
1982-83	Philadelphia	NHL	77	19	24	43	178
1983-84	Philadelphia	NHL	52	9	13	22	105
	Minnesota	NHL	11	2	5	7	46
1984-85	Minnesota	NHL	16	4	3	7	38

PLAYOFFS

Year	Team	League	GP	G	A	PTS	PIM
1975-76	Minnesota	WHA	-	-	-	-	-
	Johnstown	NAHL	-	-	-	-	-
	Philadelphia	NHL	-	-	-	-	-
	Richmond	AHL	-	-	-	-	-
1976-77	Philadelphia	NHL	10	1	1	2	25
1977-78	Philadelphia	NHL	12	1	4	5	26
1978-79	Philadelphia	NHL	8	1	5	6	22
1979-80	Philadelphia	NHL	18	10	10	20	47
1980-81	Philadelphia	NHL	12	5	9	14	49
1981-82	Philadelphia	NHL	4	1	2	3	6
1982-83	Philadelphia	NHL	3	0	0	0	0
1983-84	Philadelphia	NHL	-	-	-	-	-
	Minnesota	NHL	12	0	1	1	6
1984-85	Minnesota	NHL	3	0	0	0	8

NHL Totals

Regular Season					Playoffs				
GP	G	A	PTS	PIM	GP	G	A	PTS	PIM
527	144	179	323	1684	82	19	32	51	195

MARK HOWE

REGULAR SEASON

Year	Team	League	GP	G	A	PTS	PIM
1972-73	Toronto	OHA	60	38	66	104	27
1973-74	Houston	WHA	76	38	41	79	20
1974-75	Houston	WHA	74	36	40	76	30
1975-76	Houston	WHA	72	39	37	76	38
1976-77	Houston	WHA	57	23	52	75	46
1977-78	New England	WHA	70	30	61	91	32
1978-79	New England	WHA	77	42	65	107	32
1979-80	Hartford	NHL	74	24	56	80	20
1980-81	Hartford	NHL	63	19	46	65	54
1981-82	Hartford	NHL	76	8	45	53	18
1982-83	Philadelphia	NHL	76	20	47	67	18
1983-84	Philadelphia	NHL	71	19	34	53	44
1984-85	Philadelphia	NHL	73	18	39	57	31
1985-86	Philadelphia	NHL	77	24	58	82	36
1986-87	Philadelphia	NHL	69	15	43	58	37
1987-88	Philadelphia	NHL	75	19	43	62	62
1988-89	Philadelphia	NHL	52	9	29	38	45
1989-90	Philadelphia	NHL	40	7	21	28	24
1990-91	Philadelphia	NHL	19	0	10	10	8
1991-92	Philadelphia	NHL	42	7	18	25	18
1992-93	Detroit	NHL	60	3	31	34	22
1993-94	Detroit	NHL	44	4	20	24	8
1994-95	Detroit	NHL	18	1	5	6	10

PLAYOFFS

Year	Team	League	GP	G	A	PTS	PIM
1972-73	Toronto	OHA	-	-	-	-	-
1973-74	Houston	WHA	14	9	10	19	4
1974-75	Houston	WHA	13	10	12	22	0
1975-76	Houston	WHA	17	6	10	16	18
1976-77	Houston	WHA	10	4	10	14	2
1977-78	New England	WHA	14	8	7	15	18
1978-79	New England	WHA	6	4	2	6	6
1979-80	Hartford	NHL	3	1	2	3	2
1980-81	Hartford	NHL	-	-	-	-	-
1981-82	Hartford	NHL	-	-	-	-	-
1982-83	Philadelphia	NHL	3	0	2	2	4
1983-84	Philadelphia	NHL	3	0	0	0	2
1984-85	Philadelphia	NHL	19	3	8	11	6
1985-86	Philadelphia	NHL	5	0	4	4	0
1986-87	Philadelphia	NHL	26	2	10	12	4
1987-88	Philadelphia	NHL	7	3	6	9	4
1988-89	Philadelphia	NHL	19	0	15	15	10
1989-90	Philadelphia	NHL	-	-	-	-	-
1990-91	Philadelphia	NHL	-	-	-	-	-
1991-92	Philadelphia	NHL	-	-	-	-	-
1992-93	Detroit	NHL	7	1	3	4	2
1993-94	Detroit	NHL	6	0	1	1	0
1994-95	Detroit	NHL	3	0	0	0	0

NHL Totals

Regular Season					*Playoffs*				
GP	G	A	PTS	PIM	GP	G	A	PTS	PIM
929	197	545	742	455	101	10	51	61	34

WHA Totals

Regular Season					*Playoffs*				
GP	G	A	PTS	PIM	GP	G	A	PTS	PIM
426	208	296	504	198	74	41	51	92	48

BOB KELLY

REGULAR SEASON

Year	Team	League	GP	G	A	PTS	PIM
1970-71	Philadelphia	NHL	76	14	18	32	70
1971-72	Philadelphia	NHL	78	14	15	29	157
1972-73	Philadelphia	NHL	77	10	11	21	238
1973-74	Philadelphia	NHL	65	4	10	14	130
1974-75	Philadelphia	NHL	67	11	18	29	99
1975-76	Philadelphia	NHL	79	12	8	20	125
1976-77	Philadelphia	NHL	73	22	24	46	117
1977-78	Philadelphia	NHL	74	19	13	32	95
1978-79	Philadelphia	NHL	77	7	31	38	132
1979-80	Philadelphia	NHL	75	15	20	35	122
1980-81	Washington	NHL	80	26	36	62	157
1981-82	Washington	NHL	16	0	4	4	12

REGULAR SEASON

Year	Team	League	GP	G	A	PTS	PIM
1970-71	Philadelphia	NHL	4	1	0	1	2
1971-72	Philadelphia	NHL	-	-	-	-	-
1972-73	Philadelphia	NHL	11	0	1	1	8
1973-74	Philadelphia	NHL	5	0	0	0	11
1974-75	Philadelphia	NHL	16	3	3	6	15
1975-76	Philadelphia	NHL	16	0	2	2	44
1976-77	Philadelphia	NHL	10	0	1	1	18
1977-78	Philadelphia	NHL	12	3	5	8	26
1978-79	Philadelphia	NHL	8	1	1	2	10
1979-80	Philadelphia	NHL	19	1	1	2	38
1980-81	Washington	NHL	-	-	-	-	-
1981-82	Washington	NHL	-	-	-	-	-

NHL Totals

Regular Season					Playoffs				
GP	G	A	PTS	PIM	GP	G	A	PTS	PIM
837	154	208	362	1454	101	9	14	23	172

TIM KERR

REGULAR SEASON

Year	Team	League	GP	G	A	PTS	PIM
1978-79	Kingston	OHA	57	17	25	42	27
1979-80	Kingston	OHA	63	40	33	73	39
	Maine	AHL	7	2	4	6	2
1980-81	Philadelphia	NHL	68	22	23	45	84
1981-82	Philadelphia	NHL	61	21	30	51	138
1982-83	Philadelphia	NHL	24	11	8	19	6
1983-84	Philadelphia	NHL	79	54	39	93	29
1984-85	Philadelphia	NHL	74	54	44	98	57
1985-86	Philadelphia	NHL	76	58	26	84	79
1986-87	Philadelphia	NHL	75	58	37	95	57
1987-88	Philadelphia	NHL	8	3	2	5	12
1988-89	Philadelphia	NHL	69	48	40	88	73
1989-90	Philadelphia	NHL	40	24	24	48	34
1990-91	Philadelphia	NHL	27	10	14	24	8
1991-92	N.Y. Rangers	NHL	32	7	11	18	12
1992-93	Hartford	NHL	22	0	6	6	7

PLAYOFFS

Year	Team	League	GP	G	A	PTS	PIM
1978-79	Kingston	OHA	6	1	1	2	2
1979-80	Kingston	OHA	3	0	1	1	16
	Maine	AHL	-	-	-	-	-
1980-81	Philadelphia	NHL	10	1	3	4	2
1981-82	Philadelphia	NHL	4	0	2	2	2
1982-83	Philadelphia	NHL	2	2	0	2	0
1983-84	Philadelphia	NHL	3	0	0	0	0
1984-85	Philadelphia	NHL	12	10	4	14	13
1985-86	Philadelphia	NHL	5	3	3	6	8
1986-87	Philadelphia	NHL	12	8	5	13	2
1987-88	Philadelphia	NHL	6	1	3	4	4
1988-89	Philadelphia	NHL	19	14	11	25	27
1989-90	Philadelphia	NHL	-	-	-	-	-
1990-91	Philadelphia	NHL	-	-	-	-	-
1991-92	N.Y. Rangers	NHL	8	1	0	1	0
1992-93	Hartford	NHL	-	-	-	-	-

NHL Totals

Regular Season					*Playoffs*				
GP	G	A	PTS	PIM	GP	G	A	PTS	PIM
655	370	304	674	596	81	40	31	71	58

OREST KINDRACHUK

REGULAR SEASON

Year	Team	League	GP	G	A	PTS	PIM
1971-72	San Diego	WHL	61	18	36	54	71
1972-73	Philadelphia	NHL	2	0	0	0	0
	Richmond	AHL	72	35	51	86	133
1973-74	Philadelphia	NHL	71	11	30	41	85
1974-75	Philadelphia	NHL	60	10	21	31	72
1975-76	Philadelphia	NHL	76	26	49	75	101
1976-77	Philadelphia	NHL	78	15	36	51	79
1977-78	Philadelphia	NHL	73	17	45	62	128
1978-79	Pittsburgh	NHL	79	18	42	60	84
1979-80	Pittsburgh	NHL	52	17	29	46	63
1980-81	Pittsburgh	NHL	13	3	9	12	34
1981-82	Washington	NHL	4	1	0	1	2

PLAYOFFS

Year	Team	League	GP	G	A	PTS	PIM
1971-72	San Diego	WHL	4	1	1	2	0
1972-73	Philadelphia	NHL	-	-	-	-	-
	Richmond	AHL	3	0	1	1	10
1973-74	Philadelphia	NHL	17	5	4	9	17
1974-75	Philadelphia	NHL	14	0	2	2	12
1975-76	Philadelphia	NHL	16	4	7	11	4
1976-77	Philadelphia	NHL	10	2	1	3	0
1977-78	Philadelphia	NHL	12	5	5	10	13
1978-79	Pittsburgh	NHL	7	4	1	5	7
1979-80	Pittsburgh	NHL	-	-	-	-	-
1980-81	Pittsburgh	NHL	-	-	-	-	-
1981-82	Washington	NHL	-	-	-	-	-

NHL Totals

Regular Season					*Playoffs*				
GP	G	A	PTS	PIM	GP	G	A	PTS	PIM
508	118	261	379	648	76	20	20	40	53

REGGIE LEACH

REGULAR SEASON

Year	Team	League	GP	G	A	PTS	PIM
1967-68	Flin Flon	WCHL	59	87	44	131	208
1968-69	Flin Flon	WCHL	22	36	10	46	49
1969-70	Flin Flon	WCHL	57	65	46	111	168
1970-71	Oklahoma	CHL	41	24	18	42	32
	Boston	NHL	23	2	4	6	0
1971-72	Boston	NHL	56	7	13	20	12
	California	NHL	17	6	7	13	7
1972-73	California	NHL	76	23	12	35	45
1973-74	California	NHL	78	22	24	46	34
1974-75	Philadelphia	NHL	80	45	33	78	63
1975-76	Philadelphia	NHL	80	61	30	91	41
1976-77	Philadelphia	NHL	77	32	14	46	23
1977-78	Philadelphia	NHL	72	24	28	52	24
1978-79	Philadelphia	NHL	76	34	20	54	20
1979-80	Philadelphia	NHL	76	50	26	74	28
1980-81	Philadelphia	NHL	79	34	36	70	59
1981-82	Philadelphia	NHL	66	26	21	47	18

PLAYOFFS

Year	Team	League	GP	G	A	PTS	PIM
1967-68	Flin Flon	WCHL	-	-	-	-	-
1968-69	Flin Flon	WCHL	-	-	-	-	-
1969-70	Flin Flon	WCHL	-	-	-	-	-
1970-71	Oklahoma	CHL	-	-	-	-	-
	Boston	NHL	3	0	0	0	0
1971-72	Boston	NHL	-	-	-	-	-
	California	NHL	-	-	-	-	-
1972-73	California	NHL	-	-	-	-	-
1973-74	California	NHL	-	-	-	-	-
1974-75	Philadelphia	NHL	17	8	2	10	6
1975-76	Philadelphia	NHL	16	19	5	24	8
1976-77	Philadelphia	NHL	10	4	5	9	0
1977-78	Philadelphia	NHL	12	2	2	4	0
1978-79	Philadelphia	NHL	8	5	1	6	0
1979-80	Philadelphia	NHL	19	9	7	16	6
1980-81	Philadelphia	NHL	9	0	0	0	2
1981-82	Philadelphia	NHL	-	-	-	-	-

NHL Totals

Regular Season					*Playoffs*				
GP	G	A	PTS	PIM	GP	G	A	PTS	PIM
856	366	268	634	374	94	47	22	69	20

JOHN LECLAIR

REGULAR SEASON

Year	Team	League	GP	G	A	PTS	PIM
1987-88	U. of Vermont	ECAC	31	12	22	34	62
1988-89	U. of Vermont	ECAC	18	9	12	21	40
1989-90	U. of Vermont	ECAC	10	10	6	16	38
1990-91	U. of Vermont	ECAC	33	25	20	45	58
	Montreal	NHL	10	2	5	7	2
1991-92	Montreal	NHL	59	8	11	19	14
	Fredericton	AHL	8	7	7	14	10
1992-93	Montreal	NHL	72	19	25	44	33
1993-94	Montreal	NHL	74	19	24	43	32
1994-95	Montreal	NHL	9	1	4	5	10
	Philadelphia	NHL	37	25	24	49	20
1995-96	Philadelphia	NHL	82	51	46	97	64
1996-97	Philadelphia	NHL	82	50	47	97	58
1997-98	Philadelphia	NHL	81	51	37	89	32
1998-99	Philadelphia	NHL	76	43	47	90	30
1999-00	Philadelphia	NHL	82	40	37	77	36
2000-01	Philadelphia	NHL	16	7	5	12	0
2001-02	Philadelphia	NHL	81	25	26	51	30

PLAYOFFS

Year	Team	League	GP	G	A	PTS	PIM
1987-88	U. of Vermont	ECAC	-	-	-	-	-
1988-89	U. of Vermont	ECAC	-	-	-	-	-
1989-90	U. of Vermont	ECAC	-	-	-	-	-
1990-91	U. of Vermont	ECAC	-	-	-	-	-
	Montreal	NHL	3	0	0	0	0
1991-92	Montreal	NHL	8	1	1	2	4
	Fredericton	AHL	2	0	0	0	4
1992-93	Montreal	NHL	20	4	6	10	14
1993-94	Montreal	NHL	7	2	1	3	8
1994-95	Montreal	NHL	-	-	-	-	-
	Philadelphia	NHL	15	5	7	12	4
1995-96	Philadelphia	NHL	11	6	5	11	6
1996-97	Philadelphia	NHL	19	9	12	21	10
1997-98	Philadelphia	NHL	5	1	1	2	8
1998-99	Philadelphia	NHL	6	3	0	3	12
1999-00	Philadelphia	NHL	18	6	7	13	6
2000-01	Philadelphia	NHL	6	1	2	3	2
2001-02	Philadelphia	NHL	5	0	0	0	2

NHL Totals

Regular Season					Playoffs				
GP	G	A	PTS	PIM	GP	G	A	PTS	PIM
763	341	337	678	361	123	38	42	80	76

PELLE LINDBERGH

REGULAR SEASON

Year	Team	League	GP	W	L	T	SO	AVG
1978-79	AIK Solna	ELITE	6	-	-	-	-	-
1979-80	Swedish Olympic		5	-	-	-	-	3.60
	AIK Solna	ELITE	32	-	-	-	-	3.41
1980-81	Maine	AHL	51	31	14	5	1	3.26
1981-82	Philadelphia	NHL	8	2	4	2	0	4.38
	Maine	AHL	25	16	7	2	0	3.31
1982-83	Philadelphia	NHL	40	23	13	3	3	2.98
1983-84	Springfield	AHL	4	4	0	0	0	3.00
	Philadelphia	NHL	36	16	13	3	1	4.05
1984-85	Philadelphia	NHL	65	40	17	7	2	3.02
1985-86	Philadelphia	NHL	8	6	2	0	1	2.88

PLAYOFFS

Year	Team	League	GP	W	L	SO	AVG
1978-79	AIK Solna	ELITE	-	-	-	-	-
1979-80	Swedish Olympic		-	-	-	-	-
	AIK Solna	ELITE	-	-	-	-	-
1980-81	Maine	AHL	20	10	9	0	3.54
1981-82	Philadelphia	NHL	-	-	-	-	-
	Maine	AHL	-	-	-	-	-
1982-83	Philadelphia	NHL	3	0	3	0	6.00
1983-84	Springfield	AHL	-	-	-	-	-
	Philadelphia	NHL	2	0	1	0	6.92
1984-85	Philadelphia	NHL	18	12	6	3	2.50
1985-86	Philadelphia	NHL	-	-	-	-	-

NHL Totals

Regular Season						*Playoffs*				
GP	W	L	T	SO	AVG	GP	W	L	SO	AVG
157	87	49	15	7	3.30	23	12	10	3	3.11

ERIC LINDROS

REGULAR SEASON

Year	Team	League	GP	G	A	PTS	PIM
1988-89	Cdn. National		2	1	0	1	0
1989-90	Det. Compuware	USHL	14	23	29	52	123
	Cdn. National		3	1	0	1	4
	Ohsuwa	OHL	25	17	19	36	61
1990-91	Oshuwa	OHL	57	71	78	149	189
1991-92	Oshuwa	OHL	13	9	22	31	54
	Cdn. National		24	19	16	35	34
	Cdn. Olympic		8	5	6	11	6
1992-93	Philadelphia	NHL	61	41	34	75	147
1993-94	Philadelphia	NHL	65	44	53	97	103
1994-95	Philadelphia	NHL	46	29	41	70	60
1995-96	Philadelphia	NHL	73	47	68	115	163
1996-97	Philadelphia	NHL	52	32	47	79	136
1997-98	Philadelphia	NHL	62	30	42	72	117

PLAYOFFS

Year	Team	League	GP	G	A	PTS	PIM
1988-89	Cdn. National		-	-	-	-	-
1989-90	Det. Compuware	USHL	-	-	-	-	-
	Cdn. National		-	-	-	-	-
	Ohsuwa	OHL	17	18	18	36	76
1990-91	Oshuwa	OHL	16	18	20	38	93
1991-92	Oshuwa	OHL	-	-	-	-	-
	Cdn. National		-	-	-	-	-
	Cdn. Olympic		-	-	-	-	-
1992-93	Philadelphia	NHL	-	-	-	-	-
1993-94	Philadelphia	NHL	-	-	-	-	-
1994-95	Philadelphia	NHL	12	4	11	15	18
1995-96	Philadelphia	NHL	12	6	6	12	43
1996-97	Philadelphia	NHL	19	12	14	26	40
1997-98	Philadelphia	NHL	5	1	2	3	17

NHL Totals

Regular Season					Playoffs				
GP	G	A	PTS	PIM	GP	G	A	PTS	PIM
359	223	285	508	726	48	23	33	56	118

KEN LINSEMAN

REGULAR SEASON

Year	Team	League	GP	G	A	PTS	PIM
1975-76	Kingston	OHA	65	61	51	112	92
1976-77	Kingston	OHA	63	53	74	127	210
1977-78	Birmingham	WHA	71	38	38	76	126
1978-79	Philadelphia	NHL	30	5	20	25	23
	Maine	AHL	38	17	22	39	106
1979-80	Philadelphia	NHL	80	22	57	79	107
1980-81	Philadelphia	NHL	51	17	30	47	150
1981-82	Philadelphia	NHL	79	24	68	92	275
1982-83	Edmonton	NHL	72	33	42	75	181
1983-84	Edmonton	NHL	72	18	49	67	119
1984-85	Boston	NHL	74	25	49	74	126
1985-86	Boston	NHL	64	23	58	81	97
1986-87	Boston	NHL	64	15	34	49	126
1987-88	Boston	NHL	77	29	45	74	167
1988-89	Boston	NHL	78	27	45	72	164
1989-90	Boston	NHL	32	6	16	22	66
	Philadelphia	NHL	29	5	9	14	30
1990-91	Edmonton	NHL	56	7	29	36	94
1991-92	Toronto	NHL	2	0	0	0	0
	Asiago	Italy	5	3	3	6	4

PLAYOFFS

Year	Team	League	GP	G	A	PTS	PIM
1975-76	Kingston	OHA	7	5	0	5	18
1976-77	Kingston	OHA	10	9	12	21	54
1977-78	Birmingham	WHA	5	2	2	4	15
1978-79	Philadelphia	NHL	8	2	6	8	22
	Maine	AHL	-	-	-	-	-
1979-80	Philadelphia	NHL	17	4	18	22	40
1980-81	Philadelphia	NHL	12	4	16	20	67
1981-82	Philadelphia	NHL	4	1	2	3	6
1982-83	Edmonton	NHL	16	6	8	14	22
1983-84	Edmonton	NHL	19	10	4	14	65
1984-85	Boston	NHL	5	4	6	10	8
1985-86	Boston	NHL	3	0	1	1	17
1986-87	Boston	NHL	4	1	1	2	22
1987-88	Boston	NHL	23	11	14	25	56
1988-89	Boston	NHL	-	-	-	-	-
1989-90	Boston	NHL	-	-	-	-	-
	Philadelphia	NHL	-	-	-	-	-
1990-91	Edmonton	NHL	2	0	1	1	0
1991-92	Toronto	NHL	-	-	-	-	-
	Asiago	Italy	7	3	4	7	47

NHL Totals

Regular Season					*Playoffs*				
GP	G	A	PTS	PIM	GP	G	A	PTS	PIM
860	256	551	807	1727	113	43	77	120	325

ROSS LONSBERRY

REGULAR SEASON

Year	Team	League	GP	G	A	PTS	PIM
1964-65	Minneapolis	CPHL	2	0	0	0	0
1966-67	Oklahoma City	CPHL	46	12	10	22	83
	Boston	NHL	8	0	1	1	2
	Buffalo	AHL	7	1	1	2	4
1967-68	Boston	NHL	19	2	2	4	12
	Oklahoma City	CPHL	41	16	18	34	116
1968-69	Boston	NHL	6	0	0	0	2
	Oklahoma City	CHL	65	28	39	67	169
1969-70	Los Angeles	NHL	76	20	22	42	118
1970-71	Los Angeles	NHL	76	25	28	53	80
1971-72	Los Angeles	NHL	50	9	14	23	39
	Philadelphia	NHL	32	7	7	14	22
1972-73	Philadelphia	NHL	77	21	29	50	59
1973-74	Philadelphia	NHL	75	32	19	51	48
1974-75	Philadelphia	NHL	80	24	25	49	99
1975-76	Philadelphia	NHL	80	19	28	47	87
1976-77	Philadelphia	NHL	75	23	32	55	43
1977-78	Philadelphia	NHL	78	18	30	48	45
1978-79	Pittsburgh	NHL	80	24	22	46	38
1979-80	Pittsburgh	NHL	76	15	18	33	36
1980-81	Pittsburgh	NHL	80	17	33	50	76

PLAYOFFS

Year	Team	League	GP	G	A	PTS	PIM
1964-65	Minneapolis	CPHL	5	1	0	1	4
1966-67	Oklahoma City	CPHL	11	3	2	5	31
	Boston	NHL	-	-	-	-	-
	Buffalo	AHL	-	-	-	-	-
1967-68	Boston	NHL	-	-	-	-	-
	Oklahoma City	CPHL	7	3	3	6	22
1968-69	Boston	NHL	-	-	-	-	-
	Oklahoma City	CHL	12	4	8	12	21
1969-70	Los Angeles	NHL	-	-	-	-	-
1970-71	Los Angeles	NHL	-	-	-	-	-
1971-72	Los Angeles	NHL	-	-	-	-	-
	Philadelphia	NHL	-	-	-	-	-
1972-73	Philadelphia	NHL	11	4	3	7	9
1973-74	Philadelphia	NHL	17	4	9	13	18
1974-75	Philadelphia	NHL	17	4	3	7	10
1975-76	Philadelphia	NHL	16	4	3	7	2
1976-77	Philadelphia	NHL	10	1	2	3	29
1977-78	Philadelphia	NHL	12	2	2	4	6
1978-79	Pittsburgh	NHL	7	0	2	2	9
1979-80	Pittsburgh	NHL	5	2	1	3	2
1980-81	Pittsburgh	NHL	5	0	0	0	2

NHL Totals

Regular Season					Playoffs				
GP	G	A	PTS	PIM	GP	G	A	PTS	PIM
968	256	310	566	806	100	21	25	46	87

RICK MACLEISH

REGULAR SEASON

YR	TEAM	LG	GP	G	A	PTS	PIM
1968-69	Peterborough	OHA	50	42	92	29	54
1969-70	Peterborough	OHA	54	45	56	101	135
1970-71	Oklahoma City	CHL	46	13	15	28	93
	Philadelphia	NHL	26	2	4	6	19
1971-72	Philadelphia	NHL	17	1	2	3	9
	Richmond	AHL	42	24	11	35	33
1972-73	Philadelphia	NHL	78	50	50	100	69
1973-74	Philadelphia	NHL	78	32	45	77	42
1974-75	Philadelphia	NHL	80	38	41	79	50
1975-76	Philadelphia	NHL	51	22	23	45	16
1976-77	Philadelphia	NHL	79	49	48	97	42
1977-78	Philadelphia	NHL	76	31	39	70	33
1978-79	Philadelphia	NHL	71	29	32	58	47
1979-80	Philadelphia	NHL	78	31	35	66	28
1980-81	Philadelphia	NHL	78	38	36	74	25
1981-82	Hartford	NHL	34	6	16	22	16
	Pittsburgh	NHL	40	13	12	25	28
1982-83	Pittsburgh	NHL	6	0	5	5	2
1983-84	Philadelphia	NHL	29	8	14	22	4
	Detroit	NHL	25	2	8	10	4

PLAYOFFS

YEAR	TEAM	LG	GP	G	A	PTS	PIM
1968-69	Peterborough	OHA	-	-	-	-	-
1989-70	Peterborough	OHA	-	-	-	-	-
1970-71	Oklahoma City	CHL	-	-	-	-	-
	Philadelphia	NHL	4	1	0	1	0
1971-72	Philadelphia	NHL	-	-	-	-	-
	Richmond	AHL	-	-	-	-	-
1972-73	Philadelphia	NHL	10	4	9	13	2
1973-74	Philadelphia	NHL	17	13	9	22	20
1974-75	Philadelphia	NHL	17	11	9	20	8
1975-76	Philadelphia	NHL	-	-	-	-	-
1976-77	Philadelphia	NHL	10	4	9	13	2
1977-78	Philadelphia	NHL	12	7	9	16	4
1978-79	Philadelphia	NHL	7	0	1	1	0
1979-80	Philadelphia	NHL	19	9	6	15	2
1980-81	Philadelphia	NHL	12	5	5	10	0
1981-82	Hartford	NHL	-	-	-	-	-
	Pittsburgh	NHL	5	1	1	2	0
1982-83	Pittsburgh	NHL	-	-	-	-	-
1983-84	Philadelphia	NHL	-	-	-	-	-
	Detroit	NHL	1	0	0	0	0

NHL Totals

Regular Season					*Playoffs*				
GP	G	A	PTS	PIM	GP	G	A	PTS	PIM
846	349	410	759	434	114	54	53	107	38

BRAD MARSH

REGULAR SEASON

Year	Team	League	GP	G	A	PTS	PIM
1976-77	London	OHA	63	7	33	40	121
1977-78	London	OHA	62	8	55	63	192
1978-79	Atlanta	NHL	80	0	19	19	101
1979-80	Atlanta	NHL	80	2	9	11	119
1980-81	Calgary	NHL	80	1	12	13	87
1981-82	Calgary	NHL	17	0	1	1	10
	Philadelphia	NHL	66	2	22	24	106
1982-83	Philadelphia	NHL	68	2	11	13	52
1983-84	Philadelphia	NHL	77	3	14	17	83
1984-85	Philadelphia	NHL	77	2	18	20	91
1985-86	Philadelphia	NHL	79	0	13	13	123
1986-87	Philadelphia	NHL	77	2	9	11	124
1987-88	Philadelphia	NHL	70	3	9	12	57
1988-89	Toronto	NHL	80	1	15	16	79
1989-90	Toronto	NHL	79	1	13	14	95
1990-91	Toronto	NHL	22	0	0	0	15
	Detroit	NHL	20	1	3	4	16
1991-92	Detroit	NHL	55	3	4	7	53
1992-93	Ottawa	NHL	59	0	3	3	30

PLAYOFFS

Year	Team	League	GP	G	A	PTS	PIM
1976-77	London	OHA	20	3	5	8	47
1977-78	London	OHA	11	2	10	12	21
1978-79	Atlanta	NHL	2	0	0	0	17
1979-80	Atlanta	NHL	4	0	1	1	2
1980-81	Calgary	NHL	16	0	5	5	8
1981-82	Calgary	NHL	-	-	-	-	-
	Philadelphia	NHL	4	0	0	0	2
1982-83	Philadelphia	NHL	2	0	1	1	0
1983-84	Philadelphia	NHL	3	1	1	2	2
1984-85	Philadelphia	NHL	19	0	6	6	65
1985-86	Philadelphia	NHL	5	0	0	0	2
1986-87	Philadelphia	NHL	26	3	4	7	16
1987-88	Philadelphia	NHL	7	1	0	1	8
1988-89	Toronto	NHL	-	-	-	-	-
1989-90	Toronto	NHL	5	1	0	1	2
1990-91	Toronto	NHL	-	-	-	-	-
	Detroit	NHL	1	0	0	0	0
1991-92	Detroit	NHL	3	0	0	0	0
1992-93	Ottawa	NHL	-	-	-	-	-

NHL Totals

Regular Season					*Playoffs*				
GP	G	A	PTS	PIM	GP	G	A	PTS	PIM
1086	23	175	198	1241	97	6	18	24	124

SCOTT MELANBY

REGULAR SEASON

Year	Team	League	GP	G	A	PTS	PIM
1984-85	U. Wisconsin	WCHA	40	14	24	38	60
1985-86	U. Wisconsin	WCHA	32	21	23	44	89
	Philadelphia	NHL	2	0	0	0	0
1986-87	Philadelphia	NHL	71	11	21	32	94
1987-88	Philadelphia	NHL	75	25	26	51	185
1988-89	Philadelphia	NHL	76	21	29	50	183
1989-90	Philadelphia	NHL	57	6	17	23	77
1990-91	Philadelphia	NHL	74	20	21	41	155
1991-92	Edmonton	NHL	80	23	27	50	197
1992-93	Edmonton	NHL	69	15	17	32	147
1993-94	Florida	NHL	80	30	30	60	149
1994-95	Florida	NHL	48	13	12	25	90
1995-96	Florida	NHL	79	32	38	70	160
1996-97	Florida	NHL	82	27	29	56	170
1997-98	Florida	NHL	19	15	24	39	117
1998-99	Florida	NHL	67	18	27	45	85
1999-00	Florida	NHL	77	18	28	46	126
2000-01	Florida	NHL	40	4	9	13	46
	St. Louis	NHL	23	7	1	8	25
2001-02	St. Louis	NHL	64	15	26	41	93

PLAYOFFS

Year	Team	League	GP	G	A	PTS	PIM
1984-85	U. Wisconsin	WCHA	-	-	-	-	-
1985-86	U. Wisconsin	WCHA	-	-	-	-	-
	Philadelphia	NHL	-	-	-	-	-
1986-87	Philadelphia	NHL	24	5	5	10	46
1987-88	Philadelphia	NHL	7	0	1	1	16
1988-89	Philadelphia	NHL	19	4	5	9	28
1989-90	Philadelphia	NHL	-	-	-	-	-
1990-91	Philadelphia	NHL	-	-	-	-	-
1991-92	Edmonton	NHL	16	2	1	3	29
1992-93	Edmonton	NHL	-	-	-	-	-
1993-94	Florida	NHL	-	-	-	-	-
1994-95	Florida	NHL	-	-	-	-	-
1995-96	Florida	NHL	22	3	6	9	44
1996-97	Florida	NHL	5	0	2	2	4
1997-98	Florida	NHL	-	-	-	-	-
1999-00	Florida	NHL	4	0	1	1	2
2000-01	St. Louis	NHL	15	3	3	6	17
2001-02	St. Louis	NHL	10	7	3	10	18

NHL Totals

Regular Season					Playoffs				
GP	G	A	PTS	PIM	GP	G	A	PTS	PIM
1143	300	382	682	2109	122	24	27	51	204

BERNIE PARENT

REGULAR SEASON

Year	Team	League	GP	W	L	T	SO	AVG
1965-66	Boston	NHL	39	11	20	3	1	3.69
1966-67	Boston	NHL	18	3	11	2	0	3.64
1967-68	Philadelphia	NHL	38	16	17	5	4	2.48
1968-69	Philadelphia	NHL	58	17	23	16	1	2.69
1969-70	Philadelphia	NHL	62	13	29	20	3	2.79
1970-71	Philadelphia	NHL	30	9	12	6	2	2.76
	Toronto	NHL	18	7	7	3	1	2.65
1971-72	Toronto	NHL	47	17	8	9	3	2.56
1972-73	Philadelphia	WHA	63	33	28	0	2	3.61
1973-74	Philadelphia	NHL	73	47	13	12	12	1.89
1974-75	Philadelphia	NHL	68	44	14	10	12	2.03
1975-76	Philadelphia	NHL	11	6	2	3	0	2.34
1976-77	Philadelphia	NHL	61	35	13	12	5	2.71
1977-78	Philadelphia	NHL	49	29	6	13	7	2.22
1978-79	Philadelphia	NHL	36	16	12	7	4	2.70

PLAYOFFS

Year	Team	League	GP	W	L	SO	AVG
1965-66	Boston	NHL	-	-	-	-	-
1966-67	Boston	NHL	-	-	-	-	-
1967-68	Philadelphia	NHL	5	2	3	0	1.35
1968-69	Philadelphia	NHL	3	0	3	0	4.00
1969-70	Philadelphia	NHL	-	-	-	-	-
1970-71	Philadelphia	NHL	-	-	-	-	-
	Toronto	NHL	4	2	2	0	2.30
1971-72	Toronto	NHL	4	1	3	0	3.21
1972-73	Philadelphia	WHA	1	0	1	0	2.57
1973-74	Philadelphia	NHL	17	12	5	2	2.02
1974-75	Philadelphia	NHL	15	10	5	4	1.89
1975-76	Philadelphia	NHL	8	4	4	0	3.38
1976-77	Philadelphia	NHL	3	0	3	0	3.90
1977-78	Philadelphia	NHL	12	7	5	0	2.74
1978-79	Philadelphia	NHL	-	-	-	-	-

NHL Totals

Regular Season						Playoffs					
GP	W	L	T	SO	AVG	GP	W	L	T	SO	AVG
608	270	197	121	55	2.55	71	38	33	0	6	2.43

WHA Totals

Regular Season						Playoffs					
GP	W	L	T	SO	AVG	GP	W	L	SO	AVG	
63	33	28	0	2	3.61	1	0	1	0	2.57	

PETE PEETERS

REGULAR SEASON

Year	Team	League	GP	W	L	T	SO	AVG
1975-76	Medicine Hat	WHL	37	-	-	-	0	4.25
1976-77	Medicine Hat	WHL	62	-	-	-	1	4.07
1977-78	Milwaukee	IHL	32	-	-	-	1	3.29
	Maine	AHL	17	-	-	-	1	2.80
1978-79	Philadelphia	NHL	5	1	2	1	0	3.43
	Maine	AHL	35	25	6	3	2	2.90
1979-80	Philadelphia	NHL	40	29	5	5	1	2.73
1980-81	Philadelphia	NHL	40	22	12	5	2	2.96
1981-82	Philadelphia	NHL	44	23	18	3	0	3.71
1982-83	Boston	NHL	62	40	11	9	8	2.36
1983-84	Boston	NHL	50	29	16	2	0	3.16
1984-85	Boston	NHL	51	19	26	4	1	3.47
1985-86	Boston	NHL	8	3	4	1	0	3.84
	Washington	NHL	34	19	11	3	1	3.35
1986-87	Washington	NHL	37	17	11	4	0	3.21
	Binghampton	AHL	4	3	0	0	1	0.98
1987-88	Washington	NHL	35	14	12	5	2	2.78
1988-89	Washington	NHL	33	20	7	3	4	2.85
1989-90	Philadelphia	NHL	24	1	13	5	1	3.79
1990-91	Philadelphia	NHL	26	9	7	1	1	2.88
	Hershey	AHL	2	0	1	0	0	6.29

PLAYOFFS

Year	Team	League	GP	W	L	SO	AVG
1975-76	Medicine Hat	WHL	-	-	-	-	-
1976-77	Medicine Hat	WHL	4	-	-	1	5.00
1977-78	Milwaukee	IHL	-	-	-	-	-
	Maine	AHL	11	-	-	1	2.67
1978-79	Philadelphia	NHL	-	-	-	-	-
	Maine	AHL	6	5	0	0	2.74
1979-80	Philadelphia	NHL	13	8	5	1	2.78
1980-81	Philadelphia	NHL	3	2	1	0	4.00
1981-82	Philadelphia	NHL	4	1	2	0	4.64
1982-83	Boston	NHL	17	9	8	1	3.57
1983-84	Boston	NHL	3	0	3	0	3.33
1984-85	Boston	NHL	1	0	1	0	4.00
1985-86	Boston	NHL	-	-	-	-	-
	Washington	NHL	9	5	4	0	2.65
1986-87	Washington	NHL	3	1	2	0	3.00
	Binghampton	AHL	-	-	-	-	-
1987-88	Washington	NHL	12	7	5	0	3.12
1988-89	Washington	NHL	6	2	4	0	4.01
1989-90	Philadelphia	NHL	-	-	-	-	-
1990-91	Philadelphia	NHL	-	-	-	-	-
	Hershey	AHL	-	-	-	-	-

NHL Totals

Regular Season						Playoffs				
GP	W	L	T	SO	AVG	GP	W	L	SO	AVG
489	579	488	84	54	3.08	71	35	35	2	3.31

DAVE POULIN

REGULAR SEASON

Year	Team	League	GP	G	A	PTS	PIM
1978-79	Notre Dame	WCHA	37	28	31	59	32
1979-80	Notre Dame	WCHA	24	19	24	43	46
1980-81	Notre Dame	WCHA	35	13	22	35	53
1981-82	Notre Dame	CCHA	39	29	30	59	44
1982-83	Rogle	Sweden	32	35	27	62	64
	Philadelphia	NHL	2	2	0	2	2
	Maine	AHL	16	7	9	16	2
1983-84	Philadelphia	NHL	73	31	45	76	47
1984-85	Philadelphia	NHL	73	30	44	74	59
1985-86	Philadelphia	NHL	79	27	42	69	49
1986-87	Philadelphia	NHL	75	25	45	70	53
1987-88	Philadelphia	NHL	68	19	32	51	32
1988-89	Philadelphia	NHL	69	18	17	35	49
1989-90	Philadelphia	NHL	28	9	8	17	12
	Boston	NHL	32	6	19	25	12
1990-91	Boston	NHL	31	8	12	20	25
1991-92	Boston	NHL	18	4	4	8	18
1992-93	Boston	NHL	84	16	33	49	62
1993-94	Washington	NHL	63	6	19	25	52
1994-95	Washington	NHL	29	4	5	9	10

PLAYOFFS

Year	Team	League	GP	G	A	PTS	PIM
1978-79	Notre Dame	WCHA	-	-	-	-	-
1979-80	Notre Dame	WCHA	-	-	-	-	-
1980-81	Notre Dame	WCHA	-	-	-	-	-
1981-82	Notre Dame	CCHA	-	-	-	-	-
1982-83	Rogle	Sweden	-	-	-	-	-
	Philadelphia	NHL	3	1	3	4	9
	Maine	AHL	-	-	-	-	-
1983-84	Philadelphia	NHL	3	0	0	0	2
1984-85	Philadelphia	NHL	11	3	5	8	6
1985-86	Philadelphia	NHL	5	2	0	2	2
1986-87	Philadelphia	NHL	15	3	3	6	14
1987-88	Philadelphia	NHL	7	2	6	8	4
1988-89	Philadelphia	NHL	19	6	5	11	16
1989-90	Philadelphia	NHL	-	-	-	-	-
	Boston	NHL	18	8	5	13	8
1990-91	Boston	NHL	16	0	9	9	20
1991-92	Boston	NHL	15	3	3	6	22
1992-93	Boston	NHL	4	1	1	2	10
1993-94	Washington	NHL	11	2	2	4	19
1994-95	Washington	NHL	2	0	0	0	0

NHL Totals

Regular Season					Playoffs				
GP	G	A	PTS	PIM	GP	G	A	PTS	PIM
724	205	325	530	482	129	31	42	73	132

KEITH PRIMEAU

REGULAR SEASON

Year	TM	League	GP	G	A	PTS	PIM
1987-88	Hamilton	OHL	47	6	6	12	69
1988-89	Niagara-Falls	OHL	48	20	35	55	56
1989-90	Niagara-Falls	OHL	65	57	70	127	97
1990-91	Adirondack	AHL	6	3	5	8	8
1990-91	Detroit	NHL	58	3	12	15	106
1991-92	Adirondack	AHL	42	21	24	45	89
1991-92	Detroit	NHL	35	6	10	16	83
1992-93	Detroit	NHL	73	15	17	32	152
1993-94	Detroit	NHL	78	31	42	73	173
1994-95	Detroit	NHL	45	15	27	42	99
1995-96	Detroit	NHL	74	27	25	52	168
1996-97	Hartford	NHL	75	26	25	51	161
1997-98	Carolina	NHL	81	26	37	63	110
1998-99	Carolina	NHL	78	30	32	62	75
1999-00	Philadelphia	NHL	23	7	10	17	31
2000-01	Philadelphia	NHL	71	34	39	73	76
2001-02	Philadelphia	NHL	75	19	29	48	128

PLAYOFFS

Year	TM	League	GP	G	A	PTS	PIM
1987-88	Hamilton	OHL	11	0	2	2	2
1988-89	Niagara-Falls	OHL	17	9	6	15	12
1989-90	Niagara-Falls	OHL	16	16	17	33	49
1990-91	Detroit	NHL	5	1	1	2	25
1991-92	Adirondack	AHL	9	1	7	8	27
1991-92	Detroit	NHL	11	0	0	0	14
1992-93	Detroit	NHL	7	0	2	2	26
1993-94	Detroit	NHL	7	0	2	2	6
1994-95	Detroit	NHL	17	4	5	9	45
1995-96	Detroit	NHL	17	1	4	5	28
1998-99	Carolina	NHL	6	0	3	3	6
1999-00	Philadelphia	NHL	18	2	11	13	13
2000-01	Philadelphia	NHL	4	0	3	3	8
2001-02	Philadelphia	NHL	5	0	0	0	6

NHL Totals

Regular Season					*Playoffs*				
GP	G	A	PTS	PIM	GP	G	A	PTS	PIM
766	239	305	544	1362	97	8	31	39	177

BRIAN PROPP

REGULAR SEASON

Year	TM	League	GP	G	A	PTS	PIM
1976-77	Brandon	WHL	72	55	80	135	47
1977-78	Brandon	WHL	70	70	112	182	200
1978-79	Brandon	WHL	71	94	100	194	127
1979-80	Philadelphia	NHL	80	34	41	75	54
1980-81	Philadelphia	NHL	79	26	40	66	110
1981-82	Philadelphia	NHL	80	44	47	91	117
1982-83	Philadelphia	NHL	80	40	42	82	72
1983-84	Philadelphia	NHL	79	39	53	92	37
1984-85	Philadelphia	NHL	76	43	53	96	43
1985-86	Philadelphia	NHL	72	40	57	97	47
1986-87	Philadelphia	NHL	53	31	36	67	45
1987-88	Philadelphia	NHL	74	27	49	76	76
1988-89	Philadelphia	NHL	77	32	46	78	37
1989-90	Philadelphia	NHL	40	13	15	28	108
	Boston	NHL	14	3	9	12	45
1990-91	Minnesota	NHL	9	26	47	73	58
1991-92	Minnesota	NHL	51	12	23	35	49
1992-93	Minnesota	NHL	17	3	3	6	0
1993-94	Hartford	NHL	65	12	17	29	44

PLAYOFFS

Year	TM	League	GP	G	A	PTS	PIM
1976-77	Brandon	WHL	16	14	12	26	5
1977-78	Brandon	WHL	8	7	6	13	12
1978-79	Brandon	WHL	22	15	23	38	40
1979-80	Philadelphia	NHL	19	5	10	15	29
1980-81	Philadelphia	NHL	12	6	6	12	32
1981-82	Philadelphia	NHL	4	2	2	4	6
1982-83	Philadelphia	NHL	3	1	2	3	8
1983-84	Philadelphia	NHL	3	0	1	1	6
1984-85	Philadelphia	NHL	19	8	10	18	6
1985-86	Philadelphia	NHL	5	0	2	2	4
1986-87	Philadelphia	NHL	26	12	16	28	10
1987-88	Philadelphia	NHL	7	4	2	6	8
1988-89	Philadelphia	NHL	18	14	9	23	14
1989-90	Philadelphia	NHL	-	-	-	-	-
	Boston	NHL	20	4	9	13	2
1990-91	Minnesota	NHL	23	8	15	23	28
1991-92	Minnesota	NHL	1	0	0	0	0
1992-93	Minnesota NHL		-	-	-	-	-
1993-94	Hartford	NHL	-	-	-	-	-

NHL Totals

Regular Season					Playoffs				
GP	G	A	PTS	PIM	GP	G	A	PTS	PIM
1016	425	579	1004	830	160	64	84	148	151

MARK RECCHI

REGULAR SEASON

Year	Team	League	GP	G	A	PTS	PIM
1985-86	N. Westminster	WHL	72	21	40	61	55
1986-87	Kamloops	WHL	40	26	50	76	63
1987-88	Kamloops	WHL	62	61	93	154	75
1988-89	Pittsburgh	NHL	15	1	1	2	0
	Muskegon	IHL	63	50	49	99	86
1989-90	Pittsburgh	NHL	74	30	37	67	44
	Muskegon	IHL	4	7	4	11	2
1990-91	Pittsburgh	NHL	78	40	73	113	48
1991-92	Pittsburgh	NHL	58	33	37	70	78
	Philadelphia	NHL	22	10	17	27	18
1992-93	Philadelphia	NHL	84	53	70	123	95
1993-94	Philadelphia	NHL	84	40	67	107	46
1994-95	Philadelphia	NHL	10	2	3	5	12
	Montreal	NHL	39	14	29	43	16
1995-96	Montreal	NHL	82	28	50	78	69
1996-97	Montreal	NHL	82	34	46	80	58
1997-98	Montreal	NHL	82	32	42	74	51
1998-99	Montreal	NHL	61	12	35	47	28
	Philadelphia	NHL	10	4	2	6	6
1999-00	Philadelphia	NHL	82	28	63	91	50
2000-01	Philadelphia	NHL	69	27	50	77	33
2001-02	Philadelphia	NHL	80	22	42	64	46

PLAYOFFS

Year	Team	League	GP	G	A	PTS	PIM
1985-86	N. Westminster	WHL	-	-	-	-	-
1986-87	Kamloops	WHL	13	3	16	19	17
1987-88	Kamloops	WHL	17	10	21	31	18
1988-89	Pittsburgh	NHL	-	-	-	-	-
	Muskegon	IHL	14	7	14	21	28
1989-90	Pittsburgh	NHL	-	-	-	-	-
	Muskegon	IHL	-	-	-	-	-
1990-91	Pittsburgh	NHL	24	10	24	34	33
1991-92	Pittsburgh	NHL	-	-	-	-	-
	Philadelphia	NHL	-	-	-	-	-
1992-93	Philadelphia	NHL	-	-	-	-	-
1993-94	Philadelphia	NHL	-	-	-	-	-
1994-95	Philadelphia	NHL	-	-	-	-	-
	Montreal	NHL	-	-	-	-	-
1995-96	Montreal	NHL	6	3	3	6	0
1996-97	Montreal	NHL	5	4	2	6	2
1997-98	Montreal	NHL	10	4	8	12	6
1998-99	Philadelphia	NHL	6	0	1	1	2
1999-00	Philadelphia	NHL	18	6	12	18	6
2000-01	Philadelphia	NHL	6	2	2	4	2
2001-02	Philadelphia	NHL	4	0	0	0	2

NHL Totals

Regular Season					*Playoffs*				
GP	G	A	PTS	PIM	GP	G	A	PTS	PIM
1012	410	664	1074	698	79	29	52	81	53

JEREMY ROENICK

REGULAR SEASON

Year	Team	League	GP	G	A	PTS	PIM
1988-89	Hull	QMJHL	28	34	36	70	14
1988-89	Chicago	NHL	20	9	9	18	4
1989-90	Chicago	NHL	78	26	40	66	54
1990-91	Chicago	NHL	79	41	53	94	80
1991-92	Chicago	NHL	80	53	50	103	98
1992-93	Chicago	NHL	84	50	57	107	86
1993-94	Chicago	NHL	84	46	61	107	125
1994-95	Cologne	DEL	3	3	1	4	2
	Chicago	NHL	33	10	24	34	14
1995-96	Chicago	NHL	66	32	35	67	109
1996-97	Phoenix	NHL	72	29	40	69	115
1997-98	Phoenix	NHL	79	24	32	56	103
1998-99	Phoenix	NHL	78	24	48	72	130
1999-00	Phoenix	NHL	75	34	44	78	102
2000-01	Phoenix	NHL	80	30	46	76	114
2001-02	Philadelphia	NHL	75	21	46	67	74

PLAYOFFS

Year	Team	League	GP	G	A	PTS	PIM
1988-89	Hull	QMJHL	9	7	12	19	6
1988-89	Chicago	NHL	10	1	3	4	7
1989-90	Chicago	NHL	20	11	7	18	8
1990-91	Chicago	NHL	6	3	5	8	4
1991-92	Chicago	NHL	18	12	10	22	12
1992-93	Chicago	NHL	4	1	2	3	2
1993-94	Chicago	NHL	6	1	6	7	2
1994-95	Chicago	NHL	8	1	2	3	16
1995-96	Chicago	NHL	10	5	7	12	2
1996-97	Phoenix	NHL	6	2	4	6	4
1997-98	Phoenix	NHL	6	5	3	8	4
1998-99	Phoenix	NHL	1	0	0	0	0
1999-00	Phoenix	NHL	5	2	2	4	10
2001-02	Philadelphia	NHL	5	0	0	0	14

NHL Totals

Regular Season					*Playoffs*				
GP	G	A	PTS	PIM	GP	G	A	PTS	PIM
983	429	585	1014	1208	105	44	51	95	85

DON SALESKI

REGULAR SEASON

Year	Team	League	GP	G	A	PTS	PIM
1970-71	Quebec	AHL	72	9	7	16	51
1971-72	Philadelphia	NHL	1	0	0	0	0
	Richmond	AHL	73	22	35	57	111
1972-73	Philadelphia	NHL	78	12	9	21	205
1973-74	Philadelphia	NHL	77	15	25	40	131
1974-75	Philadelphia	NHL	63	10	18	28	107
1975-76	Philadelphia	NHL	78	21	26	47	68
1976-77	Philadelphia	NHL	74	22	16	38	33
1977-78	Philadelphia	NHL	70	27	18	45	44
1978-79	Philadelphia	NHL	35	11	5	16	14
	Colorado	NHL	16	2	0	2	4
1979-80	Colorado	NHL	51	8	8	16	23
	Fort Worth	CHL	19	9	6	15	18

PLAYOFFS

Year	Team	League	GP	G	A	PTS	PIM
1970-71	Quebec	AHL	1	0	0	0	0
1971-72	Philadelphia	NHL	-	-	-	-	-
	Richmond	AHL	-	-	-	-	-
1972-73	Philadelphia	NHL	11	1	2	3	4
1973-74	Philadelphia	NHL	17	2	7	9	24
1974-75	Philadelphia	NHL	17	2	3	5	25
1975-76	Philadelphia	NHL	16	6	5	11	47
1976-77	Philadelphia	NHL	10	0	0	0	12
1977-78	Philadelphia	NHL	11	2	0	2	19
1978-79	Philadelphia	NHL	-	-	-	-	-
	Colorado	NHL	-	-	-	-	-
1979-80	Colorado	NHL	-	-	-	-	-
	Fort Worth	CHL	14	5	6	11	20

NHL Totals

Regular Season					Playoffs				
GP	G	A	PTS	PIM	GP	G	A	PTS	PIM
543	128	125	253	629	82	13	17	30	131

KJELL SAMUELSSON

REGULAR SEASON

Year	Team	League	GP	G	A	PTS	PIM
1977-78	Tyngrsyd	Swe. 2	20	3	0	3	41
1978-79	Tyngrsyd	Swe. 2	24	3	4	7	67
1979-80	Tyngrsyd	Swe. 2	26	5	4	9	45
1980-81	Tyngrsyd	Swe. 2	35	6	7	13	61
1981-82	Tyngrsyd	Swe. 2	33	11	14	25	68
1982-83	Tyngrsyd	Swe. 2	32	11	6	17	57
1983-84	Leksand	Swe.	36	6	6	12	59
1984-85	Leksand	Swe.	35	9	5	14	34
1985-86	N.Y. Rangers	NHL	9	0	0	0	10
	New Haven	AHL	56	6	21	27	87
1986-87	N.Y. Rangers	NHL	30	2	6	8	50
	Philadelphia	NHL	46	1	6	7	86
1987-88	Philadelphia	NHL	74	6	24	30	184
1988-89	Philadelphia	NHL	69	3	14	17	140
1989-90	Philadelphia	NHL	66	5	17	22	91
1990-91	Philadelphia	NHL	78	9	19	28	82
1991-92	Philadelphia	NHL	54	4	9	13	76
	Pittsburgh	NHL	20	1	2	3	34
1992-93	Pittsburgh	NHL	63	3	6	9	106
1993-94	Pittsburgh	NHL	59	5	8	13	118
1994-95	Pittsburgh	NHL	41	1	6	7	54
1995-96	Philadelphia	NHL	75	3	11	14	81
1996-97	Philadelphia	NHL	34	4	3	7	47
1997-98	Philadelphia	NHL	48	0	3	3	28
1998-99	Tampa Bay	NHL	46	1	4	5	38

PLAYOFFS

Year	Team	League	GP	G	A	PTS	PIM
1977-78	Tyngrsyd	Swe. 2	-	-	-	-	-
1978-79	Tyngrsyd	Swe. 2	-	-	-	-	-
1979-80	Tyngrsyd	Swe. 2	-	-	-	-	-
1980-81	Tyngrsyd	Swe. 2	2	0	1	1	14
1981-82	Tyngrsyd	Swe. 2	3	0	2	2	2
1982-83	Tyngrsyd	Swe. 2	-	-	-	-	-
1983-84	Leksand	Swe.	-	-	-	-	-
1984-85	Leksand	Swe.	-	-	-	-	-
1985-86	N.Y. Rangers	NHL	9	0	1	1	8
	New Haven	AHL	3	0	0	0	10
1986-87	N.Y. Rangers	NHL	-	-	-	-	-
	Philadelphia	NHL	26	0	4	4	25
1987-88	Philadelphia	NHL	7	2	5	7	23
1988-89	Philadelphia	NHL	19	1	3	4	24
1989-90	Philadelphia	NHL	-	-	-	-	-
1990-91	Philadelphia	NHL	-	-	-	-	-
1991-92	Philadelphia	NHL	-	-	-	-	-
	Pittsburgh	NHL	15	0	3	3	12
1992-93	Pittsburgh	NHL	12	0	3	3	2
1993-94	Pittsburgh	NHL	6	0	0	0	26
1994-95	Pittsburgh	NHL	11	0	1	1	32
1995-96	Philadelphia	NHL	12	1	0	1	24
1996-97	Philadelphia	NHL	5	0	0	0	2
1997-98	Philadelphia	NHL	1	0	0	0	0

NHL Totals

Regular Season					Playoffs				
GP	G	A	PTS	PIM	GP	G	A	PTS	PIM
813	48	138	186	1225	123	4	20	24	178

DAVE "THE HAMMER" SCHULTZ

REGULAR SEASON

Year	Team	League	GP	G	A	PTS	PIM
1969-70	Quebec	AHL	8	0	0	0	13
1970-71	Quebec	AHL	71	14	23	37	382
1971-72	Philadelphia	NHL	1	0	0	0	0
	Richmond	AHL	76	18	28	46	392
1972-73	Philadelphia	NHL	76	9	12	21	259
1973-74	Philadelphia	NHL	73	20	16	36	348
1974-75	Philadelphia	NHL	76	9	17	26	472
1975-76	Philadelphia	NHL	71	13	19	32	307
1976-77	Los Angeles	NHL	76	10	20	30	232
1977-78	Los Angeles	NHL	8	2	0	2	27
	Pittsburgh	NHL	66	9	25	34	378
1978-79	Pittsburgh	NHL	47	4	9	13	157
	Buffalo	NHL	28	2	3	5	86
1979-80	Buffalo	NHL	13	1	0	1	28
	Rochester	AHL	56	10	14	24	248

PLAYOFFS

Year	Team	League	GP	G	A	PTS	PIM
1969-70	Quebec	AHL	-	-	-	-	-
1970-71	Quebec	AHL	1	0	0	0	15
1971-72	Philadelphia	NHL	-	-	-	-	-
	Richmond	AHL	-	-	-	-	-
1972-73	Philadelphia	NHL	11	1	0	1	51
1973-74	Philadelphia	NHL	17	2	4	6	139
1974-75	Philadelphia	NHL	17	2	3	5	83
1975-76	Philadelphia	NHL	16	2	2	4	90
1976-77	Los Angeles	NHL	9	1	1	2	45
1977-78	Los Angeles	NHL	-	-	-	-	-
	Pittsburgh	NHL	-	-	-	-	-
1978-79	Pittsburgh	NHL	-	-	-	-	-
	Buffalo	NHL	3	0	2	2	4
1979-80	Buffalo	NHL	-	-	-	-	-
	Rochester	AHL	4	1	0	1	12

NHL Totals

Regular Season					Playoffs				
GP	G	A	PTS	PIM	GP	G	A	PTS	PIM
535	79	121	200	2294	73	8	12	20	412

ILKKA SINISALO

REGULAR SEASON

Year	Team	League	GP	G	A	PTS	PIM
1977-78	HIFK	Fin.	36	9	3	12	18
1978-79	HIFK	Fin.	30	6	4	10	16
1979-80	HIFK	Fin.	35	16	9	25	16
1980-81	HIFK	Fin.	36	27	17	44	14
1981-82	Philadelphia	NHL	66	15	22	37	22
1982-83	Philadelphia	NHL	61	21	29	50	16
1983-84	Philadelphia	NHL	73	29	17	46	29
1984-85	Philadelphia	NHL	70	36	37	73	16
1985-86	Philadelphia	NHL	74	39	37	76	31
1986-87	Philadelphia	NHL	42	10	21	31	8
1987-88	Philadelphia	NHL	68	25	17	42	30
1988-89	Philadelphia	NHL	13	1	6	7	2
1989-90	Philadelphia	NHL	59	23	23	46	26
1990-91	Minnesota	NHL	46	5	12	17	24
	Los Angeles	NHL	7	0	0	0	2
1991-92	Los Angeles	NHL	3	0	1	1	2
	Phoenix	IHL	42	19	21	40	32

PLAYOFFS

Year	Team	League	GP	G	A	PTS	PIM
1977-78	HIFK	Fin.	-	-	-	-	-
1978-79	HIFK	Fin.	6	0	5	5	25
1979-80	HIFK	Fin.	7	1	3	4	12
1980-81	HIFK	Fin.	6	5	3	8	4
1981-82	Philadelphia	NHL	4	0	2	2	0
1982-83	Philadelphia	NHL	3	1	1	2	0
1983-84	Philadelphia	NHL	2	2	0	2	0
1984-85	Philadelphia	NHL	19	6	1	7	0
1985-86	Philadelphia	NHL	5	2	2	4	2
1986-87	Philadelphia	NHL	18	5	1	6	4
1987-88	Philadelphia	NHL	7	4	2	6	0
1988-89	Philadelphia	NHL	8	1	1	2	0
1989-90	Philadelphia	NHL	-	-	-	-	-
1990-91	Minnesota	NHL	-	-	-	-	-
	Los Angeles	NHL	2	0	1	1	0
1991-92	Los Angeles	NHL	-	-	-	-	-
	Phoenix	IHL	-	-	-	-	-

NHL Totals

Regular Season					*Playoffs*				
GP	G	A	PTS	PIM	GP	G	A	PTS	PIM
582	204	222	426	208	68	21	11	32	6

DARRYL SITTLER

REGULAR SEASON

Year	Team	League	GP	G	A	PTS	PIM
1968-69	London	OHA	53	34	65	99	90
1969-70	London	OHA	54	42	48	90	126
1970-71	Toronto	NHL	49	10	8	18	37
1971-72	Toronto	NHL	74	15	17	32	44
1972-73	Toronto	NHL	78	29	48	77	69
1973-74	Toronto	NHL	78	38	46	84	55
1974-75	Toronto	NHL	72	36	44	80	47
1975-76	Toronto	NHL	79	41	59	100	90
1976-77	Toronto	NHL	73	38	52	90	89
1977-78	Toronto	NHL	80	45	72	117	100
1978-79	Toronto	NHL	70	36	51	87	69
1979-80	Toronto	NHL	73	40	57	97	62
1980-81	Toronto	NHL	80	43	53	96	77
1981-82	Toronto	NHL	38	18	20	38	24
	Philadelphia	NHL	35	14	18	32	50
1982-83	Philadelphia	NHL	80	43	40	83	60
1983-84	Philadelphia	NHL	76	27	36	63	38
1984-85	Detroit	NHL	61	11	16	27	37

PLAYOFFS

Year	Team	League	GP	G	A	PTS	PIM
1968-69	London	OHA	-	-	-	-	-
1969-70	London	OHA	-	-	-	-	-
1970-71	Toronto	NHL	6	2	1	3	31
1971-72	Toronto	NHL	3	0	0	0	2
1972-73	Toronto	NHL	-	-	-	-	-
1973-74	Toronto	NHL	4	2	1	3	6
1974-75	Toronto	NHL	7	2	1	3	15
1975-76	Toronto	NHL	10	5	7	12	19
1976-77	Toronto	NHL	9	5	16	21	4
1977-78	Toronto	NHL	13	3	8	11	12
1978-79	Toronto	NHL	6	5	4	9	17
1979-80	Toronto	NHL	3	1	2	3	10
1980-81	Toronto	NHL	3	0	0	0	4
1981-82	Toronto	NHL	-	-	-	-	-
	Philadelphia	NHL	4	3	1	4	6
1982-83	Philadelphia	NHL	3	1	0	1	4
1983-84	Philadelphia	NHL	3	0	2	2	7
1984-85	Detroit	NHL	2	0	2	2	0

NHL Totals

Regular Season					*Playoffs*				
GP	G	A	PTS	PIM	GP	G	A	PTS	PIM
1096	484	637	1121	948	76	29	45	74	137

RON SUTTER

REGULAR SEASON

Year	Team	League	GP	G	A	PTS	PIM
1980-81	Lethbridge	WHL	72	13	32	45	152
1981-82	Lethbridge	WHL	59	38	54	92	207
1982-83	Philadelphia	NHL	10	1	1	2	9
	Lethbridge	WHL	58	35	48	83	98
1983-84	Philadelphia	NHL	79	19	32	51	101
1984-85	Philadelphia	NHL	73	16	29	45	94
1985-86	Philadelphia	NHL	75	18	42	60	159
1986-87	Philadelphia	NHL	39	10	17	27	69
1987-88	Philadelphia	NHL	69	8	25	33	146
1988-89	Philadelphia	NHL	55	26	22	48	80
1989-90	Philadelphia	NHL	75	22	26	48	104
1990-91	Philadelphia	NHL	80	17	28	45	92
1991-92	St. Louis	NHL	68	19	27	46	91
1992-93	St. Louis	NHL	59	12	15	27	99
1993-94	St. Louis	NHL	36	6	12	18	46
	Quebec	NHL	37	9	13	22	44
1994-95	N.Y. Islanders	NHL	27	1	4	5	21
1995-96	Phoenix	IHL	25	6	13	19	28
	Boston	NHL	18	5	7	12	24
1996-97	San Jose	NHL	78	5	7	12	65
1997-98	San Jose	NHL	56	2	7	9	22
1998-99	San Jose	NHL	59	3	6	9	40
1999-00	San Jose	NHL	78	5	6	11	34

PLAYOFFS

Year	Team	League	GP	G	A	PTS	PIM
1980-81	Lethbridge	WHL	9	2	5	7	29
1981-82	Lethbridge	WHL	12	6	5	11	28
1982-83	Philadelphia	NHL	-	-	-	-	-
	Lethbridge	WHL	20	22	19	41	45
1983-84	Philadelphia	NHL	3	0	0	0	22
1984-85	Philadelphia	NHL	19	4	8	12	28
1985-86	Philadelphia	NHL	5	0	2	2	10
1986-87	Philadelphia	NHL	16	1	7	8	12
1987-88	Philadelphia	NHL	7	0	1	1	26
1988-89	Philadelphia	NHL	19	1	9	10	51
1989-90	Philadelphia	NHL	-	-	-	-	-
1990-91	Philadelphia	NHL	-	-	-	-	-
1991-92	St. Louis	NHL	6	1	3	4	8
1992-93	St. Louis	NHL	-	-	-	-	-
1993-94	St. Louis	NHL	-	-	-	-	-
	Quebec	NHL	-	-	-	-	-
1994-95	N.Y. Islanders	NHL	-	-	-	-	-
1995-96	Phoenix	IHL	-	-	-	-	-
	Boston	NHL	5	0	0	0	8
1996-97	San Jose	NHL	-	-	-	-	-
1997-98	San Jose	NHL	6	1	0	1	14
1998-99	San Jose	NHL	6	0	0	0	4
1999-00	San Jose	NHL	12	0	2	2	10

NHL Totals

Regular Season					Playoffs				
GP	G	A	PTS	PIM	GP	G	A	PTS	PIM
1072	204	326	530	1340	104	8	32	40	193

RICK TOCCHET

REGULAR SEASON

Year	Team	League	GP	G	A	PTS	PIM
1981-82	Sault Ste. Marie	OHL	59	7	15	22	184
1982-83	Sault Ste. Marie	OHL	66	32	34	66	146
1983-84	Sault Ste. Marie	OHL	64	44	64	108	209
1984-85	Philadelphia	NHL	75	14	25	39	181
1985-86	Philadelphia	NHL	69	14	21	35	284
1986-87	Philadelphia	NHL	69	21	26	47	288
1987-88	Philadelphia	NHL	65	31	33	64	301
1988-89	Philadelphia	NHL	66	45	36	81	183
1989-90	Philadelphia	NHL	75	37	59	96	196
1990-91	Philadelphia	NHL	70	40	31	71	150
1991-92	Philadelphia	NHL	42	13	16	29	102
	Pittsburgh	NHL	19	14	16	30	49
1992-93	Pittsburgh	NHL	80	48	61	109	252
1993-94	Pittsburgh	NHL	51	14	26	40	134
1994-95	Los Angeles	NHL	36	18	17	35	70
1995-96	Los Angeles	NHL	44	13	23	36	117
	Boston	NHL	27	16	8	24	64
1996-97	Boston	NHL	40	16	14	30	67
	Washington	NHL	5	5	10	10	31
1997-98	Phoenix	NHL	68	26	19	45	157
1998-99	Phoenix	NHL	81	26	30	56	147
1999-00	Phoenix	NHL	64	12	17	29	67
	Philadelphia	NHL	16	3	3	6	23
2000-01	Philadelphia	NHL	60	14	22	36	83
2001-02	Philadelphia	NHL	14	0	2	2	28

PLAYOFFS

Year	Team	League	GP	G	A	PTS	PIM
1981-82	Sault Ste. Marie	OHL	11	1	1	2	28
1982-83	Sault Ste. Marie	OHL	16	4	13	17	67
1983-84	Sault Ste. Marie	OHL	16	22	14	36	41
1984-85	Philadelphia	NHL	19	3	4	7	72
1985-86	Philadelphia	NHL	5	1	2	3	26
1986-87	Philadelphia	NHL	26	11	10	21	72
1987-88	Philadelphia	NHL	5	1	4	5	55
1988-89	Philadelphia	NHL	16	6	6	12	69
1989-90	Philadelphia	NHL	-	-	-	-	-
1990-91	Philadelphia	NHL	-	-	-	-	-
1991-92	Philadelphia	NHL	-	-	-	-	-
	Pittsburgh	NHL	14	6	13	19	24
1992-93	Pittsburgh	NHL	12	7	6	13	24
1993-94	Pittsburgh	NHL	6	2	3	5	20
1994-95	Los Angeles	NHL	-	-	-	-	-
1995-96	Los Angeles	NHL	-	-	-	-	-
	Boston	NHL	5	4	0	4	21
1996-97	Boston	NHL	-	-	-	-	-
	Washington	NHL	-	-	-	-	-
1997-98	Phoenix	NHL	6	6	2	8	25
1998-99	Phoenix	NHL	7	0	3	3	8
1999-00	Philadelphia	NHL	18	5	6	11	49
2000-01	Philadelphia	NHL	6	0	1	1	6

NHL Totals

Regular Season					Playoffs				
GP	G	A	PTS	PIM	GP	G	A	PTS	PIM
1144	440	512	952	2972	145	52	60	112	471

ED VAN IMPE

REGULAR SEASON

Year	Team	League	GP	G	A	PTS	PIM
1960-61	Calgary	WHL	66	4	15	19	123
1961-62	Buffalo	AHL	70	0	19	19	172
1962-63	Buffalo	AHL	65	3	12	15	196
1963-64	Buffalo	AHL	70	4	22	26	193
1964-65	Buffalo	AHL	72	5	6	11	197
1965-66	Buffalo	AHL	70	9	28	37	153
1966-67	Chicago	NHL	61	8	11	19	111
1967-68	Philadelphia	NHL	67	4	13	17	141
1968-69	Philadelphia	NHL	68	7	12	19	112
1969-70	Philadelphia	NHL	65	0	10	10	117
1970-71	Philadelphia	NHL	77	0	11	11	80
1971-72	Philadelphia	NHL	73	4	9	13	78
1972-73	Philadelphia	NHL	72	1	11	12	76
1973-74	Philadelphia	NHL	77	2	16	18	119
1974-75	Philadelphia	NHL	78	1	17	18	109
1975-76	Philadelphia	NHL	40	0	8	8	60
	Pittsburgh	NHL	12	0	5	5	16
1976-77	Pittsburgh	NHL	10	0	3	3	6

PLAYOFFS

Year	Team	League	GP	G	A	PTS	PIM
1960-61	Calgary	WHL	5	0	2	2	16
1961-62	Buffalo	AHL	11	0	1	1	23
1962-63	Buffalo	AHL	13	1	4	5	34
1963-64	Buffalo	AHL	-	-	-	-	-
1964-65	Buffalo	AHL	9	0	0	0	26
1965-66	Buffalo	AHL	-	-	-	-	-
1966-67	Chicago	NHL	6	0	0	0	8
1967-68	Philadelphia	NHL	7	0	4	4	11
1968-69	Philadelphia	NHL	1	0	0	0	17
1969-70	Philadelphia	NHL	-	-	-	-	-
1970-71	Philadelphia	NHL	4	0	1	1	8
1971-72	Philadelphia	NHL	-	-	-	-	-
1972-73	Philadelphia	NHL	11	0	0	0	16
1973-74	Philadelphia	NHL	17	1	2	3	41
1974-75	Philadelphia	NHL	17	0	4	4	28
1975-76	Philadelphia	NHL	-	-	-	-	-
	Pittsburgh	NHL	3	0	1	1	2
1976-77	Pittsburgh	NHL	-	-	-	-	-

NHL Totals

Regular Season					*Playoffs*				
GP	G	A	PTS	PIM	GP	G	A	PTS	PIM
700	27	126	153	1025	66	1	12	13	131

JIMMY WATSON

REGULAR SEASON

Year	Team	League	GP	G	A	PTS	PIM
1972-73	Richmond	AHL	73	5	33	38	83
	Philadelphia	NHL	4	0	1	1	5
1973-74	Philadelphia	NHL	78	2	18	20	44
1974-75	Philadelphia	NHL	68	7	18	25	72
1975-76	Philadelphia	NHL	79	2	34	36	66
1976-77	Philadelphia	NHL	71	3	23	26	35
1977-78	Philadelphia	NHL	71	5	12	17	62
1978-79	Philadelphia	NHL	77	9	13	22	52
1979-80	Philadelphia	NHL	71	5	18	23	51
1980-81	Philadelphia	NHL	18	2	2	4	6
1981-82	Philadelphia	NHL	76	3	9	12	99

PLAYOFFS

Year	Team	League	GP	G	A	PTS	PIM
1972-73	Richmond	AHL	4	1	2	3	6
	Philadelphia	NHL	2	0	0	0	0
1973-74	Philadelphia	NHL	17	1	2	3	41
1974-75	Philadelphia	NHL	17	1	8	9	10
1975-76	Philadelphia	NHL	16	1	8	9	6
1976-77	Philadelphia	NHL	10	1	2	3	2
1977-78	Philadelphia	NHL	12	1	7	8	6
1978-79	Philadelphia	NHL	8	0	2	2	2
1979-80	Philadelphia	NHL	15	0	4	4	20
1980-81	Philadelphia	NHL	-	-	-	-	-
1981-82	Philadelphia	NHL	4	0	1	1	2

NHL Totals

Regular Season					*Playoffs*				
GP	G	A	PTS	PIM	GP	G	A	PTS	PIM
613	38	148	186	492	101	5	34	39	89

JOE WATSON

REGULAR SEASON

Year	Team	League	GP	G	A	PTS	PIM
1963-64	Minneapolis	CPHL	71	0	20	20	55
1964-65	Minneapolis	CPHL	65	3	23	26	38
	Boston	NHL	4	0	1	1	0
1965-66	Oklahoma City	CPHL	69	8	24	32	58
1966-67	Boston	NHL	69	2	13	15	38
1967-68	Philadelphia	NHL	73	5	14	19	56
1968-69	Philadelphia	NHL	60	2	8	10	14
1969-70	Philadelphia	NHL	54	3	11	14	28
1970-71	Philadelphia	NHL	57	3	7	10	50
1971-72	Philadelphia	NHL	65	3	7	10	38
1972-73	Philadelphia	NHL	63	2	24	26	46
1973-74	Philadelphia	NHL	74	1	17	18	34
1974-75	Philadelphia	NHL	80	6	17	23	42
1975-76	Philadelphia	NHL	78	2	22	24	28
1976-77	Philadelphia	NHL	77	4	26	30	39
1977-78	Philadelphia	NHL	65	5	9	14	22
1978-79	Colorado	NHL	16	0	2	2	12

PLAYOFFS

Year	Team	League	GP	G	A	PTS	PIM
1963-64	Minneapolis	CPHL	5	0	0	0	2
1964-65	Minneapolis	CPHL	5	0	1	1	2
	Boston	NHL	-	-	-	-	-
1965-66	Oklahoma City	CPHL	9	1	3	4	6
1966-67	Boston	NHL	-	-	-	-	-
1967-68	Philadelphia	NHL	7	1	1	2	28
1968-69	Philadelphia	NHL	4	0	0	0	0
1969-70	Philadelphia	NHL	-	-	-	-	-
1970-71	Philadelphia	NHL	1	0	0	0	0
1971-72	Philadelphia	NHL	-	-	-	-	-
1972-73	Philadelphia	NHL	11	0	2	2	12
1973-74	Philadelphia	NHL	17	1	4	5	24
1974-75	Philadelphia	NHL	17	0	4	4	6
1975-76	Philadelphia	NHL	16	1	1	2	10
1976-77	Philadelphia	NHL	10	0	0	0	2
1977-78	Philadelphia	NHL	1	0	0	0	0
1978-79	Colorado	NHL	-	-	-	-	-

NHL Totals

Regular Season					*Playoffs*				
GP	G	A	PTS	PIM	GP	G	A	PTS	PIM
835	38	178	216	447	84	3	12	15	82

BEHN WILSON

REGULAR SEASON

Year	Team	League	GP	G	A	PTS	PIM
1975-76	Ottawa	OHA	63	5	16	21	131
1976-77	Ottawa	OHA	31	8	29	37	115
	Windsor	OHA	17	4	16	20	38
	Kalamazoo	IHL	13	2	7	9	40
1977-78	Kingston	OHA	52	18	58	76	186
1978-79	Philadelphia	NHL	80	13	36	49	197
1979-80	Philadelphia	NHL	61	9	25	34	212
1980-81	Philadelphia	NHL	77	16	47	63	237
1981-82	Philadelphia	NHL	59	13	23	36	135
1982-83	Philadelphia	NHL	62	8	24	32	92
1983-84	Chicago	NHL	59	10	22	32	143
1984-85	Chicago	NHL	76	10	23	33	185
1985-86	Chicago	NHL	69	13	37	50	113
1986-87	DID NOT PLAY						
1987-88	Chicago	NHL	58	6	23	29	166

PLAYOFFS

Year	Team	League	GP	G	A	PTS	PIM
1975-76	Ottawa	OHA	12	3	2	5	46
1976-77	Ottawa	OHA	-	-	-	-	-
	Windsor	OHA	-	-	-	-	-
	Kalamazoo	IHL	-	-	-	-	-
1977-78	Kingston	OHA	2	1	3	4	21
1978-79	Philadelphia	NHL	5	1	0	1	8
1979-80	Philadelphia	NHL	19	4	9	13	66
1980-81	Philadelphia	NHL	12	2	10	12	36
1981-82	Philadelphia	NHL	4	1	4	5	10
1982-83	Philadelphia	NHL	3	0	1	1	2
1983-84	Chicago	NHL	4	0	0	0	0
1984-85	Chicago	NHL	15	4	5	9	60
1985-86	Chicago	NHL	2	0	0	0	2
1986-87	DID NOT PLAY						
1987-88	Chicago	NHL	3	0	0	0	6

NHL Totals

Regular Season					Playoffs				
GP	G	A	PTS	PIM	GP	G	A	PTS	PIM
601	98	260	358	1480	67	12	29	41	190

LARRY ZEIDEL

REGULAR SEASON

Year	Team	League	GP	G	A	PTS	PIM
1951-52	Detroit	NHL	19	1	0	1	14
	Indianapolis	AHL	43	6	17	23	99
1952-53	Detroit	NHL	9	0	0	0	8
	Edmonton	WHL	59	4	22	26	114
1953-54	Chicago	NHL	64	1	6	7	102
1954-55	Edmonton	WHL	70	10	40	50	142
1955-56	Hershey	AHL	56	5	27	32	128
1956-57	Hershey	AHL	64	9	19	28	211
1957-58	Hershey	AHL	58	2	16	18	152
1958-59	Hershey	AHL	67	8	24	32	129
1959-60	Hershey	AHL	66	5	19	24	293
1960-61	Hershey	AHL	70	4	25	29	149
1961-62	Hershey	AHL	70	3	19	22	146
1962-63	Hershey	AHL	66	4	29	33	127
1963-64	Seattle	WHL	66	5	19	24	163
	Cleveland	AHL	2	0	1	1	2
1964-65	Seattle	WHL	64	2	12	14	202
1965-66	Cleveland	AHL	72	3	12	15	162
1966-67	Cleveland	AHL	72	5	24	29	124
1967-68	Philadelphia	NHL	57	1	10	11	68
1968-69	Philadelphia	NHL	9	0	0	0	6

PLAYOFFS

Year	Team	League	GP	G	A	PTS	PIM
1951-52	Detroit	NHL	5	0	0	0	0
	Indianapolis	AHL	-	-	-	-	-
1952-53	Detroit	NHL	-	-	-	-	-
	Edmonton	WHL	15	2	6	8	26
1953-54	Chicago	NHL	-	-	-	-	-
1954-55	Edmonton	WHL	9	2	5	7	2
1955-56	Hershey	AHL	-	-	-	-	-
1956-57	Hershey	AHL	7	0	5	5	21
1957-58	Hershey	AHL	11	0	6	6	20
1958-59	Hershey	AHL	13	4	6	10	59
1959-60	Hershey	AHL	-	-	-	-	-
1960-61	Hershey	AHL	8	0	2	2	8
1961-62	Hershey	AHL	7	0	1	1	20
1962-63	Hershey	AHL	14	1	6	7	51
1963-64	Seattle	WHL	-	-	-	-	-
	Cleveland	AHL	9	0	4	4	12
1964-65	Seattle	WHL	7	1	2	3	2
1965-66	Cleveland	AHL	12	1	3	4	14
1966-67	Cleveland	AHL	5	0	1	1	2
1967-68	Philadelphia	NHL	7	0	1	1	12
1968-69	Philadelphia	NHL	-	-	-	-	-

NHL Totals

Regular Season					Playoffs				
GP	G	A	PTS	PIM	GP	G	A	PTS	PIM
158	3	16	19	198	12	0	1	1	12